THE GIVING AND TAKING OF LIFE

The Giving and Taking of Life

ESSAYS ETHICAL

James Tunstead Burtchaell, C.S.C.

UNIVERSITY OF NOTRE DAME PRESS

NOTRE DAME, INDIANA

46292

Library of Congress Cataloging-in-Publication Data

Burtchaell, James Tunstead.
    The giving and taking of life : essays ethical /James Tunstead
Burtchaell.
      p. cm.
    Includes index.
    ISBN 0-268-01018-8
    1. Christian ethics—Catholic authors. 2. Life and death,
Power over—Religious aspects—Catholic Church. 3. Catholic
Church—Doctrines. I. Title.
BJ1249.B87 1989
241'.042—dc20   89-40023

For

MARION MURPHY BURTCHAELL

who gave me life
and
in ways herein described and others indescribable
initiation into Christian ethics

Contents

Preface

IT WAS EARLY IN THE AUTUMN of 1968, and we had about four dozen bishops gathered quietly at Notre Dame for one of their annual theology seminars. Quietly, because no one had a comfortable public explanation of what those men, graced with the plenitude of faith-understanding, stood to learn from theologians over whom they were placed as teachers. In virtue of just having become chairman of the Department of Theology I was the bishops' host. But since I had sat in that chair not yet one month, I was present as an onlistener, contented that my predecessor who had planned the affair was actually presiding.

Contented, that is, until a Canadian friend invited as a speaker was explaining to us "The Salvation of the Unbeliever according to Karl Rahner." Now anything according to Karl Rahner is pretty murky, but as the speaker was striving quite competently to make light shine in that particular darkness it came clear that unbelievers were to be saved by some unwitting tie-up with the church. Salvation came only through Jesus Christ; Jesus could be got at only through faith; faith was a copyrighted element of the church's rescue program; and hence those unfaithed who were fortunate enough to make it *had* to be beholden somehow, through some mystical association at least, to Jesus and to us, his card-carrying believers. It was the old stuff about crypto-Christians, anonymous believers, people-who-would-belong-if-only-they-got-the-call-ungarbled. The gist of it, though tortuously extended by Rahner (you tended to forget his beginning by the time you arrived, spent, at his conclusion), was familiar. Basically, a person cleaves to

ix

God by doing something religious, whether the person knows it or not.

As the presentation proceeded I grew fidgety, and at its close I violated hospitality by saying in front of all the bishops that Rahner's view sounded like a lot of malarkey. Unbelievers are rescued the same way believers are: by emerging from their native selfishness into love, something we do by generous and faithful service of neighbors in need, and something for which our limp spirits are unready and need the quickening and favoring of God's breath, not to mention much human hoisting. Basically, we cleave to God by cleaving to one another, by doing something serviceable, the works of duty that transform us: diapering babies and stopping wars and keeping our heavy thumb off the shop scales. Faith of itself does not make us safe. It reveals to us the things which do. It reveals how sacred is the seemingly secular; it discloses the eternal significance of the daily services by which we are called to work out our salvation.

I owe much to that moment, and to reflections on it later. This book presents some of those reflections.

We Christians respect our elders. We hold ourselves answerable to the more durable insights our ancestors in faith left us from their graced experience. But we think that we too have the Spirit, and that we have never maturely learned what the tradition has to teach us until we can see and say it sensibly shown in our own experience. Bad theology comes when we say in ancient words what ancients told, but cannot say it as something we relearned ourselves (at their cue). Sacramental character, grace of state, original sin, magisterium (all that theospeak which puts glaze on the eyes of those in the pews)—teachers tell us of the nature of these things and their worth, but one sometimes has the notion they couldn't really point one out in a crowd. There is also bad theology when one construes the "signs of the times" without the interpreting wisdom which only the tradition can give. This sociospeak can put a lot of hop in an audience with talk of structural oppression and self-actualization and participatory decision-making, but you may never learn from it why Jesus had to die.

Sound theology must close the synapse between what ancients said to us and what we have then seen for ourselves. In the matter of salvation, we had heard it from our forebears closest to Jesus that he had rescued them, that faith had brought them out of estrangement into peace. Ignoring, then, the obvious sight of goats milling among sheep on both sides of the faith-fence, we carelessly concluded that God offers reconciliation only through Jesus-things: creed, sacraments, clergy, commandments, and the like. If we gave as much reverence to what we have seen with our own eyes as to what the earlier disciples saw with theirs, we would perceive more wholly that Jesus-faith offers us a vision. What the vision sees is that the vision does not save. It incites but does not accomplish what we long for: union with the Father. Faith sends us to do the works of love and to be refashioned through the doing of them. And such works lie at hand also to those without faith, who often take them up with more relish and pluck and grace than we whose faith has told us of their concealed worth.

It is in giving and sustaining life that we come to life. It is in denying and depleting life that we become moribund. These essays on Christian ethics, though they deal with only a few of the specific issues, will probably be more helpful as elaborating a general approach than as resolving specific questions. I find that I return habitually to the nature of moral goodness, the way in which the faith community articulates and grooms its moral wisdom, and the interplay between behavior and character. These are great matters, and I hope that those who hear me out will find here some coordinates to orient their further search into them. The Mystery we try to unpuzzle is the best of mysteries, so delightfully deep that we can never get to the bottom of it: not because it is radically unintelligible but because it never ceases to yield further insight.

The Metamorphosis
6 August 1988
Princeton

Moral Wisdom and the Christian Faith

1

Community Experience as Source of Christian Ethics

A PRIMARY WELLSPRING OF Christian ethical wisdom is the believing community's reflection on human experience and on the personal aftermath of that experience. That is the proposition I want to expound.

MORAL WISDOM, NOT MORAL LAW

I speak of wisdom, not law, because of the impediments Christians have tended to find when using "law" as their analogy for moral norms. Law requires obedience to another's stated will, under pain of estrangement and punishment. I say obedience, not just conformity, for law implies a conscious relation between lawgiver and subject: a known command, announced sanctions for disobedience, and intentional submission to the command. Now Christians have no awkwardness in understanding God as a sovereign. Both as creator and as re-creator, God is presented in the scriptures as establishing a long-hoped-for reign beyond all hopes: over the disciples of Jesus, over all humankind, and indeed over all creation. Nor is it confusing for Christians to suppose that immoral behavior incurs inexorable penalties. Jesus' teaching gains its urgency from his warning that if we do not repent and extricate our-

3

selves from sin we shall be dead even before our obituaries appear. Right behavior is a matter of life and death.

The risky element in the analogy of law is its implication that our good or evil behavior will determine God's attitude towards us. Quite naturally (and quite contrary to the gospel) when we construe our moral performance as obedience to God's law or as violation of divine law, we infer that God will cherish and bless those who submit, and that God will take offense at those who take the law into their own hands. But Jesus who dies for those that kill him reveals a love that defies defiance, that is persistent to the point of wrathlessness, that is determined to cherish us quite beyond our ability to alienate him. He consummates our understanding of the character of his Father, the God of Abraham and Sarah, Isaac and Rebecca, and Jacob and Leah and Rachel. That God, we finally can see, has no wrath, no curse, no doom. It is not we who control God's stance towards us, for that is fixed and fast in love beyond all telling.

How, then, if there be no wrath in the God that Christians know, is the course of human behavior a matter of life and death? In our passage through this time-life, while change is possible, we must grow from selfishness into love. Our failure to do that will not bring reaction from the Lord but will leave us unredeemably incapacitated to clasp that love, to take it in, to be God's (or anyone else's) intimate. The tragedy of being fixed in selfishness is not that God will cease to love us but that we shall have stifled our capacity to enter the eternal embrace.

It is more illuminating, then, to speak of moral wisdom, which does not require obedience to another's will to avoid that person's wrath, but allows one to benefit from another's mind. This conforms to the Christian notion of Good News as revelation rather than statute; urgent invitation rather than command. When your physician pleads with you that three packs of cigarettes a day will tend to give you emphysema until you contract lung cancer, no matter how peremptory her mood and voice are, she is giving you wisdom, not orders. You ignore her at your risk, but it is not she who will penalize you. Doctors tell patients about their bodies and about what favors their bodies and thus their selves. If they are right and we ignore them, what ensues is not of their doing, only of their telling.

The church is a community of moral wisdom accumulated, passed on, challenged, and revised. The primary font of that savvy is our own experience and observation. Experience, of course, does not consist in merely being there. Inspector Clouseau is always in the right spot at the right time, yet he never gets the point. He hath eyes yet seeth not. Experience consists in figuring out what is going on.

A young graduate, formerly my student, returned to campus to tell me of his work. As a precinct worker from high school days he easily found patronage work in the city assessor's office while he was earning money to go to law school. His task was to explain to the walk-in public the mysteries of property evaluation and taxation. It was with special warmth that he recounted how helpful he had been to an elderly Italian couple that week, taking more than an hour to explain to them the whys and wherefores of the recent upward assessment of their home. "They were so grateful," he beamed, "that when they were leaving the old man slipped a ten-dollar bill into my hand!" It was at this point in our visit that the sun refused to give its light and the moon turned to blood. I stormed at him for having just made his entry into the sleaze and graft of the Chicago underworld, for taking bribes and extorting the savings of the poor. How did he imagine big-time dishonesty started? I was not warning him of criminal indictments or threatening him with my anger. I was telling him what becomes of the souls of public servants on the take. Ours was a transaction of ethical wisdom.

It put me in mind of an incident when I was five years old and told my mother a lie. I distinctly recall a savage right uppercut that sent me cannonading across the room into the far wall. Our explanatory conversation is less clear in my memory, but somehow I understood that it was not her fist but my weakness I had to fear. Moral wisdom was being conveyed.

How does the community evaluate any kind of act as good or evil? By seeing what that action does to us. The gospel, for instance, cues us about wealth: wealth carries a high risk. Taking the tip, the community takes a long look at the affluent and develops an even more trenchant and shareable conviction that few of us are strong enough to survive wealth. The same with marijuana, dictatorship, red-lining, slavery, embezzlement, and child abuse. If we share or if we dispute the received ethical assessments of such activities, it is primarily because of our own moral appraisal of what they do to people: most of all, to those who engage in them. And the evidence most influential for us comes from those who have made a life out of these kinds of behavior and then looked back on it with dismay.

We begin by being told, by listening to the tradition, whether it comes to us from the gospel, the clergy, wise Uncle Harry, Miss Manners, or the *Tribune*'s resident anthropologist. They tell us what's what. But just listening is passive. As we leave childhood behind it is our need to look about us (and within us) as closely as did those whose wisdom has been passed on to us like a sourdough starter, so to speak, and to make the tradition our own. As that happens, we no longer have moral guidance by hearsay. We come to the point where we can vouch for it ourselves. That is an act of judgment, not one of mere memory and acceptance. It is moral maturity.

In our anxiety to persuade others how to live rightly we sometimes offer them motives why they should not do thus or so. Stealing violates property rights and persons' integrity; bribery violates the law; pollution violates the environment. Promiscuity will get you VD. Drunkenness will lose you your job. Or: hard study will get you into Cal Tech. Fair wages will hire you a steady workforce. Meditation will lower your pulse and skin tension. Now all of that may be true, but it is secondary. In fact, it may eclipse what is primary.

Our primary moral concern must be: How do certain courses of behavior tend to make us thrive or induce us to wither . . . personally, spiritually, in our character, our self?

The ultimate outcome of your life is your self, and it is the course and pattern of what you have done and what you have withheld that will be most of the making of you: acts coalescing into traits combining to develop your self.

Christians have a chronic handicap in understanding a graced ethical wisdom, for Christians believe they benefit from a revealed faith, a faith that includes our moral doctrine. And

Christians often have crude ideas about revelation. They imagine that their faith emerges from some specially inspired persons or gatherings, say, from Moses and Paul and their like; or from Augustine and Kierkegaard and Barth and their like; or from the bishop of Rome who has no like; or from their charismatic prayer meeting which may be like nothing else you ever saw. What may underlie (and compromise) their appeals to revelation is the supposition that certain privileged persons were visited by direct inner disclosures entrusted to them to be shared with us.

Revelation better understood is neither so passive nor so exotic. Revelation, in Israel and in the church, comes as an insight into experience on the strength of the God who capacitates someone. Consider the paragons of revealing inspiration, the classical prophets of Israel and Judah. Their rivals, the prophets on the royal payroll, delivered oracles to order in some sort of induced ecstasy, oracles that were respected as divine because the prophets' normal mode of thinking and speaking had been deactivated. The classical prophets, by contrast, were not professional seers and they had no truck with all the dance and trance of prophecy-for-hire. They were persons so acutely aware of Israel's calling and of the inevitable outcome of national life as it unfolded before their muck-raking eyes, that they blurted out what was at stake: loudly, articulately, antagonizingly. It was only by hindsight that the community—the sadder but wiser girl was she—came to treasure those oracles as coming from Yahweh's true visionaries: men and women who had eyes to see. Their divine disclosures came when their powers of thinking and speaking and authorship were at full alert, not when they were shut down. It was not their process of learning but their message of prophetic insight that convinced Israel of its divine origin.[1]

Revelation is graced insight into experience. Moses came by it the same way we do, only more abundantly. What we inherit under the byline of Moses is a code of law. It was not delivered, it was derived—from some especially graced leaders of the clans of Israel who had great wisdom: that knack of settling disputes and setting rules that enabled touchy families and competitive tribes to dwell beside one another in peace.

What we have from Paul is not so much what came to him during his solitary meditation in the Syrian desert as it is the convictions he acquired when he was shouting in those toe-to-toe arguments with Peter over who should eat at whose house. It is the same with any great person in the church: divinely given insight emerges from graced yet energetic scrutiny of what is really going on and what it is really worth, in the prospect of death and the perspective of eternity.[2]

GROOMS OF THE TRADITION

Revealed moral wisdom is uncommon insight into common events. It is cumulative, in that we are always starting from what our predecessors saw and said. It is also current, for we have never appropriated the wisdom tradition until we have tried it out ourselves to the point where we can pass it on, not as hearsay or in quotes, but as a complex of insights we vouch for in our own name. John Cassian, the Gaul who visited late fourth-century Egypt to see for himself the communities of ascetic monks in the desert there, reported that they gathered in large caves during long stretches of the night to praise God with the Psalms, led by one singer who read by a single lampflame. So often had they chanted those 150 Psalms, he observed, that they sang as if composing them extemporaneously as they went along. That is a fit image for a community of faith, which makes the wisdom it receives its very own. No matter how many scores or hundreds of forebears had a hand in shaping its contours and picking out its highlights, we learn it well and then put it to the test in our own time. Then we can utter it as if it were our own fresh discovery. Which, by that time, it is.

It is inevitable that some elements of the wisdom handed down would give us pause, and that a few might even stick in our throats. It is inevitable, and it is good. For as grooms of a vital tradition we must reconstrue and improve on those few matters on which our particular generation may have been given further light. The tradition is not inert. But our reconsideration of it is a nervous task, for it is as likely to be astigmatism or blindness which puts us in stress with our elders in the faith as it is their backwardness and our enhanced vision. Still, we must take our misgivings out to the plaza of human experience for newly inquisitive study. If it goes well we shall either disagree more articulately with the tradition because we know better why we must revise it, or we shall appreciate the older wisdom more than ever because we did take a second look.

The authentic and sound Christian tradition would insist that ethical truth must be discerned, not decided. And that discernment, I am claiming here, is primarily an act of the believing community which remembers what happens to us in the aftermath of certain ways of living.

PASTORS AND SCHOLARS

By now it must be obvious that this exposition has gone out of its way to omit any reference to a privileged role in this moral endeavor for two kinds of person who have been prominent in Christian norm-making: the officers of the church and its experts: the hierarchy (or clergy) and the scholars. They do have special services to offer, but those services have not always been carefully understood.

The task of the cleric (within any tradition), and its corresponding charism, is to preside. Whether any individual officeholder in the church actually possesses the requisite charism or empowerment, the duty of office is to preside, to convene the community, to call it to listen to the gospel, to provoke it to respond, to orchestrate its care and service, to cultivate its peace. To preside is not always to lead. Actually, few of those ordained to preside seem to have been chosen for their manifest graces of leadership. They are rarely learned in the faith, rarely the ones whose imagination is strongest in keeping the community on the *qui vive*, or the ones whose courage and candor help others to see through the legerdemain of current fashion. But if those and the other essential gifts are at the community's disposition in other members, the one who presides can call on them for the common benefit.

In this matter of moral discernment most church officers

will not be so possessed of the prophetic spirit that their insights will revitalize the tradition. But those who preside will commonly have to review or summarize or recite the tradition. That is an important task, and there are more articulate ways and less articulate ways of doing it. When it goes wrong it is often because the presiding official fancies himself, not to be enunciating what the community and its predecessors have worked to elaborate, but to be in the position of giving orders which others should obey. This, of course, is the authority of the scribes. It is exactly the same as when a pastor of a church treats the congregational bank account as his own money.

As one who presides, the cleric enjoys no *ex officio* insight, save possibly a presidential concern lest any sector of the community not find its voice or be squelched. But since, in the Christian tradition, the officers who preside are also charged with pastoral care, this other role can and should advantage the cleric with a privileged exposure to the consciences and experiences of the community. It is especially providential that by ancient tradition the presbyter who is deputed to preside at the eucharist and expound the gospel is also entrusted with the initiatives of forgiveness. The one who calls the community into the fire of the Lord's summons is the same one who must look each one lovingly in the eye when he fails that call. Thus the gospel is more realistically preached and forgiveness less sentimentally transacted for their both having the same minister. A cleric who is energetically and effectively active in pastoral ministry has an extraordinary opportunity to elicit and study and witness to prophetic insight in the church. But one who presides without that experience is quite disadvantaged, and must have it all on hearsay. In fact, pastoral involvement is so essential to effective presidency in the church that one who holds office without it may do much mischief without being aware.

This interpretation is allied to that expounded by Newman's essay, "On Consulting the Faithful in Matters of Doctrine." Though he construes faith as tenacity in holding what has descended from the apostles more than as inquiry into what those ancient insights might mean further and later, Newman argues that in a season of most urgent crisis, that of the Arian controversy, it was not the bishops but the laity who by instinct and stubbornness held fast to the orthodox faith.[3]

The other special role in moral inquiry belongs to the scholar. A tradition that is historical, scrutiny of human behavior that is systematic, and constructive reflection that is principled are all activities that scholars should be able to assist with skill and method. In Christian moral inquiry scholars are essential. They could, I suppose, be considered the sheep dogs of the flock, running from side to side and barking and biting. Yet everything the theological scholar does is derivative, for the communal inquiry cannot be monopolized out of the hands of the church. In the end it will probably be the scholar that writes it all up. But it is always "as told to" him or her. The scholar is the ghost writer of faith, not its hero.

The moral inquiry of the church is crucially assisted by these two ministries, so that it can move from learning to expounding, from description to prescription, from what they see happens to people who behave in certain ways to conclusions about how we must all live in order to live well.

RECOGNIZING SAINTS

Now I would like to illustrate this by some examples. The first is the largest, for it entails the most tested ethical wisdom in the long centuries of Christian experience. It begins in the apostolic age itself and is still incomplete: it is the designation and veneration of saints.[4]

There is an inveterate question that has occupied some theologians and canonists ever since the Roman see reserved to itself the prerogative of canonization: Is a solemn declaration of sainthood an infallible act, guaranteed free from error? By and large canonists have said no and theologians have said yes.[5] Those who have held for infallibility have argued that too much is at stake in the church for God to allow the pope to err in such a decree. Their concern, typically, has been that papal teaching would be worthless were it fallible. No one seems to have noted the much more significant matter at stake: that the identification of a specific person as a saint is perhaps the most fundamental moral statement that the church has occasion to make. It is the validity of the statement, more than the reputation of the one who utters it, that counts most here.

What I should like to propose is that the designation of saints is not merely a specific application of all that the Christian community knows about good and evil; it is a major source for our ethical doctrine. It is popularly believed ("popularly" means that this is a misunderstanding of the learned to which the unlearned seem more immune) that we hold and study a body of knowledge about good and evil human behavior which we then apply to individuals. It is more radically true to say that we derive any reliable general notions about ethical value from our exposure (either personally or through stories) to very virtuous and very sinful people, and to no one more significantly than to the saints. We come to know about sanctity by meeting saints.

It will be helpful to review two evolutions in the Christian cult of the saints: a progression in the church's ability to identify various ways of life with sanctity, and a change in the procedures for designating individual saints. These developments in categorization and canonization are distinct but not unrelated.

The first saints were martyrs. The New Testament already presents them to us as those who most radically followed their master by willingly accepting a violent death for their commitment. Stephen, one of the Greek-speakers recruited as a deacon for that aggrieved sector of the Jerusalem Christians, is the first of the new community to meet death after Jesus. Luke's account is carefully crafted to present the episode in parallel with the story of Jesus: Stephen in the course of his work is filled with grace and power and performs prodigious signs and wonders among the people; he is confronted antagonistically by unsympathetic Jews (scribes and elders) who hale him before the Sanhedrin; perjured witnesses are put forward to accuse him of destructive designs on the Temple; he gives an account of God's historic works and of Israel's repeated resistance to the prophets as climaxed in their killing of Jesus; when they are manifestly infuriated he claims to behold the Son of Man, the heavenly judge sent to close down history, poised to commence his assize; Stephen is hustled out of town to be lynched; in his dying gasp he asks the Lord not to hold their sin against his killers.[6] It is the master's own story all over again, reenacted now by the disciple.

The literature shortly to follow the New Testament tells us of Peter and Paul, James the apostle and James the chief of the Jerusalem church, then Ignatius of Antioch and Polycarp of Smyrna and a host of others encountering death in such a way that they come to be called *martyres* [witnesses].[7]

The martyrs were the analogies for Christian discipleship, and they brought the presence of the Lord Jesus by their memories and their bodies into the midst of the local churches. Just as in ancient Israel there were locations made sacred by great events, and each locale was usually provided with its myth or legend or chronicle and a resident seer to recite the tale to passers-by, so the Christian martyr was given a special tomb and feast and story. It became customary to consider burial in the earth as unworthy of the martyrs, and they were exhumed and buried above the ground, and later still were moved and interred in a shrine or a church. They were remembered by narrative. The *acta* of a martyr sometimes included even the transcript of the Roman court notary with the dialogue between the accused and the official. Or the local community might compose a *martyrion/passio* of the saint: a devout recollection of his or her death. Later, when the status of a deceased was at issue and a church was presenting evidence for the authenticity of its veneration, a *libellus de vita et miraculis* would be drawn up as a brief on behalf of the saint.[8] The cult of the martyr would include, locally, the celebration of his or her *natalitia* [birthday] (anniversary of rebirth to heaven through martyrdom) and, throughout the other churches, inclusion in the anaphorae and litanies, or lists of saints who were invoked in prayer. The "birthday" could, in later discipline, be supplemented or replaced by celebration of the *elevatio* [exhumation] or *translatio* [transfer] of the body to a shrine. As the veneration of relics became more popular, in the expectation of miracles, recollection of the day of translation when the martyr's remains were first brought into their midst might understandably replace for a local church the anniversary of birth/death.

Near the end of the second century Clement of Alexandria was already pointing out that there might be other ways of life than that of the martyr which were exemplary of Christ.[9] Yet it awaited later centuries for a second category of saint to emerge. The third century, in the waning days of pagan Rome, witnessed the most widespread and persistent persecutions of Christians. Among the increasing numbers who were identified as Christians and imprisoned for torture and eventual execution, some came to escape violent death because of a change of regime or by being mistakenly left for dead, or by exile to slavery in the imperial mines. Anyone who stood up as a Christian in the face of capital punishment was classified by the Christians as a *homologêtês* [confessor], or one who had made public profession of his or her faith. The church held itself obligated to provide food and comfort to a confessor in prison, and the expectation of martyrdom gave confessors the privilege of requesting and securing amnesty and reconciliation for Christians of more feeble faith who had flinched before persecution and were in disgrace and estrangement from the church. "Confessor" began as a synonym for "martyr" used for those who made the ultimate act of public loyalty. As its usage developed it came to designate only those who emerged alive.

But when some began to survive torment and death, they were held in high honor. They were given an annual stipend from the community payroll, commensurate with the various ranks of clergy and their own manifest levels of endurance. They were also accorded the conventional courtesies owed to these clerical orders, and could claim ordination to the rank itself upon request.[10] When they died their tombs were occasionally revered and their intercession credited with miracles. It must be noted, however, that the literature suggests that confessors who faced but eluded death were awkward to have around. The church seems to find that when a person faces martyrdom it is better for the rope not to snap, for a surviving hero is a great moral temptation to himself and to others. It is not insignificant that these first confessors were rarely honored by published narratives of their exploits or *passiones*.[11]

With Constantine the church emerged from what had become a regular rhythm of persecution, and the fourth and fifth centuries were the occasion for a third category of sainthood to emerge. Ardor and intensity would no longer be manifest in courageous readiness to brave a violent death. Now a new appreciation of the church was fastened upon the ascetics. This mode of heroic sanctity was accepted, however, because of its perceived parity with the previously accepted categories. Martyrdom had been accepted by dint of its likeness to Christ, and confessors had been venerated because of their undeniable similarity to the martyrs. The first ascetics to be venerated had to embody a similar discipleship, by self-denial on a par with what the emperors and magistrates had imposed on the gallant heroes of an earlier age. The continuity was displayed also by nomenclature: the saintly ascetics were called confessors (males) or widows or virgins (females): titles of traditional honor from the persecutions or from the New Testament.

Only after this innovation had been accepted, of persons venerated for their lives more than for their deaths, was the new category of peacetime confessor enlarged to include men notable for their pastoral dedication. Yet the first bishops admitted tended to be those who had been roughed up violently during their ministry. It took time for the church to recognize heroism in the nonviolent self-expenditure of the pastoral office. Later still, men and women of the nobility were enrolled because of single-minded solicitude for their subjects, especially the destitute. And by now the hagiography was published in the form of "lives" rather than "sufferings." The ancient *Acts of Justin and his Companions,* the *Letter of the Churches of Lyons and Vienne,* and the *Passion of Perpetua and Felicitas* were succeeded now by the *Life of Anthony* by Athanasius, the *Life of Martin* (of Tours) by Sulpicius Severus, the *Life of Felix* by Paulinus of Nola, the *Life of Hilarion* and the *Life of Paul* (of Thebes) by Jerome. These in turn gave way to the compilations of saintly lives by Palladius of Helenopolis and Theodoret of Cyr and Sozomen of Gaza and Gregory of Tours.

With the passage of time the eye of the church gained further perspective, and other categories were added to the fellowship of the saints. In the early Middle Ages mystics came to honor, followed later by scholars (both pastoral and polemical), and as the Middle Ages turned into the Renaissance, by missionaries and founders of vowed, celibate orders. But along the way, many popes had to be honored as martyrs, queens as widows, and founders as virgins, because their other status had not yet been recognized as an avenue of sanctity. For the same reason, perhaps, all the apostles whose destiny was historically unremembered had been given the honors of martyrdom, for that was the only category people first understood as saintly. That this process of progressive authentication of heroic forms of discipleship is still incomplete seems clear from the fact that there is as yet hardly a single person venerated as a saintly parent or a saintly merchant or a saintly politician or a saintly professor (except, of course, of theology). Nor has the Catholic Church yet reached beyond the palisade of its own communion to venerate the charism of sanctity within other Christians. If the future is faithful to the past, sanctity will be acknowledged in some individuals before their generic life-path is identified as a divine calling. That already befell a number of holy women who were canonized before there was a category available, and for centuries they had to be listed as "neither a virgin nor a martyr."

The lesson within all of this is that the faith community has been learning about Christian discipleship. The church has been moving slowly from a time when holiness was stylized and discernible in but a few walks of life, to a later time when a more sensitive scrutiny sees the Spirit invested in so many forms of service.

The fact, however, that Zita the housemaid and Henry of Bolzano the laborer and Joan of Arc the patriot and Benedict Joseph Labre the vagrant and Maria Goretti the rape-victim and Simeon the Stylite and many other uncategorizable saints were lofted to veneration before the church authorities could quite figure out what to make of their ways of life suggests that there is in the cult of the saints an impulsive and vehement element that somehow transcends the method and science of official procedures. To appreciate how and why that is so we must review the evolution of those procedures.

The earliest saints were appraised, acclaimed, and venerated by a process that was populist, spontaneous, and immediate. A person was hailed as saint almost in the aftermath of death by those most intimately acquainted with his or her enduring fidelity. Today the procedures for canonization are papal rather than populist, scholarly instead of spontaneous, and methodically deliberate instead of abrupt. A person is hailed as a saint by persons as detached as possible from his or her enduring fidelity.

Stephen was venerated as one who had followed the Lord to the end by the witnesses who had seen his service to the widows and orphans, heard his prophetic confrontation with the literati of Jerusalem, and watched his ecstatic beauty while being assassinated. They had *seen* his sanctity. They did not argue for it; they simply testified to it. To this they added stories of the still greater signs and wonders he wrought after his death. It was not the case that they knew beforehand what sanctity or immortal witness were, and then found them embodied in Stephen. It was his life and death that taught them what sanctity and martyrdom were. The specific instance gave them their category.

In time sanctity was vouched for by the local community, as in the testimonies of Smyrna, Vienne, and Lyons. Later still the presiding officers emerged as more saliently active in that process, for a variety of reasons. In the fourth and fifth centuries controversy attended the discernment of "true martyrs." Those of the Catholic faith had to reject veneration of Donatist martyrs (who were said to invite death a bit too enthusiastically, having caught the scent of glory). The twin temptations of money and pride were inducing some churches and monasteries to honor martyrs of questionable credentials and phony relics. And prelates of churches peopled largely by newcomer Christians converted abruptly from their ancestral heathenism could consolidate their followers' new allegiance by bringing the bodies of the most potent saints into their cathedrals. The bishops increasingly took personal charge, then, over both the designation of saints and the custody of their remains.

In the centuries after the collapse of the empire and the new missionary undertaking to introduce Christianity throughout the Goths and Franks and Gauls and Celts and Slavs of Europe, there were new martyrs. And then when the invader peoples had been inducted into the church they not only venerated the intrepid missionaries who had been their own victims, but developed a yen for a supply of saintly patrons in every locality. The seventh and eighth centuries saw a remarkable evacuation of the Roman catacombs and trafficking in holy remains to faraway northern churches. By this time the local bishops had made local synods and regional councils the venue for controlling the cult of the saints. When the hostilities of Europe had interrupted the open roads and posts of the old empire, church governance by councils was supplemented by a new network of codified decretals and statutes gathered from the many councils of the past. The canon lawyers were a powerful network that systematized the western church in the early Middle Ages. Included in the legislation that was copied and widely deferred to throughout the area were two canons that dealt with the cult of the saints.

Sixth Council of Carthage (401)

Likewise the Council agrees that altars set up here and there in the fields or along the roads as memorials to martyrs, but which are found to contain no body or relics of martyrs, should be destroyed by the local bishops whenever possible. If that is not possible because of the public disturbance it would arouse, the people should nevertheless be warned not to visit those places so they will be wise enough to avoid being drawn into superstition. And let no shrine to a martyr be approved unless the body or some relics be there, or there be hard evidence that it was the martyr's own home or possessions or the spot where he or she suffered. Altars that have no basis except somebody's dream or absurd revelations should somehow be discredited.[12]

Council of Mainz (813)

Canon 51. Henceforth no one should presume to move bodies of saints without agreement by the ruler or permission of the bishops and the holy synod.[13]

By the tenth century there is a lively tradition of cautious supervision. Bishops refuse to consider petitions for canonization without carefully compiled *libelli* including evidence from eyewitnesses. Then, possibly to ensure the *cachet* of greater authority, or to prevent later challenge by rival claimants to saintly relics, bishops begin in the tenth century to send their decisions to Rome for apostolic confirmation. The eleventh and twelfth centuries are a period of energetic consolidation of papal prerogative by activist reforming popes, and it was natural that authority over the causes and cult of saints would be one of the issues drawn to Rome. By the twelfth century popes were willing to adjudicate such matters outside the context of a general council. Two distinguished canonists, Alexander III and Innocent III, decreed respectively that it was customary for all such causes to come before the pope and that only he could authenticate relics. It was only shortly afterwards that the decretals of Gregory IX in 1234 finally and explicitly reserved canonization to the pope.

The Roman curia inexorably imposed a juridical order on the procedure. Both certain evidence of a consistent life of high virtue and sworn testimony to intercessory miracles were required. But whereas out in the field the miracles tended to have a higher evidentiary value, in the curia that was less so. The devil could counterfeit miracles, but virtue under stress was not so readily forged. Also, Rome seems to have been more conscious that a saint venerated throughout the universal church had to serve as a model for the Christian life anywhere, not merely as a hometown favorite; hence the account of heroic morality was more crucial than that of cures and resurrections. Rome regularized the position of the *promotor fidei* (the "devil's advocate"), the official who would systematically criticize all petitions. In fact, it might be said that the procedures for the causes of saints were the first serious undertaking of critical scholarship by the See of Rome, centuries before the hagiographical research of the Bollandists was begun[14] and nearly a millenium before Rome was to smile on the scholarly study of scripture.

The papal takeover by canonist popes might appear to have been complete. Yet custom has a way of evading canons. Eric Kemp writes:

> It is evident, however, that the practices of popular religion were far from conforming to the theories of canonists and theo-

logians. The fact that the Council of Trent found it necessary to pass a decree defining the control to be exercised over images and relics shows that abuses were prevalent. . . . Any reform which resulted, however, was little more than local or temporary, for in the early years of the seventeenth century much scandal was caused in Rome and other parts of Italy by the popular veneration of a number of persons who had died in the odour of sanctity but had not yet been beatified or canonized.[15]

It was in the seventeenth century that Urban VIII issued two massive decrees which bid fair to make the cult of the saints a fastidious and thoroughly bureaucratized Roman monopoly. In the very midst of this legislation, however, Urban enacted a massive grandfather clause in favor of popular cults:

> Decree 1, par. 4. It is meanwhile clear that the above provisions are not designed or intended to call into question saints who have been venerated either by broad consensus throughout the church or from time immemorial, or on the strength of what the fathers or saints have written, with the ancient and conscious acquiescence of the Apostolic See or the local bishop.[16]

Some scholars, like André Vauchez, have perceived a conflict between the elitist attitude towards sainthood developed in sophisticated clerical circles and the popular attitudes and intuitions displayed by the laity. Others, like Peter Brown, have vigorously opposed any theory that discounts the pervasive and dominating intuitions and control of popular piety. Even under modern church legislation which governs both canonization and cult, it is important to realize that the driving force in the entire veneration of saints is essentially popular. It is the familiars of a deceased person who have been struck by his or her single-minded generosity, that have petitioned for a consideration of his or her life and charmismatic evidences. It is the laity who, in the absence of recognized categories, press for acknowledgment of any new sort of saint. It is the reflective and assertive experience of the appreciative lay witnesses which is the driving force in the entire process.

No matter who is exercising jurisdiction—a local bishop,

a synod, a regional council, a pope or his curia or a general council—the role of presidency is less to initiate than to preside: to discipline, to challenge, to look for conflicts of interest or superstition or inconsistency. It is a superficial and incomplete observation that the cult of the saints has been enlarged in its perspective at the same time it has been taken over by the clergy from the laity. It is certainly the case that procedure has evolved. As Kemp puts it, "Canonization in the age of the martyrs was a spontaneous act of the local community."[17] No one imagines that this is true today. Yet the basic ecclesiastical act of recognizing signal holiness and distinguishing it from sham and mediocrity remains within the popular grasp. Scholars and pastors may through their keen questioning induce the community to scrutinize more closely, for that is the proper relationship of scholars and pastoral officers to the community. But the prophetic insight that discerns heroic sanctity belongs to the membership as much as to the officers or scholars.

Hippolyte Delehaye the Bollandist, who is this century's most authoritative scholar on the veneration of the saints, has this to say:

> The saint is a servant of God venerated by public cult. What people honor the saint for is holiness. And what is holiness?
>
> The answer will be framed differently depending on who is asked: the average Christian, theologians, or church officials officially charged with these matters.
>
> As saints have increased in the church, the concept of holiness has become increasingly well defined. In the minds of believers enlightened by their faith, and by the sight of the virtues practiced by the best among them, it has emerged as an ideal that is both refined and precise. This ideal is a spontaneous insight of Christian reflection, and it does not derive from any scholarly analysis. It is a concept we could willingly call popular and instinctive. It is basic, more basic that any academic construct, and it should be the primary object of our study. One must not fail to observe how deeply the speculation of intellectuals about the essence of holiness is grounded on the instinct of the Christian people. Since, after long experience the church

has authoritatively decided the conditions under which her children can be raised to the honors of the altar, it is appropriate to follow up these definitions—first intuitive, and then scholarly—with canonical formulae regarding sanctity.[18]

The concept of sanctity which Christians share is grounded on tradition from the past: the teaching of the gospel and the example of the saints. It arises, not from study, but from an intuitive insight. It is the task of theology to accept these concepts as given, and to give them clearer definition, correct them where necessary, integrate their various elements, and especially to differentiate what is essential from what is marginal or optional.[19]

People may mistakenly suppose that the church has an analytic checklist of the qualifications required for sanctity, against which it examines the recorded lives of the candidates: certain virtues, a rigorous consistency of character, the potency of miracles, and the like. In actuality, our process has been the reverse of that. We have beheld saints. We have seen them with our eyes and touched them with our hands and heard them with our ears and been awestruck at their luminous likeness to Jesus. Only after beholding them did we begin to reflect on what we saw and recognized. That reflection led eventually to the criteria which later authorities could use to verify sanctity in others who come along. But if you have seen a saint, and are a believer yourself, you should know her for a saint. It may take you some time and some care to portray her adequately. But your knowledge of what a saint is comes from your exposure to that person and to her intense dedication, not to theological treatises or sociological surveys. And this manifests what I have been trying to illustrate: that sanctity is in the eye of the beholder, and the primary beholder is the believing community.

Now let me offer two other illustrations of how moral wisdom is enacted and managed in the Christian tradition. The first is the controversy one century ago about the legitimacy of belonging to the Knights of Labor. The second is much more recent: the dispute over the moral acceptability of contraception.

THE KNIGHTS OF LABOR DISPUTE

To assess the conflict regarding the Knights of Labor in North America one must first be knowledgeable about the odium visited upon secret societies by the Roman See.

The origins of Freemasonry are usually dated back to 1717, but that era begat numerous fraternal organizations offering alternative allegiance to aristocrats, professionals, and bourgeois who were disaffected towards the increasingly activist exercise of authority by both national sovereigns and the established churches. Those who looked for a religion more amenable to rational discourse without priestcraft and dogma found these new societies refreshing, as did those who aspired to more popular forms of government with or without monarchy. Often it was the same men whose thoughts ran to both those restive hopes and looked for comrades with whom to ventilate their ideas more freely, beyond the ears of civil or ecclesiastical orthodoxy. As sometimes happens, the fraternities were organized into more levels of rank and honor than any sovereign's court, and created a pastiche of borrowed mystical lore and costume and ritual more exotic than anything to be seen in church.

The Freemasons found soaring success in both northern and southern Europe. By 1735 they were being outlawed in Holland; two years later Louis XIV forbade them in France; and in 1738 Pope Clement XII issued the first, fierce papal condemnation.[20]

Clement itemized four reasons why Freemasonry was a threat to both church and state. First, their mixed composition put Catholics indiscriminately into fellowship with members of many religious affiliations (all heretical). Second, the Deism which pervaded the organization refused to countenance divine revelation, church authority, or even divine intiatives towards humankind; its adherents saw no need for dogmatic belief so long as a sound morality was fostered. Third, members bound themselves by a solemn oath which created an allegiance so strong it overrode prior obligations to princes and prelates. Lastly, the aims and doings of the Masons were surrounded by a palisade of sworn secrecy. Catholics were forbidden on pain of excommunication either to join or to associate with the Freemasons, and Catholic rulers were instructed to suppress the organization with the rigor appropriate to a virulent heresy.

Clement's apostolic constitution was brief and to the point. It made clear that what made the masonic lodge so seditious civilly and so impious religiously was the creation, by solemn compact and closely shared secrecy, of a comradeship that competed with both state and church for their members' primary loyalty.

Ten years later the great jurist-pope, Benedict XIV, published his own prohibition. It was being noised about that since he had never explicitly reiterated the action of his predecessor it was no longer in force. Rumor went further to suggest that perhaps the pope himself had joined the Lodge on the sly. Benedict ratified the clementine constitution and reprinted it word-for-word. His summary of Clement's bill of particulars, however, alters its lineaments somewhat. He makes little of masonic religious tenets or rituals, but much of their secrecy. They clearly have something to hide, he infers, quoting the adage from Minucius Felix: "Decency can always take a public bow, but crime has to enjoy its satisfactions out of sight." The oath of solidarity is odious, he says, because it prevents legitimate authorities from exercising any scrutiny or control.[21]

By the early nineteenth century there were many fraternal societies gaining in size and influence. Their membership was broader and less elite, and they were especially successful in recruiting from populations that were restive under foreign rule. Italy was an ideal venue, with nationalist sentiment high in regions occupied by French or Austrian troops. The Papal States were also vulnerable to democratic discontent. The Carbonari and Giuseppe Mazzini's Young Italy were two rival societies appealing to Italian patriots. And this provoked fresh disapproval from Rome. Pius VII, once he was free from abuse by Napoleon, issued an apostolic constitution excommunicating the Carbonari in 1821.[22] He spoke more broadly, however, of numerous "secret and clandestine sects." Their secrecy was reminiscent of the underground style of heretics. Their rancor against lawful authority (an understandable issue in a Europe heading imminently towards riot and revolt) is more explicitly deplored than in the papal documents of the previous century. The clandestine movements, Pius warns, have branded all rulers as tyrants to be overthrown. Besides invoking the penalties of Clement and Benedict, Pius adds that no one enrolled in forbidden secret societies may be reconciled as a penitent until he identifies the rest of the membership to his local bishop. Also, now that the secret societies have gone public, at least for recruitment and propaganda purposes, Catholics will incur excommunication even by reading their printed literature.

Four years later Leo XII reprinted all the preceding condemnations along with his own.[23] Secret sects, he warns, are pledged to destroy the lawful power of the Catholic religion. Along with their great success (some estimates reckon more than a half-million adherents in Italy at that time) has come a strident insolence. Their oath of secrecy—sanctioned by a death penalty, the pontiff claims—is especially derisory since it is sworn by a god who, by their sectarian doctrine, does not exist. Leo then pursues a new line of criticism. The societies have undertaken an astute appeal for public respect. Their program, they say, is one of social welfare and philosophical inquiry. That goes down well with the public, and as far as members at the lower degrees are aware, it is why they joined. But the ulterior agenda of the governing elites is ruthlessly and aggressively dedicated to the overthrow of the social order, civil and religious.

The next two popes echoed this refrain in their inaugural encyclicals: Pius VIII in 1829 and Gregory XVI in 1832.[24] Gregory in particular begins to show that it is the rejection of papal superintendence by both totalitarian rulers and secular republican governments that makes the secret societies' independence all the more galling. He and his successors, Pius and Leo, all deplore the prospect of states where the Catholic Church is not officially established. Princes, of course, had always done as they pleased, but not since Philip the Fair and John of Paris in 1302 had theoretical claims to independence been so bluntly formulated.

Only two years before the convulsions of 1848 Pius IX

contributed his anathema.[25] Later, in 1884, a date quite significant for our interests, Leo XIII devoted an entire encyclical
letter, *Humanum Genus,* to the Freemasons whom he vilified as
the leadership of a worldwide coalition of united, vehement
malice "pernicious no less to Christendom than to the State."[26]
Leo was the first to see the secret societies with an economic
agenda, which he linked to socialism and communism.

He repeats all the old themes but it is clearer now how the
entire clandestine movement (of which he sees Freemasonry
as but one element) is, by its oath of unquestioning obedience,
a direct antagonist of the church.

> As a convenient manner of concealment, they assume the
> character of literary men and scholars associated for purposes
> of learning. They speak of their zeal for a more cultured refine-
> ment, and of their love for the poor; and they declare their one
> wish to be the amelioration of the condition of the masses, and
> to share with the largest number all the benefits of civil life.[27]

But to exact from its membership a disciplined, servile
obedience in order to achieve the utter overthrow of the religious order only shows that its social program is mere camou-
flage. By denying the possibility of dogma or religious authority
they attempt to delegitimate the officers of the church as actors
in the public forum. Their repudiation of eternal life yields a
moral doctrine that is religion-free and naive about original sin
and the handicapped state of the human will. They assert that
marriage is a matter for the state, not the church, and that it is
a contract dissoluble at will. They believe that political power
resides in the people, who have the right to depose rulers they
no longer desire.

As alternatives to these godless associations the pope suggests the Third Order of St. Francis, a lay movement associated
with the spirituality of the Poverello, or workmen's associations "under the auspices and patronage of the bishops."[28]

What we behold here is a classic instance of a moral judgment articulated by church authority. It is rooted in an evidentiary assessment of character. The pontiffs go out of their way
to insist that despite the secluded and private nature of these
societies they, the popes, had familiarized themselves with

their constitutions and rituals, and that disclosures by defectors had laid bare the ultimate designs of the leadership. It deserves to be said that the papacy was quite accurate in perceiving in the Freemasons, especially in the Latin countries, an abiding and active hostility to the Christian religion. The matter of interest here is how Rome came to present its case to the laity.

One cannot avoid noticing that the outlawed associations are increasingly depicted as rivals. They offer alternatives to all of the elements of the Catholic Church: a competing, sworn allegiance; a bonding ritual; a dogmatic account of the human situation in the world; a moral code; an exclusive claim to authority which resists any other, especially any which claims divine establishment; a system of discipline and sanction; a social program overshadowed by transcendent purposes. The church is alarmed by a popular challenger, competing for the primary allegiance of the burgesses of Christendom.

What had begun, however, as the condemnation of one specific society eventually targeted a *kind* of institution.[29] As the grievance becomes more generic, opposing first an institution and later a movement, it is typical that among the various elements or traits of the offending entity, one or two would emerge as definitory. Specific condemnations need reasons; but generic condemnations need definitions as well. This inevitably affects both the rhetoric and the vocabulary of the moral doctrine. In this case it was the oath and the secrecy that became highlighted as essential.

This identification of telltale signs of evil is all the more needful because later popes were insisting that the subversive sects were so cunning that the average Catholic would tend to be deceived when confronted by their publicity. The two elements that adequately betray sinister character and intent became the oath (which commits a member to unquestioning obedience) and the secrecy (which insulates that obedience from supervision by any lawful authority). Thus the long and articulate condemnation becomes known as "the church's outlawing of secret societies." If they are covert, you know enough to be sure they are godless and subversive.

It is significant that in its origins the moral assessment of these fraternal organizations spread its findings on the page:

the reader was asked to take note of the data which give rise to the papal judgment. But at a certain point that changed. The popes instructed the faithful that they were no longer to try to join in the assessment; they needed only to obey. For the movement had proven too cunning and deceptive for the public to be able to judge it capably. It was precisely at this point (Leo XII in 1825) that the tradition was transformed. Until then the character and purposes and drift of the brotherhoods were presented alongside the account of their tactics. Thereafter the evidence was separated from the conclusion. The faithful were no longer enjoined to observe how these indicators embodied those pursuits. It would now be enough to verify that the indicators (the oath and secrecy) were present for a Catholic to reject an organization as seditious and diabolic.

This was the traditional message of official Catholic moral doctrine in 1884, the year of Leo XIII's encyclical, *Arcanum*. It was an eventful year for fraternal societies in North America. The senior Catholic churchman in Canada was waiting for Rome to issue the judgment he had requested on the Knights of Labor. The Knights of Labor had an oath of membership and a sworn obligation to secrecy. They thus encountered a *prima facie* suspicion of being an organization forbidden to Catholics. That same year all the Catholic bishops in the United States assembled in the Third Plenary Council of Baltimore and decided not to condemn the Knights of Labor.[30]

Fraternal organizations came to America in the nineteenth century and found an eager welcome. Arthur Schlesinger estimates that between 1880 and 1890 there were perhaps 490 secret societies established in this country, with a membership that would swell to six millions.[31] Just as their elder counterparts in Europe had appealed to the aspirations of the aggrieved and oppressed, there was a ready constituency for secret fraternities among the American Irish, whose resentment of British occupation (and perhaps of all rulers) had not been left behind by the emigrants. There was also an interest in such organizations among the labor force, as industrial conflict grew. The Fenians and the Ancient Order of Hibernians were two of the many groups that rallied Irish sentiment, while the Molly Maguires were both Irish and laborite. Catholic clergy in America, alarmed by Gaelic insubordination and industrial violence, grew nervous. Rome was appealed to and the Fenians were condemned. Investigations were opened into the acceptability of the Modern Woodmen, Knights of the Maccabees, Improved Order of Red Men, Knights of Pythias (condemned), Odd Fellows (condemned), Sons of Temperance, Knights of St. Crispin (a shoemakers union), the Grand Army of the Republic, and others. Perhaps more authoritative than papal condemnations were those by parish priests from their local pulpits, bringing high feelings to many local churches.

The Noble and Holy Order of the Knights of Labor of America stood at the confluence of several traditions. They were a labor union with Irish-Americans notable among the leadership. Organized in 1869, their growth was prodigious: from 20,000 members in 1879 to over 700,000 in 1886. Two-thirds were said to be Catholics. Terence Vincent Powderly, the mayor of Scranton, was elected in 1879 as their chief executive—Grand Master Workman—an office he would hold for the fourteen most turbulent years of the Knights' existence.

The Order had an oath committing members to obedience and to secrecy, a ritual faintly reminiscent of those of Freemasonry and the Knights of Pythias, and an inclination to irreverence for established authorities. Some Catholic clergy quickly smelled the scent of the Lodge and refused the sacraments to parishioners who belonged.

This led to a major factional conflict among the Catholic hierarchy, of which only the broad course of events is germane to our inquiry here. Archbishops Taschereau (later Cardinal) of Quebec, Kenrick of St. Louis, Salpointe of Santa Fe, and (though ambivalently) Corrigan of New York, and bishops Healy of Portland (Maine), McQuaid of Rochester, and Chatard of Vincennes sought an explicit condemnation of the Order as a secret society. Archbishops Gibbons (later Cardinal) of Baltimore, Lynch of Toronto, and Ireland of St. Paul, and bishops Keane of Richmond and Gilmour of Cleveland argued against any condemnation. Rome at first ruled (in 1884, responding to Taschereau's inquiry) that membership was forbidden and later, after Gibbons' presentation of a strong majority stance by the U.S. bishops, receded to the point of decreeing that membership in the Knights could be tolerated, provided the Order amended its constitutional documents somewhat.[32]

That the Knights never did revise their documents to suit the Vatican, but for other reasons entered thereafter into a swift decline, is incidental to our interest. The episode was significant for two reasons that quite transcended the fortunes of that fraternal union. The position defended by Gibbons and his allies put the United States hierarchy aggressively on record in behalf of the right and need of workers to act collectively in their own interests. Although Rome gave them scant satisfaction in their specific effort, their advocacy was to be a major influence on the perspective of Leo XIII, whose previous encyclicals (somewhat like those of his predecessor) in defense of the lawful social order were to be followed by *Rerum novarum* (1891) which pleaded eloquently that no social order could be tolerable unless workers had standing and institutionalized power to secure their own rightful welfare.

The second outcome of the Knights of Labor conflict has received no mention in studies of the controversy, but it has relevance to our inquiry into the way the church elaborates its moral wisdom. The conflict was an instance of a moral judgment that had originated in community experience, then had been codified for transmission through the tradition in a way that eventually severed it from its original insight, and finally encountered challenge by observant churchmen who could not square it with their moral estimate.

The two groups of bishops differed, of course, in their moral judgments, but more interesting than their respective conclusions on the merits of the case were their very different modes of proceeding.

The critics of the Knights began with the conviction that their people needed a decision from them, and must not be left without pastoral direction. Elzéar-Alexandre Taschereau, years before he was aware of a single member of the Knights of Labor in his archdiocese of Quebec, prevailed upon Rome for a ruling which he forthwith published. The record abounds in Irish pastors burdened by the obligation to decide whether to permit their parishioners to become members. Gibbons, by contrast, sought to slow down the rush to judgment by what he called a "masterly inactivity."[33] His party did not want to decide whether laypeople could or could not enroll. Also, while the critics thought such an issue ought be decided by the Holy See, the advocates preferred to have it resolved at home by those directly involved. There was this wide gulf between their estimates of how determinative their pastoral office should be.

There is further significance in the evidence on which the two parties grounded their arguments. The critics went by the book. Taschereau submitted the current constitutions of the Order (actually they were already outdated) as his only exhibit. To assess that booklet against the various papal statements would have to be an act of documentary analysis, a legal judgment.

Gibbons' *plaidoyer* was quite different. Yes, it was a fact that Catholics were in fellowship with Protestants in the Order. The actual result, however, was not religious indifference but a helpful influence by the Catholics on the Protestant minority. Yes, it was a fact that there were rituals that smacked of masonic hokum. In practice, though, they were not the carriers of Deism or any other religion. They were simply quaint solemnities no one would ever confuse with what he did in church. Yes, there was an oath and a commitment to secrecy. But the oath had been changed to a promise in order to allay ecclesiastical misgivings, and Knights were permitted to breach their secrecy in the privacy of the confessional. Knowledge of the people, Gibbons argued, must govern interpretation of the facts: it showed that the oath and promise were, in the case of the Knights, no evidence of impiety or sedition. The Order required solidarity and confidentiality, not to put it beyond the reach of church or state, but as a protective measure against reprisals by employers. Yes, they sometimes resorted to the strike and the closed shop and the boycott, but as countervailing measures against punitive dismissal, the lockout, and unfair wages. They were not to be condemned by a different standard than had been imposed on ownership and management. Gibbons offered a personal appraisal of the religious sincerity and practice of Powderly and other union leaders as evidence of the character of the organization itself. Yes, the Order was not a Catholic association run by the church, but Gibbons stated sternly that that was just as well:

> I sincerely admire the efforts of this sort which are made in countries where the workers are led astray by the enemies of religion; but thanks be to God, that is not our condition. We find that in our country the presence and explicit influence of the clergy would not be advisable where our citizens, without distinction of religious belief, come together in regard of their industrial interests alone.[34]

In brief, one group of bishops was using naked documentary evidence to show that the papal excommunication devised against Freemasonry applied to the Knights of Labor. The other group appealed to its immediate, pastoral acquaintance with the workers and their leaders as the appropriate pivot of interpretation on which any moral appraisal of their organization should turn. Archbishop Riordan of San Francisco said it plainly: "The majority are honest men who apart from this association know no other means of attaining their rights."[35] The advocates of the Knights were nineteenth-century prelates, and were surely disposed to reverence a tradition of papal teaching. They were emboldened to confront that tradition because what they knew of these people obligated them to reexamine the received wisdom of the past. The men they saw did not qualify for the odium of popes.

A procedure that is authoritarian and canonical stands over against one that rests on a pastoral assessment of character. James Healy of Portland, the most persistent foe of the labor union, said not untypically that his was a policy "of obeying first, and asking questions afterwards."[36] By contrast, Frenchman Benoît-Marie Cardinal Langénieux, who had received his red hat with Taschereau and Gibbons, praised the latter's initiative: "What an honor it is for the church which finds itself so officially and publicly become again the protectress of the humble and the poor, of those above all whom modern industry has thrown so cruelly into wretchedness through the excesses of its prosperity."[37] Gibbons insists that the Knights may be judged only after consideration of their context:

> It may suffice to mention only that monopolies on the part of both individuals and of corporations, have already called forth not only the complaints of the working classes, but also the opposition of our public men and legislators; that the efforts of these monopolists, not always without success, to control legislation to their own profit, cause serious apprehension among the disinterested friends of liberty; that the heartless avarice which, through greed of gain, pitilessly grinds not only the men, but particularly the women and children in various employments, makes it clear to all who love humanity and justice that it is not only the right of the laboring classes to protect themselves, but the duty of the whole people to aid them in finding a remedy against the dangers with which both civilization and the social order are menaced by avarice, oppression and corruption.[38]

Gibbons implies that the decrees repudiating clandestine fraternities, which had come to be generically understood as a condemnation of secret societies, were inapplicable to this labor union although it was a secret society. A ruling passively accepted from the tradition and legally applied without making active moral appraisals in the present is bound to go wrong. In a word, Gibbons' argument provoked his contemporaries to honor the tradition of moral judgment by becoming its active trustees and by engaging in the same kind of experiential appraisal when applying a point of moral wisdom that had led its originators to formulate it in the first place. It is as strenuous and discriminating a task to apply moral wisdom from the past as it is to enact it for the future.

Clement XII and his successors perceived the church threatened by an upbeat Freemasonry with a power struggle for the primary loyalties of the more willful classes in the Old and New Worlds. James Gibbons and those pastors who supported him were stating on their own say-so—that is, they were vouching for what they had witnessed—that despite *prima facie* appearances, this was not at stake in the Knights of Labor.

THE BIRTH CONTROL CONTROVERSY

Our final story is not yet complete. The lessons it yields for our purposes arise from the history of a relatively small papal advisory group that met from 1963 to 1966. The issue contemplated was the morality of contraception.

The birth control commission, as it was commonly known, had the attendance and advice of John Noonan just as he was publishing his great historical study, *Contraception*.[39] The commission's own chapter in that ongoing serial which has as yet no finale is capably told by Robert Kaiser, one of the two or three most effective journalists at Vatican II. His account, *The Politics of Sex and Religion*,[40] is the other documentary source for our inquiry.

Let Noonan's masterful (one should say magisterial) reconstruction suffer here a summary. The earliest Christians had few developed convictions about sex. The esteem for fecundity inherited from Israel had been doubly moderated by the Old Testament's wariness of some features of sex (e.g., incest, adultery, homosexuality, bestiality) and the New Testament's innovative appreciation for widowhood and virginity. The rabbinical prohibitions of certain sexual practices (such as intercourse during menstruation, or withdrawal), though without counterpart in Christian moral lore of the early years, may reflect a tradition not entirely dormant in the synagogue's cousin, the church.

That community was goaded to elaborate its own sexual ethic, however, by two attitudes it found repulsive: Roman society's indifference to promiscuity and to the unborn, and Gnosticism's distaste for procreation. Gnosticism, an elusive amalgam of austerity and licentiousness, was anti-marriage, anti-fertility, and anti-law. In their reaction the Christian intellectuals of the second century drew on the slender resources of scripture, but found readier help in the Stoic teaching that marriage was for procreation. The Stoics' premium on rationality had obliged them to resolve how an act as passionate as sexual intercourse could be licit. Their answer was that procreation was what made sex good. Christians came to adopt that view, and to frown therefore on intercourse disabled by infertility (during pregnancy or after menopause or through contraception). Their fierce opposition to abortion, at a time when biological competence could not distinguish accurately between it and contraception, was an added reason for them to disallow the latter. Thus it was that explicit repudiations of contraception first emerged in the Christian literature of the third century.

Two centuries later that doctrine was called up to oppose the anti-sexual preaching of the Manichees. The borrowed Stoic rule found new eloquence in the polemics of Augustine. Against an anti-procreational ethic he found both sex and procreation good—by being utterly identified with each other. And among the three benefits of marriage—offspring (*proles*), fidelity (*fides*), and indissolubility (*sacramentum*)—it was the first he usually designated as fundamental.

It was Augustine's awesome usage of the Stoic doctrine that the only purpose of conjugal intercourse was procreation which gave it authority for ages to follow. Noonan observes that the teaching had little occasion to draw on personal and pastoral experience, with the obvious exception of Augustine's eleven-year liaison with his mistress, an experience he never regarded as one of unselfish love on his part. Augustine's doctrine failed to incorporate major themes of the faith. Neither love nor friendship nor affection, for instance, was related to sexuality. Had Chrysostom, who taught that it was love which validated sex, become the classical authority instead, or even been remembered as a valuable supplement to an incomplete presentation, the Christian moral teaching might have developed differently.

For centuries this doctrine was handed on by the monks, who were both the pastors and the scholars of Christian Europe. They evinced little appreciation for marriage and much distrust of sex. The tradition made its way thither into the penitentials and thence into the codifications of canon law, acquiring along the way an apparatus of penalties for every manner of sexual misbehavior intended to avoid pregnancy.

The threat of the Cathars (or Albigensians), who in the

twelfth century revived the old repugnance to marriage and sex, put the traditional Catholic doctrine in bold face. Procreation was good: so good that it made sex good and even mitigated the sinfulness of the attendant enjoyment and pleasure (for which the still-Stoicized tradition could find no other apology). It seems amazing that a church so persistently in favor of sex should have been so ill at ease with its carnal joy.

A change set in. The schoolmen of the High Middle Ages began to pursue insights at odds with the Augustinian synthesis. Albert the Great put forth a little-noticed suggestion that intercourse to reinforce the bond of marriage might be licit without reference to fecundity. Something other than procreation was being proposed as validating sex. His pupil Aquinas caused a bigger stir when he defended Aristotle's dictum that delight which proceeds from any act shares the moral value of the act itself. This new sympathy to sexual pleasure found a following among other scholars like Bonaventure.

> All of this rearrangement of values into a synthesis permitting or favoring contraception was possible.... The doctrine on sexuality, as it stood, was a balance—not the logical projection of a single value, but a balance of a whole set of competing values. The balance was weighted at a particular point which excluded contraception. If it held where it did at the height of the Middle Ages, the influence of St. Augustine, the reaction to the Cathars, and the mating habits of the age were together responsible. It was not inevitable that the balance remain so. In what follows we shall see a gradual shift.[41]

Denis the Carthusian in the fifteenth century wrote *The Praiseworthy Life of the Married*, with positive regard for sexual enjoyment. Noonan introduces us to a remarkable contemporary, Martin Le Maistre, who bolted radically from the Augustinian doctrine. Virtue being moderation, he says, conjugal chastity must pursue a middle course between incontinence and insensibility. It is quite right to relish pleasure, provided it does not obliterate other considerations. The older doctrine, he grieves, had done harm. Though Martin made no disciples, his was "a sweeping legitimation of the nonprocreational purposes of marriage." Noonan sees here a shift in method.

The key is the experience of Christian couples. When Augustine found in his acquaintance not a single couple who had intercourse only for procreation, he was not in the least deterred from stamping all nonprocreative purpose as sinful. In the different Christian community of fifteenth-century France—much more established in its traditions than that of fifth-century North Africa, and innocent of advocates of Manicheanism—a different approach is valued. On another subject of much importance to the laity, usury, Christian moralists were beginning to look to the custom and practice of good Christian merchants in determining whether a particular contract was sinful. Similarly Le Maistre ... invoke[s] the experience of Christian married folk to determine workable rules for intercourse, and urge[s] the perils of negative reaction that an unrealistic harshness may engender.[42]

Eventually the new view became established. The old pessimism inherited from Augustine waned even more among Catholics because of the favor he enjoyed among the Reformers. The Augustinian revival among the Jansenists only fortified the new theory among the Catholics, which found an authoritative new synthesis in the work of Alphonsus Liguori, the experienced pastor who made it settled doctrine that the purposes of marriage were the purposes of marital intercourse. Writers began to relate sex to pleasure, to health, even to love.[43]

The thinkers who were freeing marital intercourse from its single-purpose destiny, however, were still continuing to hand on intact the ancient ban on contraception.

At the close of the seventeenth century the Holy See began to criticize and sometimes to condemn some of the innovations, but speculation continued. It was in that century that authors for the first time opined that economic need might justify denying the marital debt to one's spouse in order to avoid pregnancy.

The seventeenth and eighteenth centuries were notable, not for any further development of doctrine but for the increasing frequency with which confessors were advised they need not interrogate or disturb penitents whom they supposed were using contraception. This was, at the least, a policy of pastoral diffidence.

The last episode in Noonan's narrative, one as decisive as Augustine or Aquinas or Liguori, was inaugurated by the nineteenth century birth control movement, the abrupt population increase due to public health improvements, and the advances in contraceptive technology. Catholic clergy went out to meet this "godless materialism" as belligerently as they had campaigned against the Gnostics, Manichees, and Cathars. This eventually culminated in *Casti Connubii*, the enyclical letter of Pius XI in 1930. The document was faithful to the primitive sexual doctrine but not to its historical development. All the themes were there: the Hebrew favor for procreation, the anti-Gnostic teaching, Augustine's marital goods with offspring still in first place, Thomas on the biologically determined nature of intercourse, and Onan as the founder and namesake of birth control.

The rigor of *Casti Connubii* was attenuated twenty years later when Pius XII countenanced rhythm for medical, eugenic, economic, or social motives. It was the development of chemical anovulants in the 1960s that was destined to push Rome beyond its theological supply lines.

When bishops throughout the world were submitting their requests for agenda items to be considered at Vatican II, not a single one asked for the birth control ban to be reconsidered. This may have been an indicator, however, not of low interest but of low expectation. For it was during the conciliar years that bishops, theologians, pastors, and articulate laypeople displayed impatient and restive dissatisfaction with the papal teaching.

Those voices were heard in St. Peter's basilica, and the bishops there drafted an astonishingly permissive enactment. Pope Paul VI succeeded in having the document docked on the strength of his commitment to a thorough study by an expert commission. Before considering what transpired within that group let us give ear once more to John Noonan, whose narrative leaves off just at that point.

The lay voice on marriage was never entirely lost after the fifteenth century, when it played a part in framing the new doctrine on the purposes of marital intercourse. It was not much listened to. When Bishop Bouvier [in the early nineteenth century] cited the belief of younger couples of Le Mans that contraception was not a sin, the testimony of the laity never rose to the dignity of an argument that contraception was lawful, but was used to support the plea that their good faith not be unsettled. The laity spoke, but their testimony was individual, oral, unsystematic, and not expressed in theological categories. To most theologians it failed to be persuasive or even relevant.[44]

John XXIII had quietly appointed an advisory group shortly before he died. Called eventually the Commission for the Study of Population, Family, and Birth, it was put to use by Paul VI and met for five sessions between October 1963 and June 1966. Paul added members at every gathering. The charter group of six European social scientists grew to an international crowd of seventy-one: demographers, psychologists and sociologists, physicians, moral and systematic theologians, diocesan bishops, officials of the curia, and three married couples.[45]

When the commission met first in 1963, no Catholic prelate or theologian or lay leader anywhere in the world had yet stated publicly that contraception judiciously used was morally acceptable. That was true of these people as well. Yet when they submitted their report to Paul VI less than three years later they had, by a substantial and vigorous majority, determined that contraception was not intrinsically illicit, that the position taken by *Casti Connubii* should be rescinded, that birth control could be integrated with the most abiding Christian values of marriage and childbearing, and that the misdirection of official Catholic teaching on this subject should swiftly be corrected. How then was it that so varied and responsible a task force underwent so unforeseen and drastic a change?

First, one must note that they claimed for their deliberations a free and frank exchange. In early sessions members assumed their participation would be limited by the discreet deference due to any explicit papal policy. Soon they resolved that they must send up their own best convictions as advice and no longer calculate how the pope was going to receive it. From that day the commissioners not only spoke their minds, they found their minds. In the very liberty of debate they came to clarify and affirm convictions long held subliminally but never openly known or shared.

Second, each category of member functioned in its characteristic way. There were no mere layfolk present. Even the three married couples were each centrally involved in large marriage-related enterprises. Pat and Patty Crowley from Chicago, for instance, were founders and leading couple of the international Christian Family Movement, the first organization in the Catholic Action movement in which spouses belonged and functioned as couples. These three couples came less for witness to their own marital experience than as persons with intense and confidential exposure to many Catholic households. All the other professionals (mostly lay but some clerical) thought and spoke as persons giving access to vast human experience and opinion.

It is noteworthy that this mostly lay group was not the source of initiative in the commission. That came from the theologians. It was the theologians more than either the secular professionals or the bishops who were familiar with the history and official pronouncements of the past. It was these scholars of the tradition who questioned its inadequacies, re-articulated the question as it lurched forward, and at the end produced a position paper that could speak for the group. The theologians were, so to speak, the engineers of the commission's work.

But once prompted, the lay professionals gave the project most of its impetus. Pierre van Rossum, a Belgian physician from the original membership of six, was quick to criticize the clerical bias of the magisterium. "'You think of sex as something you must avoid in order to be faithful to your vocation. That's all right for you. But our vocation is to love one another.' They all knew what he meant by 'love.' "[46]

Albert Görres, a psychologist from Frankfurt, spoke more bitingly of a "celibate psychosis" that had rendered some moral theologians emotionally handicapped by unconscious reactions of resentment, envy, and aggression.[47] The Crowleys brought in two surveys they had conducted of their CFM membership: activist, devout, and procreative couples (average children per family: six). The evidence showed that most had tried rhythm valiantly but found it stunted their marital intimacy. About half had moved on to using the pill, which they did with no sense of wrongdoing.[48]

Washington psychiatrist John Cavanagh then displayed an extensive survey of his own in which 71 percent of the women responding (2,300 users of rhythm) asserted that their sexual desire was greatest precisely at the time of ovulation. Rhythm, he observed, is more psychologically harmful than other methods because it deprives a woman of the sexual embrace during the time of her greatest natural desire. "Abstinence as the only means of controlling conception has left Catholics immature emotionally and impoverished financially. . . . Serious psychiatric disorders have arisen as a result."[49] Demographers pointed out that abortion tended to be most used where contraception was least accessible.[50] One entire meeting was given to frank and moving testimony by women on the commission about how integral and effective sexual intercourse was as a nourishment of their marital affection.[51] The psychologists deplored what they perceived as a dualist view of sex as an animal act to be controlled by the spirit.[52] Had the Manichees emerged victorious after all? The lay evidence was especially sharp in accusing the church officials of combining an irrationally rigorous public standard with a private pastoral indulgence that kept couples on an infantile level. Lay believers were not asking for a permissive or lenient norm, only a valid one.[53]

It took this dam-burst of lay testimony to persuade the theologians that the conscientious, experienced convictions of the faithful are evidence of high authority in moral inquiry, and especially on the subject of marriage.[54]

The participation of the hierarchy in the commission was also characteristic. They proved not to be cogent defenders of the official teaching; few of them knew much of the history or the theology. But once exposed to the momentum of the lay participants (which was well underway by the time the bishops were added for the final session), and put at their ease by the finding of the theologians that the papal policy was modifiable, the cardinals and bishops reverted from prelates to pastors. Shehan of Baltimore, Döpfner of Munich, Dupuy of Albi, Zoa of the Cameroun, Dearden of Detroit, Reuss of Mainz, Suenens of Malines—they testified to their experience in the confessional, their canvass of parish priests, what they had learned from couples, and how that had led them to suspect the pope had somehow got it wrong, though they had never before said it to themselves in so many words. By contrast, the few prelates who held back from the gathering consensus were either in the pontifical establishment or dismayed at the prospect of approving a practice for which they had so willingly consigned offenders to hell in the past.[55]

It was not the bishops, in fact, who had the most stressful change to undergo. It was the theologians. At their first meeting (the commission's second) there was no convergence. At the next they rejected contraception: nine to five. At the fourth session they looked over the brink and then drew back. It was only at the extensive final session that, by a decisive majority, the theologians at last saw their way clear to accepting contraception as licit and responsible.

What made their journey so toilsome was that, while the lay experience of the present commanded immediate respect and the pastoral assessment of the lay testimony rather swiftly ratified those lay insights, for the scholars those experiences and appraisals of the present were insufficient. The scholarly calling was to submit that evidence to a twofold test. They had to see whether it was both coherent and inclusive: whether it honored all the major faith-insights about marriage, fidelity, and childbearing and did so without inner contradiction. And they had to verify that this conviction in the present was in communion with those haunting and prophetic insights of the past, which had marked the road of doctrinal development.

One might have expected the hierarchy to be slowest and most reluctant to accept a reversal of doctrine, but it was not so. Once freed from fear of reprisal for free thought and free speech (Vatican II had initiated this emancipation), their pastoral orientation made them quickly and honestly ready to reconsider.[56] Cardinal Heenan said it was the seeming abruptness of the theologians' reversal that made him hesitate.[57] But Heenan misperceived. The bishops who joined the new consensus did so through the course of one month at the last session; the theologians had needed three years to cover the same distance. The theologians had rightly heeded the lay testimony and that of the pastors. Those who lead valiant lives of service under the gospel are presumed to know what they are talking about, and the good shepherd must heed their voices. But the scholar must then apply critical and historical analysis. What unnerved Heenan was being present only at the finale when the scholars finally saw it all fall into place.

Together the commissioners gave their advice to the pope:

> The morality of sexual acts between married people takes its meaning first of all and specifically from the ordering of their actions in a fruitful married life: that is, one which is practised with responsible, generous and prudent parenthood. It does not then depend upon the direct fecundity of each and every particular act. Moreover, the morality of every marital act depends upon the requirements of mutual love in all its aspects. . . .
>
> More and more clearly, for a conscience correctly formed, a willingness to raise a family with full acceptance of the various human and Christian responsibilities is altogether distinguished from a mentality and way of married life which in its totality is egotistically and irrationally opposed to fruitfulness.[58]

THE COMMUNITY AND ITS SERVANTS

These have been three quite different stories: the recognition of sanctity, the vindication of independent working people keeping their own counsel, and the struggle to reconstrue conjugal sexuality. All three illustrate in helpfully distinct ways how moral wisdom emerges from the church's primal moral experience: assessing what becomes of people—ourselves and others—when they act in certain ways.

Pius IX, in the last days of heated dispute before the conciliar definition of papal infallibility when some cautioned that such a doctrine lacked adequate grounding in the tradition, was reported to have said: *La tradizione son' io,* "I am the tradition!"[59] For a pope, the statement is perhaps extravagant. But for the people, the church, it may not be.

The community's gaze will often be whistled up by those rare individuals called prophets: foretopmen who see first and far. But the community has its own inspiration and will follow the prophets with their sight and their insight. The saints will be there first. Pastors who preside will be reminding the community of its store of tried insight from the past. But the past is cue, not script, for the present. The tradition is dangerous in the hands of any generation that can only quote it without vouching for it. As any generation puts its ancestral moral wisdom to the test there will be new insights—or so it will seem. The scholars have their service especially at these moments of stress, to construe to the community the landscape and inscape of the older wisdom, to help them be humble enough to acquiesce in the abiding truth others left to them, and humble enough to accept as well those moments when they, and no one prior to them, must utter moral insights that give the tradition new nourishment.

There are, then, these three gifts that groom the ancestral wisdom: the charisms of prophecy, pastorate, and scholarship. But the title to ownership of the tradition is communal, never private. The primary wellspring of Christian ethical wisdom is the believing community's reflection on human experience and on the personal aftermath of that experience.

NOTES

1. James Tunstead Burtchaell, C.S.C., *Catholic Theories of Biblical Inspiration Since 1810: A Review and Critique* (Cambridge: Cambridge University Press, 1969), 289–294.

2. This point is most effectively expounded in George Lindbeck, "Scripture, Consensus, and Community," *This World* 23 (Fall 1988): 5–24.

3. Newman writes:

It is not a little remarkable, that, though, historically speaking, the fourth century is the age of doctors, illustrated, as it was, by the saints Athanasius, Hilary, the two Gregories, Basil, Chrysostom, Ambrose, Jerome, and Augustine, and all of these saints bishops also, except one, nevertheless in that very day the divine tradition committed to the infallible Church was proclaimed and maintained far more by the faithful than by the Episcopate.

Here, of course, I must explain:—in saying this, then, undoubtedly I am not denying that the great body of the Bishops were in their internal belief orthodox; nor that there were numbers of clergy who stood by the laity, and acted as their centres and guides; nor that the laity actually received their faith, in the first instance, from the Bishops and clergy; nor that some portions of the laity were ignorant, and other portions at length corrupted by the Arian teachers, who got possession of the sees and ordained an heretical clergy;—but I mean still, that in that time of immense confusion the divine dogma of our Lord's divinity was proclaimed, enforced, maintained, and (humanly speaking) preserved, far more by the "Ecclesia docta" than by the "Ecclesia docens"; that the body of the episcopate was unfaithful to its commission, while the body of the laity was faithful to its baptism; that at one time the Pope, at other times the patriarchal, metropolitan, and other great sees, at other times general councils, said what they should not have said, or did what obscured and compromised revealed truth; while, on the other hand, it was the Christian people who, under Providence, were the ecclesiastical strength of Athanasius, Hilary, Eusebius of Vercellae, and other great solitary confessors, who would have failed without them.

John Henry Newman, *On Consulting the Faithful in Matters of Doctrine*, ed. John Coulson (London: Collins, 1961 [first published 1859]), 75–76.

4. For what follows, see Peter Brown, *The Cult of the Saints: Its Rise and Function in Latin Christianity* (Chicago: University of Chicago Press, 1981); Hippolyte Delehaye [S.J.], *Sanctus: Essai sur le culte des saints dans l'antiquité* (Brussels: Société des Bollandistes, 1927); idem, *Les origines du culte des martyrs*, 2nd ed. (Brussels: Société des Bollandistes, 1933); idem, *Les passions des martyrs et les genres littéraires*, 2nd ed. (Brussels: Société des Bollandistes, 1966); Ludwig Hertling, S.J.,

"Materiali per la storia del processo di Canonizzazione," *Gregorianum* 16 (1935): 170–195; Eric Waldram Kemp, *Canonization and Authority in the Western Church* (London: Oxford University Press [Geoffrey Cumberledge], 1948); André Vauchez, *La sainteté en occident aux derniers siècles du moyen age d'après les procès de canonisation et les documents hagiographiques* (Rome: École Française de Rome, 1981).

5. Kemp, 151–170.

6. Acts 6–7. The first similar account published after the New Testament, the *Martyrdom of Polycarp* (+155 or 156) written as a letter by the church of Smyrna to the church of Philomelium and all the churches, likewise presents the death of the old bishop with many allusions to that of Jesus.

7. In the first story, that of Stephen, the only *martyres* mentioned by Luke are the perjurers who left their cloaks with Saul when they did their task of casting the first boulders, Acts 6:13, 7:59. But the New Testament knows Jesus himself as the great *martyr*, and it is he, not Stephen, who is the prototype.

8. It is interesting that just as the gospels began as accounts of Jesus' death and resurrection appearances, then were expanded by reminiscences of his ministry, and finally (in Matthew and Luke) by infancy and childhood narratives that bespoke his divine mission, so the first martyrdom narratives developed backwards, so to speak: the first accounts concentrated on the heroic death, and later accounts expanded to include the extraordinary dedication of the person's life.

9. *Stromateis*, 4:4.

10. There is also some evidence, though ambiguous, that confessors ranked with presbyters could actually function as such without ordination.

11. There is an interesting parallel between the apostles and prophets of the New Testament and the martyrs and confessors of the persecutions: the second party to each dyad was theoretically the peer of the first, but in practice seems not to have been treated so.

12. "Item placuit, ut altaria quae passim per agros, aut vias, tanquam memoriae martyrum constituuntur, in quibus nullum corpus, aut reliquiae martyrum conditae probantur, ab episcopis qui praesunt eisdem locis si fieri potest evertantur; si autem hoc per tumultus populares non sinitur, plebes tamen admoneantur ne illa loca frequentent, ut qui recte sapiunt nulla ibi superstitione devincti teneantur. Et omnino nulla memoria martyrum probabiliter accepetetur, nisi ubi corpus aut aliquae reliquiae sunt, aut origo alicujus

habitationis vel possessionis, vel passionis fidelissima origine traditur. Nam quae per somnia et inanes quasi revelationes quorumlibet hominum ubicumque constituuntur altaria, omnimodo improbentur." Christophorus Justellus, *Codex Canonum Ecclesiae Africanae* (Paris: Pacard, 1614), 212–213; Giovanni Domenico Mansi, *Sacrorum Conciliorum Nova et Amplissima Collection*, 2nd ed. (Florence: A. Zatta, 1759–1798 [photocopy: Paris: Welter, 1901–1927]) 3:972; *Concilia Africae: A. 345–A. 525*, ed. C. Munier, *Corpus Christianorum*, Series Latina 144 (Turnhout: Brepols, 1974): 204.

13. "LI. Deinceps vero corpora sanctorum de loco ad locum nullus transferre praesumat sine consilio principis, vel episcoporum, et sanctae synodi licentia." Mansi, 14:63. For the wide currency of these canons see Kemp, 15,38–42.

14. Hippolyte Delehaye, *The Work of the Bollandists through Three Centuries, 1615–1915* (Princeton: Princeton University Press, 1922).

15. Kemp, 145.

16. 13 March 1625: "1,4. Declarans, quod per suprascripta, praejudicare in aliquo non vult, neque intendit iis, qui aut per communem Ecclesiae consensum, vel per immemorabilem temporis cursum, aut per Patrum, virorumque Sanctorum scripta, vel longissimi temporis scientia, ac tolerantia Sedis Apostolicae, vel Ordinarii coluntur," C. Cocquelines, *Magnum Bullarium Romanum: Bullarum, Privilegiorum ac Diplomatum Romanorum Pontificum Amplissima Collectio* (Rome: Mainard, 1739–62 [photocopy: Graz: Akademische Verlag, 1964–66] 5,5 (318).

17. Kemp, 7.

18. Delehaye, *Sanctus*, 233.

19. Ibid., 244.

20. Clement XII, Apostolic Constitution *In Eminenti*, 28 April 1738; *Bullarum Diplomatum et Privilegiorum Sanctorum Romanorum Pontificum Taurinensis Editio*, ed. A. Tomassetti 24 (Turin: Vecco, 1872): 366–367.

21. Benedict XIV, Apostolic Constitution *Providas*, 18 March 1751, *Benedicti Papae XIV Bullarium* 3,8 (Mechlin: Hanicq, 1827): 417–425.

22. Pius VII, Apostolic Constitution *Ecclesiam*, 15 September 1821; *Bullarii Romani Continuatio*, ed. Andreas Barberi & Rainaldus Segreti, 15 (Rome: 1853): 446–448.

23. Leo XII, Apostolic Constitution *Quo graviora mala*, 13 March 1825; ibid., 16 (1854): 345–355.

24. See Pius VIII, Encyclical Letter *Traditi humilitati Nostrae*, 24

May 1829, par. 6, ibid., 18 (1856): 18–19; Gregory XVI, Encyclical Letter *Mirari vos*, 15 August 1832, par. 13–14,21, ibid., 19 (1857): 129–131.

25. See Pius IX, Encyclical Letter *Qui pluribus*, 9 November 1846, par. 10, *Acta Pii IX* 1 (Rome, 1854): 32–37.

26. Leo XIII, Encyclical Letter *Humanum Genus*, 20 April 1884, *Acta Sanctae Sedis* 16 (1884): 417–433. See par. 5.

27. Ibid., par. 9.

28. Ibid., par. 35.

29. This can be seen in the document which, in a way, brought to a close this series of documents: the 1918 *Code of Canon Law*. Canon 2335 prescribes: "Those who enroll in a masonic sect or in other associations of the same sort which conspire against the church or lawful civil authorities incur *ipso facto* an excommunication reserved simply to the Apostolic See."

30. For what follows, see Henry J. Browne, *The Catholic Church and the Knights of Labor* (Washington, DC: Catholic University of America Press, 1949); John Tracy Ellis, *The Life of James Cardinal Gibbons, Archbishop of Baltimore 1834–1921*, 1 (Milwaukee: Bruce, 1952): 439–546; Marvin O'Connell, *John Ireland and the American Catholic Church* (St. Paul: Minnesota Historical Society, 1988), 229–239; Fergus Macdonald, C.P., *The Catholic Church and the Secret Societies in the United States*, ed. Thomas J. McMahon, (New York: U.S. Catholic Historical Society, 1946).

31. Quoted in Ellis, 1:439.

32. The ruling read, in part: "In view of the latest statement of the case, the Society of the Knights of Labor may be allowed for the time being, provided whatever in its statutes is improperly expressed or susceptible of wrong interpretation shall be corrected. Especially in the preamble of the constitutions for local assemblies words which seem to savor of socialism and communism must be emended in such a way as to make clear that the soil was granted by God to man, or rather the human race, that each might have the right to acquire some portion of it, by use however of lawful means and without violation of the right of private property." Browne, 324.

Gibbons was meticulous in restricting his advocacy to the Knights in the United States; he specifically disclaimed any desire to interfere with the Canadian church and its discipline. This was his adroit way of rebuking Taschereau for having published his ruling from Rome as one that should apply below the border as well.

33. Ibid., 165.

34. Ibid., 370. This document, Gibbons' formal memorandum

to the Holy See, is also available in *Documents of American Catholic History*, ed. John Tracy Ellis, 2 (Wilmington: Glazier, 1987): 444–457.

35. Browne, 212.

36. Ibid., 257.

37. Ibid., 316–317.

38. Ibid., 368; Ellis, *Documents*, 448.

39. John T. Noonan, Jr., *Contraception: A History of Its Treatment by the Catholic Theologians and Canonists* (Cambridge, Mass.: Harvard University Press, 1965). An enlarged edition, adding an essay written in 1980, has been issued in 1986 by the same press.

40. Robert Blair Kaiser, *The Politics of Sex and Religion: A Case History in the Development of Doctrine, 1962–1984* (Kansas City, Mo.: Leaven, 1985).

41. Noonan, 300.

42. Ibid., 312.

43. In noticing how absent pastoral experience was from this tradition, Noonan remarks that any serious attention to the experience of married couples would have uprooted the entire Augustinian outlook, ibid., 24.

44. Ibid., 489.

45. Only a select number of the full commission was convoked for the decisive final session, however, so that the final statement was actually considered by a cohort comprising less than half the membership.

46. Kaiser, 45.

47. Ibid., 139. Görres was following up a remark made at the Council by Maximos IV Saigh, the Melkite Patriarch, when expressing dissatisfaction with the birth control ban: "And are we not entitled to ask if certain positions are not the outcome of outmoded ideas and, perhaps, a celibate psychosis on the part of those unacquainted with this sector of life? Are we not, perhaps, unwittingly setting up a Manichean conception of man and the world, in which the work of the flesh, vitiated in itself, is tolerated only in view of children? Is the external biological rectitude of an act the only criterion of morality, independent of family life, of its moral, conjugal and family climate, and of the grave imperatives of prudence which must be the basic rule of all our human activity?" ibid., 65–66. There was an exquisite irony that a doctrine originally established to combat the Manichees should now be diagnosed as suffering from their same affliction.

48. Ibid., 92–95, 135–136.

49. Ibid., 136–137.

50. Ibid., 150–151.

51. Ibid., 140–142.

52. Ibid., 151.

53. Ibid., 142–143.

54. Ibid., 57,137,142,158.

55. Ibid., 164–174.

56. This is not to say they did not need help. Kaiser records this sharp encounter, ibid., 167–168:

> [Cardinal] Heenan had already mentioned the Pope's fear: that a change in the church's teaching might damage the church's credibility. How, Heenan had asked, could the church change its stand and avoid losing its moral influence. Or, if the church did not change, how could it preserve its authority over couples? Now [Thomas Burch, a population expert from Georgetown University] stood up and called Heenan's stand "hypocrisy." Almost 20 years later, Burch told . . . about his feelings at the time. "I think my very strong reaction was, 'What the heck's going on here? You guys are saying that you might have been wrong for nigh on thirty to forty years on some details about methods; you've caused millions of people untold agony and unwanted children; brought on stresses and strains and tremendous feelings of guilt. You've told people they were going to hell because they wouldn't stop using condoms, and now you're saying maybe you're wrong. But you want to say it in such a way that you can continue to tell people what to do in bed?"

57. "Although my heart tells me that at almost any cost, we must bring relief to the magnificent Christian couples who are finding the discipline of the church intolerable, my head warns me against accepting too readily the arguments of converted theologians who now argue against the accepted doctrine. . . . theologians who until a few months ago, not twenty or thirty years ago, dogmatically taught the old doctrine," ibid., 167.

58. Ibid., 252. That the pope rejected the commission's work, and commissioned some of the minority to draft an encyclical much in line with *Casti Connubii*, does not diminish the significance of what transpired within the commuission. For comment upon the emergent encyclical, *Humanae Vitae*, see chapter four below.

59. The source is highly questionable: Johann Joseph Ignaz von Döllinger, writing from Rome under the pseudonym "Quirinus."

2

The Defining Ethic of the Earliest Church

THE ABORTION DEBATE in the United States that has centered around the 1973 decisions of the Supreme Court (*Wade*-and-*Bolton*) that voided all federal and state laws regulating abortion and, in effect, made abortion on demand legal at any time during pregnancy, has been carefully studied by scholars curious about the influence of religion on the various positions taken. There were surprises.

RELIGION RELATED TO ABORTION VIEWS

The popular assumption was that Catholics would be most opposed to the national consensus. That commonplace proved, on inspection, to be erroneous in several ways. The national consensus for nearly three decades now has, by a strong majority that varies from three-fifths to four-fifths, rejected abortion on demand. Since polls have been surveying public opinion on this question, the position set forth by the Supreme Court has never enjoyed the agreement of a national majority. A further disclosure was that Catholics varied only insignificantly from the consensus on abortion in general, and in particular on the acceptability of abortion under various circumstances, such as when a mother's life is imperiled, or when pregnancy has resulted from sexual crime, or in order to eliminate a handicapped child. Catholics have been at variance with the Court but in harmony with the national consensus. If one is intent on finding a religious group that polls found to be at odds with the consensus—consistently and by an almost polar opposition—it turns out to be not the Catholics but the Jews.

Judith Blake, the UCLA social scientist whose analyses of public opinion surveys on abortion during the 1960s and 1970s are the most authoritative, has drawn attention to another unanticipated result. The basic conflict of opinion among religionists, she has noticed, does not correspond simply to denomination. It is, of course, true that in recent years virtually every sizeable Protestant, Catholic, and Jewish community has issued its official statements of ethical doctrine and legal policy regarding abortion. Opinion surveys have repeatedly suggested that these policy utterances formulated by activist committees or headquarters staffs were sometimes noticeably at odds with the convictions of the memberships at large. But what Blake found is that religious affiliation is not a very reliable predictor of trenchant ("polar") prochoice or prolife convictions. The variable that counts most is religious practice, whatever one's denomination. Consistently prochoice people are typically inactive or marginal in their religious commitments, whereas determinedly prolife people tend to be active in the practice of their faith.[1]

A third departure from the anticipated correlations between religion and abortion has been provided by dissent and controversy among Catholic ethicists themselves. Contrary to common expectation and official teaching, there have been Catholic academics who seriously defend the moral acceptability of abortion.[2]

Among ethicists arguing from shared religious premises, reconstruction of the beliefs of the past is very significant. A community of belief that is in continuity and communion with its inspired ancestry requires of those who challenge any settled consensus that they present evidence and argument that appeal somehow to what is most abiding in the normative past. Theological history is being cited in this case by Catholic dissenters, not so much to allow abortion as to allow dissent. They argue from an old in-house Catholic rule which held that a body of respectable dissent could cast into doubt certain moral obligations on which there had otherwise been a firm and settled consensus. They have rummaged through history, cited miscellaneous exceptions to the continuing revulsion against abortion, and concluded that the church's past doctrine is not unanimous or unqualified enough to impose itself on our consciences today. For want of moral unanimity, it is now being argued, there can be no moral imperative. As Daniel Maguire sums it up: "Now, as ever, there is no one Christian view of the morality of abortion."[3]

Under close scrutiny that plea labors under at least three confusions. The first is evidentiary. Most misgivings in the Christian tradition regarding the morality of abortion have pivoted on the status and living integrity of the unborn. Once nineteenth-century discoveries of the process of conception and of gestational development dispelled the primitive uncertainties that dated back to classical Greek biology, Christian moralists forthwith set aside those earlier doubts. Another confusion is hermeneutical. For those who defer to a tradition as normative, the mere presence (or absence) of dissent cannot discredit (or certify) the received view. Not until one has interpreted the grounds for a doctrine's development and accounted historically for the swerve and the shunt of its trajectory can dissent be weighed and appraised. A third confusion is procedural. Partisans of this prochoice position have appealed to past dissent, not so much for its wisdom about abortion as for its procedural value as evidence that the question is still unresolved. It remains to be seen, by a closer examination of the way they are drawing on the past, whether their plea on behalf of abortion is actually derived from some persisting (though not yet ascendant) insight rooted in the inveterate insights of the community, or whether divergent opinions of the past are only being used to give cover of respectability to a doctrine that is really quite deviant from the tradition's native direction.

Those are questions I do not wish to explore further here. If one be guided by rules of method alone, such as the procedural rule used to assert that the abortion issue has never been settled within the Christian community, there is probably enough dissent scattered on the pages of the past to neutralize any Christian tenet or commitment you might choose. My inquiry is not procedural but substantive: What are the merits of the case? How authentic and how profoundly rooted in the normative documents of the Christian past is moral repugnance for abortion?

A Fourfold Imperative of the Earliest Christian Ethic

The men and women who first tried to follow the risen Jesus were Jews. They were not entirely unprepared for the moral demands their new allegiance would make on them. The Christian road followed terrain already familiar to Jewish moral teaching. Infidelity was to be avoided in all its forms: adultery, incest, and idolatry. They were never to take crafty advantage of others, by perjury or sorcery or usury. And they were to restrain themselves from all violence, whether by drunkenness, gossip, or murder. This ethical standard rests as firmly on rabbinical teaching as on the New Testament, which shows what a direct lineage there is from biblical and Hellenistic Judaism to early Christianity.

In the Sermon on the Mount Jesus invites his followers to go even further along this Way. It was not enough to spare your neighbor's life; you must not even hurl insult at him. If adultery was wrong, then so was lustful intent. And there was scant advantage from being a person of your sworn word if you were a chiseler whenever you were not on oath. Yet this prophetic summons to a righteousness higher than that of the scribes and Pharisees would have found strong endorsement in many of the better synagogues around Judaea or Galilee.

Christian moral doctrine showed from the first its direct descent from Jewish ethics. It was fitting, then, that its great breakaway point of departure would be a further pursuit of one of the teachings they most closely shared. Both synagogue and church taught that authentic religion meant coming to the aid of women and children deprived of breadwinners, and of those two other categories of the helpless: the indigent and the stranded aliens. Nothing could be more traditional for a Jew or more fundamental for a Christian than this ancient commitment to provide for the widow, the orphan, the pauper, and the stranger. Yet it was precisely here, on this point of ancient and familiar obligation, that the young Christian community found a distinctive vigor and vision, and set forth from its mother's house on a moral journey of its own.

The alien and the pauper, the widow and the orphan, classic beneficiaries of preferential sustenance since the Torah, were suggestive to the Jesus people of four other forlorn categories that they must safeguard: the enemy and the slave, the wife and the infant—unborn or newborn.

The resident alien had to be guaranteed shelter, for he dwelt defenseless within the national enclosure of the land and trusted its people. But the Christian was bidden to go far beyond protecting the nearby alien. He was charged to cherish the distant enemy. He had heard it said that he must love his neighbor and hate his enemy. Jesus told him he must love his enemy even at the risk of receiving hatred from both countryman and enemy. A disciple was to set no more bounds to her bounty than the Father who lavished sunshine and rainfall on all fields alike. Their pattern was the Lord Jesus who had loved to the death those who betrayed and denied and deserted and condemned and crucified him.

The poor were always a special charge on the Christian's conscience. But their endless needs suggested another, even more vulnerable, group. The novice Christians were told forthwith that for those "in the Lord," no one was any longer to be demeaned as mere property of another. Even slaves had to be dealt with as brothers and sisters in the Lord.

Every man was to join in supporting the wives his fellow believers had left behind as widows. But now he was startled to be told that he no longer had a male's freedom of choice to dismiss his own wife. Jesus' rejection of divorce affected men and women differently, since only husbands had previously been free to reject their partners. Now women could no longer be chosen and then discarded by their men. Both alike must now be faithful throughout life, if they loved and married in the Lord.

There were four radical, prophetic imperatives that the

new Christian faith set before those who would live in the
Spirit and fire of Christ: four disconcerting duties that would
distance them from Jews and Romans alike. First: the command
to love their enemies struck down forever their exclusionary
allegiance to a single race or nation. Second: the command to
acknowledge slaves and masters as brothers and sisters condemned slavery to a long and sullen retreat, and ultimately to
extinction. Third: the command that husbands and wives were
to pledge an equal fidelity was a first yet crucial rejection of the
corruption of men and women by their respective domination
and acquiescence. These were thunderclaps of moral exclama-
tion that bound the small and scrappy new fellowship to make
the very purpose of their lives the liberation of those most at a
loss.

CONDEMNATION OF ABORTION AND INFANTICIDE

And there was a fourth point of radical conversion, for
there was a fourth group of victims they had to embrace. Beyond the children orphaned by their parents' deaths were
those still more helpless children whom their parents slew
themselves.

The Jewish scriptures seem to have regarded the unborn
as paternal property. A monetary indemnity was due to the
father from anyone who caused his wife to abort. The rabbinical tradition, which sired the long legal continuity of later Judaism, is also relatively silent on the subject of abortion.

But at the time of Jesus there was an alternative Jewish
tradition, associated with the Greek idiom, that was articulat-
ing a strenuous prohibition against both abortion and infanticide. It was this Hellenistic Jewish moral tradition that was in
many respects to be both parent and sibling of the nascent
Christian belief.[4] Jews and their sympathizers were commonly
enjoined not to abort or to expose their children, but to bear
and rear them: the defense and nurture of the unborn and
newborn was put forth as a notable moral duty.

Hecataeus of Abdera writes:

[Moses] required those who dwelt in the land to rear their children [in contrast with the Greeks who exposed unwanted newborns].[5]

Pseudo-Phocyclides concurs:

A woman should not destroy the unborn babe in her belly; nor after its birth throw it before the dogs and the vultures as a prey.[6]

Philo of Alexandria gives this injunction:

He must not make abortive the generative power of men by gelding nor that of women by sterilizing drugs and other devices. . . . no destroying of their seed nor defrauding their offspring.[7]

Flavius Josephus deals with the same theme:

The Law orders all offspring to be brought up, and forbids women either to cause abortion or to make away with the foetus; a woman convicted of this is regarded as an infanticide, because she destroys a soul and diminishes the race.[8]

A Jewish portion of the *Third Sybil* joins the doctrine:

Foster your offspring instead of killing them: for the fury of the Eternal threatens one who commits such crimes.[9]

Roman law in the same era offered no protection against either abortion or infanticide, both of which were within the prerogatives of the male head-of-household. Neither tradition offered a protection for infants reliable enough to suit the first Christians, and they soon stated their own conviction which was to the point.

The most ancient Christian document we possess, besides the New Testament, is *The Didache, The Instruction of the Twelve Apostles.* Already in this first century catechism, the obligation to protect the unborn and the infant was included within the roster of essential moral duties:

You shall not commit murder; you shall not commit adultery; you shall not prey upon boys; you shall not fornicate; you shall not deal in magic; you shall not practice sorcery; you shall not murder a child by abortion, or kill a newborn; you shall not covet your neighbor's goods. You shall not break your oath; you shall not give perjured evidence; you shall not speak damagingly of others; you shall not bear a grudge.[10]

In a later passage the instruction describes what it calls "the way of death":

It is the path of those who persecute the innocent, despise the truth, find their ease in lying . . . those who have no generosity for the poor, nor concern for the oppressed, nor any knowledge of who it was who made them; they are killers of children, destroyers of God's handiwork; they turn their backs on the needy and take advantage of the afflicted; they are cozy with the affluent but ruthless judges of the poor: sinners to the core. Children, may you be kept safe from it all![11]

The Greek is as straightforward as my translation, bluntly choosing words like "kill" (*apokteinein*) and "murder" (*phoneuein*). Its word for abortion, *phthora*, means, literally, "destruction," and the one destroyed is called "child," *teknon*, the same gentle word used in the final sentence to address the readers themselves.[12]

Shortly before or after the turn of the second century, the *Letter of Barnabas* repeats the *Didache's* injunction against abortion and infanticide in virtually the same words, and laments that they destroy small images of God.[13]

The second century had not advanced far before the Christian movement had achieved momentum enough to arouse antagonism from Roman society. Some of the most articulate writers of that age were apologists defending their fellow Christians against libel. And one of the slanders that outraged them most was the rumor that Christians slew infants to obtain blood for their eucharistic rites. What made the lie particularly galling was the fact that protection of the young had become such a Christian priority. They did not conceal their contempt for the surrounding pagan society that was willing to destroy its young by choice.

One early apologist, writing in the *Letter to Diognetus*, notes that his fellow Christians stand out from their neighbors, not by citizenship or language or social style, but by their moral convictions.

> Every foreign land is their home, and every home a foreign land. They marry like all others and beget children; but they do not expose their offspring. Their board they spread for all, but not their bed. . . . They obey the established laws, but in their private lives they go well beyond the laws.[14]

Minucius Felix, a Roman attorney of African origin, states the contrast even more irascibly.

> There is a man I should now like to address, and that is the one who claims, or believes, that our initiations take place by means of the slaughter and blood of a baby. Do you think it possible to inflict fatal wounds on a baby so tender and tiny? That there could be anyone who would butcher a newborn babe, hardly yet a human being, who would shed and drain its blood? The only person capable of believing this is one capable of actually perpetrating it. And, in fact, it is a practice of yours, I observe, to expose your own children to birds and wild beasts, or at times to smother and strangle them—a pitiful way to die; and there are women who swallow drugs to stifle in their womb the beginnings of a human on the way—committing infanticide even before they give birth to their infant.[15]

The same rumor was challenged by Athenagoras of Athens. How could Christians be accused of murder when they refused even to attend the circus events where humans perished as gladiators or as victims of wild beasts? Christians consider, he wrote, that even standing by and tolerating murder is much the same as murder itself. He then continues:

> We call it murder and say it will be accountable to God if women use instruments to procure abortion: how shall we be called murderers ourselves? The same person cannot regard

that which a woman carries in her womb as a living creature, and therefore as an object of value to God, and then slay the creature that has come forth to the light of day. The same person cannot forbid the exposure of children, equating such exposure with child-murder, and then slay a child that has found one to bring it up. No, we are always consistent, everywhere the same, governed by the truth and not coercing it to serve us.[16]

Tertullian, a teacher in Rome, was perhaps the most eloquent of the second century apologists. He repeatedly opposed the teaching of the Stoics that children are not yet alive in the womb, and that their soul is given them at birth. Arguing from philosophical more than biological grounds, he insisted that the body and soul grow together from the beginning.

We have established the principle that all the natural potentialities of the soul with regard to sensation and intelligence are inherent in its very substance, as a result of the intrinsic nature of the soul. As the various stages of life pass, these powers develop, each in its own way, under the influence of circumstances, whether of education, environment, or the supreme powers.[17]

Abortion, he said, was not only homicide, it was parricide: the slaying of one's own flesh and blood.

With us, murder is forbidden once for all. We are not free to destroy anyone conceived in the womb, while the blood is still being absorbed to build up the human being. To prevent the birth of a child is simply a swifter way to murder. It makes no difference whether one destroys a soul already born or interferes with it on its way to birth. It is a human being and one who will be a human being, for every fruit is there present in the seed.[18]

Even in the case of a child whose uterine presentation makes birth impossible, when Tertullian would accept dismemberment to save at least the mother's life, he bluntly says the child is being "butchered by unavoidable savagery" (*trucidatur necessaria crudelitate*).[19]

Those were statements which Christians apologists were

making to outsiders. Among themselves, abortion continued to be reviled as a procedure unthinkable for believers. Clement of Alexandria, perhaps the leading theologian of the second century, wrote:

> If we would only control our lusts at the start, and if we would refrain from killing off the human race born or developing according to the divine plan, then our entire lives would be lived in harmony with nature as well. But women who resort to some sort of deadly abortion drug slay not only the embryo but, along with it, all human love (*philanthropia*).[20]

Early in the next century Hippolytus of Rome condemned bishop Callistus for his readiness to encourage marriage, legal or otherwise, between affluent women and lower-class or slave-class men. Such unions, he observed, had only tended to encourage abortion.

> Women who pass for believers began to resort to drugs to induce sterility, and to bind their abdomens tightly so as to abort the conceptus, because they did not want to have a child by a slave or lower-class type, for the sake of their family pride and their excessive wealth. Look what abuse of duty this lawless man has encouraged, by inciting them both to adultery and to murder. And after such outrageous activity they have the nerve to call themselves a Catholic church![21]

Those were forthright voices from the first and formative Christian years, all arguing that the destruction of the child, unborn or newborn, is infamy for those who follow Christ.

THE CHARACTER OF THIS CONVICTION

One is confronted by five facts: five aspects of that early Christian conviction which must in some way be foundational for Christian ethics.

First, the repudiation of abortion was not an isolated or esoteric doctrine. It formed part of an obligation by all believers to protect the four categories of people whom they now saw as peculiarly exposed to the whim and will of their fellow hu-

mans: the slave, the enemy, the wife and the infant, unborn
or newborn. These were at great risk, as were the four traditional protégés: the pauper, the alien, the widow, and the orphan. And this fourfold obligation was preached across the full
expanse of the church: from Carthage to Egypt and up into
Syria, then across Greece and in Rome.

Second, this was not a program for the more strenuous.
It was presented as the imperative agenda for the church, the
test for all discipleship. Believers were warned away from abortion just as they were from adultery, murder, greed and theft:
they were all ways to spiritual death. The four Christian innovations were offered as the classic new signs of authenticity. If
theirs was not a community where Jew and gentile (divided
by such ancient hostility), where man and woman, where slave
and free could show forth as one, then it had failed as Christian. That was their test. Paul sends Onesimus the slave back
to his master Philemon and tells him to receive him as a
brother, and then charges him: "So if you grant me any fellowship with yourself, welcome him as you would me." That was
their test. If this be heroism, it is a heroism exacted of every
person who would walk the new Way.

A third thing one must observe is that though these exhor-
tations show a sensitive and compassionate sympathy for the
victims, their principal moral concern is for the oppressors. It
is the husband that bullies his wife whose person dwindles
even more sadly than hers. The master or mistress who abuses
the slave sustains an injury even greater than what the slave
experiences. It is the mother who eliminates her son that Clement cares about, because she must destroy her *philanthropia* as
well, her love for humankind, in order to do it. The disease of
character that follows from exploitation of others was seen, in
Christian perspective, to be more hideously incapacitating than
the worst that befell the victims. It could be a death far worse
than death. Even when they enter the contemporary dispute
over the animation of the unborn, these writers dismiss it as a
quibble when it comes to abortion: it is the same ruthless willingness to eliminate unwelcome others that shows itself in the
slaying of the unborn, the newborn, or the parent. In truest
Christian perspective, it is the oppressor that is destroyed.

Fourthly: these writers know well that any true protection of the helpless and exploited calls for a stable empowerment, so that those same people would not continue to be victimized. This means that the Christian moral agenda demands a price. Oppressors must give up their advantage. It little matters whether the advantage was seized purposefully or inherited unwittingly. There is a forfeiture to be accepted by those in power if the disadvantaged and helpless are to be afforded true protection.

But there is a further sacrifice to be made. The victims must accept suffering as well. The price they must pay—if they are to be Christians—is that they must forgo resentment and hatred. Empowerment cannot be grasped as the means to take revenge or, still worse, as the way to begin to be an exploiter oneself. The victims must gaze directly upon those who had taken advantage of them, and recognize them as brothers and sisters who themselves may have been pressed by distress of one kind or another. So there is no moral accomplishment possible unless reconciliation extends the hand of fellowship across the battleline of suffering. There will be heavy and sometimes bitter things to accept if hatred is to be extinguished, and not merely aimed in a new direction.

Fifth, we must note that this was a rigorous duty presented to the church's Christian ancestors. The light was dazzling, and they often preferred to draw back into the cover of darkness. Christians have sinned against that light and continued to relish and even to justify hatred against their enemies. They did not set the slaves free. Women were not welcomed into full and equal status. And parents continued to destroy their young.

A FOURFOLD MORAL MOVEMENT TODAY

Yet every person interested enough to follow this debate must be aware that we live in an extraordinary age in the life of the world and the church. Four great movements have stirred the church round the world:

1: a movement for world peace that is more than a weariness of war; it is making bold and positive ventures towards the reduction of enmity and distrust.
2: another movement for the relief of bondage of every kind: freedom from slavery and from racial subjection, dignity for the worker, status for the migrant.
3: another movement for equality of women and a more integrated companionship with men, so that family and work can be humanized for each and for both together.
4: and a fourth movement to rescue the children from abortion, prenatal neglect, infanticide, infant mortality, and every sort of abuse and predatory danger.

In the trough of some of the most genocidal carnage and oppressive bondage and degradation of women and slaughter of children, our era may be unusual in the readiness of some to listen to that bold and visionary Christian age whose teaching I have been holding up for recollection.

Each of these movements is bent on empowerment. If the exploited do arise and claim their rightful places, will they take power like Spartacus or Robespierre or Pol Pot? Or will they take power like Mahatma Gandhi or Nelson Mandela . . . or like Jesus? Christians may make the difference. This fourfold phalanx of conscience on the march is only partly Christian in origin. But Christians will mean much to these movements of grace, and these movements must mean much to the Christian community.

Christians, possibly more than others, should immediately recognize that these various struggles are in alliance with each other. None can be pitted against another. The United States, for instance, must never imagine that enmity between nations will be subdued if our neighbors are in bondage to us. Enslavement and enmity must both vanish; one must never be forfeited for the sake of the other. Likewise, the movement of enhancement for women must never be furthered by making their children expendable. In America today abortion is said to resolve a conflict of rights, a conflict of interests between women and their children. But a Christian must hold suspect any human right which must be guaranteed by another human's elimination.

Another Christian contribution will be to tell all those who stand to lose bully power that it is in their highest interest to do so. For they have truly withered under the weight of their exploitative advantages. To say this to them with any credibility, one must first be utterly persuaded that oppressors suffer an even more tragic injury than their victims. Are we really ready to believe that the staff of Auschwitz perished in a worse tragedy than those they exterminated? Do you mourn more for the 2,000 or so abortionists in America than for the 20,000,000 or so infants they have efficiently destroyed? Were you more dismayed about Bull Connor than about Martin Luther King, Jr.? Only if you do believe that can you say believably that it is the mothers who destroy their unborn children you care much for, for they stand to lose even more than do their tragically destroyed offspring.

A CHARACTERISTICALLY CHRISTIAN INSIGHT

There is another characteristic Christian insight needed in the abortion dispute. Christians must see and say how often it is that women who victimize their children are themselves handicapped by never having enjoyed control over their own lives. They are victims—even though they are victims who destroy others.

How often it is that some helpless group is savaged by aggressors who have themselves been victims. They are survivors of outrage, and they now seek to relieve their stress and suffering by turning on others who are weaker still. Victims exploiting victims.

Who are those who want to close the nation's gates against impoverished and threatened refugees? Those groups who have long been trampled underfoot by the economy, and who fear new rivals just as they see for themselves a hope for betterment and security at last. Victims pushing aside victims.

What is the background of parents who abuse and batter their children? A childhood of violence, incest, contempt. Victims lashing out at victims.

And who are aborting their daughters and sons today?

Women and men who are alienated, abused, spoiled, poor, who are at a loss to manage their own lives or intimacies. Victims destroyed, destroying victims.

Hate them—hate any victimizers—and you are simply cheering on the cycle of abuse and violence. Suppress your rage well enough to look closely and humanely at drug dealers, at rapists, at pathological prison guards, and you may see it there too: the same pathetic look of the battered spirit, preying on others wantonly.

Women who are desperate or autistic enough to destroy their children are among society's most abused victims. We owe them every help. But a truly compassionate support could never invite them to assuage their own anger by exterminating those more helpless still. It is by breaking the savage cycle of violence that victimization is laid to rest.

When you grasp the uplifted hand to prevent one injured person from striking out at another, you must do so in love, not in anger, for you are asking that person to absorb suffering rather than pass it on to another. And, to be a peacemaker, you must be as ready to sustain as you are to restrain. One must be more than just to accept undeserved injury, yet deal out undeserved favor.

The church's belief is in a Lord who was the innocent victim of injustice. Yet Christ caught the impact of that injustice in his own body, his own self. He deadened it and refused to pass it on; he refused to let the hatred go on ricocheting through humankind. If we truly follow him we are committed to doing the same. And the truest test of that faith is whether we have the gumption to share it with others, with those who are treating others unjustly, but especially with people who are victims. Christians must prevail upon them to let us help them catch the impact of their distress in their own bodies, and in our own selves alongside theirs, without permitting the cycle of violence to carry on.

The fire of Pentecost rapidly enflamed the Christian community to a sense of what they were about. They were in so many ways an observant Jewish movement: in their worship, their hopes, their moral way of life. But in two great matters they burst forth as men and women possessed by a new Spirit.

They witnessed to the resurrection: Jesus, during whose unjust execution they had been inert and disengaged, was risen to power as Messiah and Lord. That was the first great matter. The second was like it. They too had been raised to unexpected power, and they stated with vehemence that they would no longer be passive before affliction. That determination was embodied in the distinctive and innovative moral commitment to befriend the enemy, to embrother the slave, to raise up the wife, and to welcome the child. Their own lives were at stake, for these Christians believed that they would perish in their persons if they proved nonchalant about the suffering of any of these most vulnerable brothers and sisters. But they rushed to their task, for many lives depended on them: the lives of those so powerful they could crush others without noticing; and the lives of their victims—unnoticed, undefended, even unnamed.

I have been asking whether recent developments and reflection give us authentic reasons to reconsider what the *Didache* and Athenagoras and Tertullian and other ancestors in faith held to be essential. We have never had more reasons to reconsider their teaching. And I say that their teaching has never rung more defiantly as the prophetic call of Christ.

The revolt against abortion was no primitive and narrow dogma that a more sophisticated church has now outgrown. It was in the very nucleus of the moral insight by which the church first defined itself before the Lord and before the world. The community has not yet approached it, while some speak of having surpassed it. Those first disciples who reverenced every unwanted child, born or unborn, would have been stupefied by the sight of their own children in the faith gainsaying this or any of that fourfold commitment. Were that community to forswear the hated enemy, the enslaved laborer, the subjected woman, or the defenseless infant, and do that in his name, Christ would have died in vain.

NOTES

1. On opinion surveys, see Judith Blake and Jorge Del Pinal, "Predicting Polar Attitudes toward Abortion in the United States," in James Tunstead Burtchaell, ed., *Abortion Parley* (Kansas City, Kan.: Andrews & McMeel, 1980), 29–56; Burtchaell, *Rachel Weeping and Other Essays on Abortion* (Kansas City, Kan.: Andrews & McMeel, 1982), 96–121. Parallel findings were made by Kristin Luker, *Abortion and the Policies of Motherhood* (Berkeley: University of California Press, 1984).

2. See, for instance, Daniel Maguire (with James Tunstead Burtchaell, C. S. C.), "The Catholic Legacy and Abortion: A Debate," *Commonweal* 114,20 (20 November 1987): 657–680.

3. Maguire, 661.

4. John J. Collins has described this pre-Christian development in Hellenistic Judaism which framed ethical duty in less particularist ways: *Between Athens and Jerusalem: Jewish Identity in the Hellenistic Diaspora* (New York: Crossroad, 1983) 142–148.

5. Hecataeus of Abdera (reported by Diodorus Siculus, *Library of History* 40,3,8); see *Diodorus of Sicily*, trans. Francis R. Walton, 12 (Cambridge, Mass.: Harvard University Press, 1967): 284.

6. Pseudo-Phocylides, *Sentences* 184–185; see *The Sentences of Pseudo-Phocylides*, P. W. van der Horst (Leiden: Brill, 1978), 232.

7. Philo of Alexandria, *Hypothetica*, 7:7; see *The Works of Philo of Alexandria*, ed. Francis Henry Colson et al. (New York: Putnam, 1929–62) 9:428.

8. Flavius Josephus, *Contra Apionem* 2:202; see *The Works of Flavius Josephus*, ed. Henry St. John Thackeray et al. (Cambridge, Mass.: Harvard University Press, 1962–65) 1:372–374.

9. *Sibylline Oracles* 3:765–766.

10. *Didache* 2:2–3.

11. Ibid., 5:2.

12. This vocabulary carries over from the hellenistic Jewish documents quoted above.

13. *Letter of Barnabas* 19:5; 20:2.

14. *Letter to Diognetus* 5:6–7,10.

15. Marcus Minucius Felix, *Octavius* 30:1–2.

16. Athenagoras of Athens, *Embassy for the Christians*, 35.

17. Tertullian, *De Anima* 38:1; see also 37.

18. Idem, *Apologeticum* 9:8; see also 9:4–7

19. Idem, *De Anima* 25:4.

20. Clement of Alexandria, *The Pegagogue*, 96.

21. Hippolytus of Rome, *Refutation of All Heresies* 9:12:25.

3

The Torah as Obsolete for Christian Ethics

"THE CHRISTIAN COMMUNITY of those who are witnesses to the Resurrection is a community marked by a new perception of the possibilities of human life and human community. Human beings need no longer live under compulsions and restraints that long have bound and sometimes enslaved them. . . . Is there," asks Walter Harrelson, "any place for the Ten Commandments in such a community of the Resurrection?"[1]

What obedience, if any, should the Ten Words, or the entire Torah, or indeed the full extent of Israel's moral injunctions, exact from those who identify themselves as a New Israel?

IS THE OLD TESTAMENT OBSOLETE?

The question has had a keen bite for the communities of the Reformation. The same founders who revived so learned a reverence for the Bible had also made Romans and Galatians the rate of exchange for the whole of scripture. All that was authentically Christian was seen as innovative, and as a breakaway from its Jewish antecedents. On this view of the gospel as a revolt, it was difficult not to follow Marcion's example and regard the code of Israel as utterly obsolete: inspired but archaic, like the leather-bound family Bible reverently displayed in the living room, reverently unread.

The evangelical and fundamentalist traditions have had an especially vexed relationship with Old Testament law. Assuming that all divine teaching is to be found in the Bible (not in germ alone, but in full fruit and flower), and convinced as well that this revelation has conveyed a moral doctrine to be received attentively, Christians of this persuasion have had to go to the Hebrew scriptures to find much of their ethical program. Since it is not really there, they have had to ignore some commands that are there in full sight, and impose a sense of their own upon others. Thus the Christians who confess most dependence upon the closely read biblical text have sometimes hearkened least to its original imperatives.

A more scholarly tradition has sought other ways to evaluate the ancient laws. Reinhold Niebuhr has portrayed the older ethic, unlike the newer, as one that is possible of fulfillment. "The social justice which Amos demanded represented a possible ideal for society. Jesus' conception of pure love . . . transcends the possible and historical."[2] Jesus' command to forgive the aggressor, for example, which forbids prudent self-defense and ignores natural impulses and social consequences, can have only a transcendent meaning for us, not a normative instruction. "Surely this is not an ethic which can give us specific guidance in the detailed problems of social morality where the relative claims of family, community, class, and nation must be constantly weighed. One is almost inclined to agree with Karl Barth [something Niebuhr never did eagerly] that this ethic 'is not applicable to the problems of contemporary society nor yet to any conceivable society'."[3]

But Niebuhr's erstwhile colleague at Union, Dietrich Bonhöffer, brought a starkly different interpretation to the same text: "You have heard how it was said: 'Eye for eye and tooth for tooth.' But I say this to you: offer no resistance to the wicked" (Mt 5:38–39):

> In the Old Testament personal rights are protected by a divinely established system of retribution. Every evil must be requited. The aim of retribution is to establish a proper commu-

nity, to convict and overcome evil and eradicate it from the body politic of the people of God. . . . The Church is not to be a national community like the old Israel, but a community of believers without political or national ties. The old Israel had been both—the chosen people of God *and* a national community, and it was therefore his will that they should meet force with force. But with the Church it is different: it has abandoned political and national status, and therefore it must patiently endure aggression. Otherwise evil will be heaped upon evil.[4]

Unlike Niebuhr, Bonhöffer thinks nonresistance should be practiced in public life, but he believes that only a Christian living forthrightly under faith in the Cross will be empowered to do so. Despite their differing applications of scripture, both master and pupil were in agreement that an authentic Christian ethic was to be found only in the documents of the new covenant, not in the old.

Walter Harrelson, standing about as far from them as Alexandria stands from Antioch, argues that the absolute prohibitions of the Ten Commandments can indeed yield divine guidance to the Christian, provided that they are taken as guidelines, not as explicit norms.

The Ten Commandments are much more akin to statements about the character of life in community than they are to cases of violation of the law of the community and what punishment is to be dealt out when violations occur. Put in constitutional terms, the Ten Commandment are much more like the Bill of Rights and its amendments than the United States Code.[5]

Combining exegetical precision with pastoral shrewdness, he sees the Commandments as suggestive first principles which, when put into Christian service, become the outline of a moral guide for life. My concern about this proceeding, which Harrelson pursues as eloquently and persuasively as any I have read, is that in the end it seems to rescue the Old Testament from obsolescence by bleaching out of it the original concerns of the authors, which were very explicit, normative, particular, and grounded on suppositions far more primitive than we could accept. My counterproposal is to accept not only the entire Old Testament in its original sense as obsolete for Christians, but the New Testament as well.

CREED CREATES CANON

In the final scenes of both *The Merchant of Venice* and *A Comedy of Errors* the chaos of previously confused identities is handsomely resolved. Portia and Nerissa, and the two pairs—Amphibolus and Dromio—of Ephesus and of Syracuse are discerned at last. What really happens in each finale is not simply that the characters disclose who they are, but that they reconstrue what they all mean to each other. I want to suggest a way to reconstrue the continuous Jewish and Christian tradition of moral injunction, not by altering its content, stringency, or definition, but by proposing a more helpful understanding of what these ancient yet normative teachings, underwritten by God, might require of the Christian community in a much later day.

Christians are the heirs of a continuity in community and inquiry, both of which we trace back to Abraham and Sarah. Along that journey we have beckoned strangers into fellowship with us: companions in both our inquiry and our community. There were other times when some of our comrades broke away and walked with us no longer. The account of those mergers and those disengagements has left its geological record, so to speak, in our ancient documentation.

The construction of the canon has been a function of realignments among the biblical people. The tribal unity between the tribes had been sundered at the death of Solomon, when Judah went his own way from the other brothers. Eventually the Jews received the narratives and oracles of the prophets into their sacred collection, while the Samaritans would add nothing to the Torah. Evidence suggests that the later rifts between the Pharisees and the Sadducees, and between the houses of Hillel and Shammai, were reflected in differing lists of books "that defile the hands."[6] The separation of Christians from Jews entailed acceptance by the former and repudiation by the latter, not only of the new Christian writings, but of earlier Jewish documents: books thought to have been written in Greek, and particularly essential to the Christian sense of continuity because of their testimony to the late-developing belief in resurrection and after-life for the just in the heavenly court. Gnostics later canonized many gospels and apocalypses which the Catholics repudiated, and this confirmed those two communities as going their separate ways. On every one of those occasions when the community drew itself closely together on matters of crucial identity, it determined at the same time which books it would hold sacred.

Canon-making is community-making. The selection of which writings are to be read aloud before the community in God's name is an act of self-definition by a family of faith. It is a primal loyalty test whereby a people identifies itself by its narrative and liturgical and moral and doctrinal antecedents.

Yet the chosen corpus of sacred writings—selected at great cost of membership—is no testimony to uniformity. While the books were honored as the ground of the newly defined faith, they did not embody a homogeneous or synoptic view among themselves. The Christian Bible retains (wittingly or unwittingly) much diversity—and disagreement as well. Genesis, which retains long documents partisan to the northern kingdom and to Joseph, its dominant tribe, is revered alongside the Early Prophets, whose final loyalties were truculently for Judah. Joshua gives a different account of the conquest than that of Judges. Ruth and Jonah were written with an eye to contradicting the message of Ezra. Jesus' teaching about response to enemies is hardly that of the Psalmist. The attitudes towards civil authorities ascribed to Peter and to Paul are certainly more benign than those which scorch the Book of Revelation.

The canonical scriptures, despite the tendentious process which led to their selection, do not provide the community with a creed. They are a mosaic, an amalgam of the early past that the community must always be unpuzzling in order to formulate its contemporary beliefs. The individual elements in scripture each represent a viewpoint particular to its author, stress, and context. But the collection, as a selective composite of those elements, is enacted from the much later viewpoint of the canonical moment. Scripture, then, is a retrospective archive of the earliest remembered trajectory of the traditional faith. Like all archives, it is of little use and possibly even some misunderstanding to laypersons unless learned scholars versed in the ancient ways of thought help them unroll and expound the canonized books: both in their original sense and in their contribution to the ongoing perspective.[7]

Crises over the long past have provoked the community to isolate and disavow various equivocations, misunderstandings, and misjudgments. The community has nevertheless retained various inconsistencies and insufficiencies. They will either stymie the believing community, or somehow spur it on to play its own needful, contemporary part in drawing the tradition further along into restatement. To remain alive in faith the community must both hold fast to the conclusions of the past and reach new surmises and resolutions and insights of its own. The growing tip of the tradition must be alive with new growth for it to have a strong enough draw on its root system for nourishment.

The most honored records of the past show us that our contemporary conclusions will sometimes diverge from those of our forebears, but that need not mean we break faith with them. As present inquiry telescopes out of past understanding, the process requires a discerning initiative by the community. Beholden to the inspired meditations of the past, the present church believes that she too has the same Spirit that spoke through the prophets and apostles, and that she is a coactive party to the making of the never-closed creed.

Christians are therefore unable to say simply, "It says here . . ." because the church, who has already decided repeatedly which sayings count most, must continue to reflect actively upon her own past sayings, and frame a sequel which is faithful to that foundation, not by mere repetition but by development. As I have already mentioned, it is those who imagine that the Spirit guides them to find in scripture a library of one single perspective and doctrine who are in fact the most prone to subject the documents of revelation to their own perspective, fancy, and doctrine.

Since the canon represents early editions of the continuing faith, they have to be read first of all exactly as they were meant, in the sense and force of their original authorship. They need not be allegorized or spiritualized or forced to fit any more current edition of the faith. The same community, led by the same Spirit, is inspired by those earlier accounts of faith, and then endeavors to do for its generation what those seers did for theirs. The scriptures provide the inspiration, but not the text, of our creed. Consulting the sacred writings is therefore an active undertaking. In the biblical sense, one hearkens in order to hear; one must be creative to be receptive.

Two Testaments in One Trajectory

A common assumption among Christians is that the flash of brilliance marking the arrival of Jesus paled and darkened all that had gone before.

When the moon shone, we did not see the candle.
So doth the greater glory dim the less.[8]

All of Israel became preamble, archive, ancient history, obsolete. But I want to argue that it is obsolete in much the same way the Christian scriptures are also obsolete.

Faith and scholarship have been at cross purposes in their estimate of the relative worth of what is older and what is later. Church doctrine has usually assumed that when comparing Jewish with Christian scriptures it is the ancient that must be read in light of what followed. But when scholars examine individual passages, they often value the more ancient over the more recent. In studying the New Testament documents, higher critics have tended to distrust the later developments in favor of the most primitive traces. A dogmatic *Ur*-fixation has turned every exegete into an archaeologist, shoveling away all the debris and clutter to get back to the pure faith closest to the source. This method may rest on a theological motive more than a scholarly one, however.

The presupposition, of course, has been that utterances of Jesus enjoy a higher clarity and credibility than utterances of his disciples. And among the discipleship, priority must go to the eye-witnesses, with a supposed cooling-off of charism the further one got from Galilee. The handicap in this theory is that we probably never do get to Jesus himself. All that we have is from the disciples. And there is abundant evidence in the New Testament to suggest that whatever they heard that was radical, explosive, and *bouleversant* fell on dull and unprepared ears. Faith came through hearing . . . but the disciples were hard of hearing. The witnesses admitted that his teaching, his mission, and his character had all gone right past them in a blur. It was only after he had been tortured, slain, raised, and exalted that they began to reflect on what they had heard. And then it began to dawn on them. We have good reason to believe that it was a long dawn. But the disciples were getting better, not worse, at unpuzzling the drift of Jesus' teaching with the passage of time. Thus the later layers of literary evolution may not be all shards and debris. The documents may have gained in perspective. Some may also on occasion have regressed, but each editorial adaptation must be surveyed on its own to determine that.

If one accepts this view that the community of faith has generally, by divine assistance, looked back and gained an enhanced understanding, one then sees faith as following a trajectory, with a beginning but not yet an end. Though the scriptures give us access to the founding times, our venture of understanding has never come to a standstill. The canonical books are normative, not by being the Last Word, but by being the First. They are annunciation and gestation to the faith, not myrrh and aloes. It derogates not a bit from our confession that the full face of the Father—or as much sight of it as we could bear—has shone upon us in Jesus, if we admit that it was more than the first disciples could make full sense of, and that we have been deciphering their ecstatic blurtings ever since.

The Christian scriptures do represent an abrupt innovation in the tradition, but it was already a tradition in which abrupt innovations were conventional. Christians see in Jesus an apocalypse without precedent. But Israel was not unfamiliar with being yanked into disclosures that made all things new. When every token of divine predilection had been annihilated—royal house, holy city, promised land, and temple-home for the ark and the glory—and this devastation then gave birth to a young, new faith of even greater tenacity: it took their breath away. And when in their deepest disgrace they heard their prophets making mockery of all rival gods, and proclaiming that their Yahweh was the only god, the creator of the heavens and the earth and therefore—this was what really sent them gagging—he was also the fond father of the Assyrian and Babylonian slaughterers: this too took their breath away. And when in the very teeth of butchery by the effete cosmopolites of Syria they first heard it whispered that God's great life-and-death promises were not all to be cramped and squeezed into Judah and into three-score-and-ten years, but that those who walked honorably before the Lord would laugh at their tormentors from within the divine retinue in heaven: this seemed to leave them with no breath at all. No matter how strong our sense of innovation in Christ, the Jewish scriptures prepare us for the unanticipatable by establishing the expectation of the unimaginable. And the unimaginable came, repeatedly.

Dramatic permutations of faith were already traditional in Israel long before Jesus. And the New Testament in its turn discloses not one but several convulsive new disclosures. The acknowledgment of Jesus as Messiah was tumultuous, but it was followed a while later by the unthinkable admission of Gentiles to table-fellowship, and later still by recognition of Jesus as the Only-begotten. It is not the case that transfiguration of faith is peculiar to the Christian scriptures; only that its tempo had picked up. There is then a continuing itinerary of development that wends its way through both Testaments.

The history of the people of Abraham numbers certain very privileged witnesses to more enlightened discoveries in faith. Those who accept the Bible as inspired should have no difficulty honoring some of the ancient seers as more intensely exposed to the Mystery than others—and Jesus as invested with its fullness. But the rate of absorption by which the believing community took in those insights, integrated them with all it knew from beforehand and otherwise, and then drew revised conclusions from them; the rate at which Israel, Old and New, metabolized those disclosures, was spiked by the surges of high charism in peak individuals but overall it followed a more steady climb. And what we have in the Bible is more a residual account of what the community was absorbing than an account of what God had to disclose. Thus the textual community might take considerable time to digest and take the benefit of its greatest visionaries. The Bible exposes us to the greatest, most insightful prophetic leaders in those early ages. But the trajectory of understanding faith resolutely gained in perspective such that its steady, fitted curve absorbed those sometimes scattered points above and below.

The elements of faith were being reconsidered, recast, and reapplied from Canaan to Corinth. From Genesis to Revelation (or, perhaps, from Exodus to the Pastorals) that faith was constantly developing—though not always in an upward vector, for there were times of regression and eddies of confusion. Jesus may be the flashpoint of God's revelation, but the faith neither then nor now reached its apogee. The revelation may be definitive but the faith is not. The community and the inquiry move on, and so too does the absorption of revelation into faith.

MORAL DUTY IN THE SIGHT OF A WRATHLESS GOD

How might this bear on the applicability of Israel's ethics for Christianity? There are two different relationships those ancient moral and legal codes bear to the Christian faith in its contemporary moment. In one sense that ancient material is primitive and obsolete; in another, it is invaluable.

The New Testament does convey a radically new perspective on ethical obligation. Jesus, presented as our best glimpse of the Father, displays his own character and that of the Father when he dies for those who kill him: Judaean establishment, Jerusalem populace, forsworn Peter, treacherous Judas, craven disciples, Pilate, Herod, Roman cohort. As Peter in Acts puts it more cosmically: it was done by those under the Law and those outside it. In a word, by everyone. Readers of the gospel are given to understand that they too would have had a hand in it had they been there. Jesus would fare as badly in Jacksonville, Jakarta, or Johannesburg as he did in Jerusalem. We are all standing there at Calvary with silver in our purses and hammers in our hands.

What Jesus reveals is a relentless love for those who relentlessly kill him. And he reveals a Father who loves sinners. His love is not like ours, we being so handicapped. He loves, not for the goodness he finds in us, but for that which is in him. He cherishes us regardless of our behavior. There is no wrath in him. As Jesus dies stubbornly cherishing those who for every sort of expediency or malice shifted around aimlessly in their efforts to rid themselves of his compelling presence, he reveals a Father whose love is not a response but entirely initiative. His is an originating love, fastened upon us like that of the Prodigal Father, whether we serve or whether we renege.

The Father of Jesus cannot be offended. Nor can he be pleased. He is disclosed to us as One whose attitude towards us is not governed by our characters but by his own. His attitude does not swivel on our performance. It is we who swivel. He cannot turn his back on us, but we are inveterate in turning our backs on him and on one another. Or, to put it all in John's terse way, God is love.

If this be so, it quarrels with the notion of a God who will punish those who violate his law. This was put well enough by a Louisville foundry worker who, as a folk philosopher, was interviewed by a local journalist.

> Crowe's view of the hereafter is beautiful. His God is a good guy who eats chicken, drinks beer, loves moonlight on the river and would even smoke a joint if you offered it to him. "I can't believe what churches and so-called religious people say," says Crowe. "I had eight or 10 people tell me that the tornado of '74 was God's warning. My God isn't in charge of tornadoes. He wouldn't throw one at you just for kicks. My God's waiting over there with a table laid for me. When I get there, he's going to say, 'I'm God, and I love you. Forget all the bull you heard on earth'."[9]

His theology is anthropomorphic, but no more so than what biblical scholars should be comfortable with. What makes

Crowe interesting is that he is criticizing Christians for behaving like they left the tradition sometime back.

The New Testament is every bit as concerned about right moral behavior as is the Old. But it is incompatible with the gospel's disclosure of the Father of Jesus for us to portray God as threatening with wrath and punishment those who disobey his law. Whatever the sense of the New Testament, it cannot imply that failure before the law will cause God to reject us. What we do see is that wrongful behavior will cause *us* to reject *God*.

The pay-off in the teaching remains very much what it was before: that if we act in certain ways we shall surely die. But it will be at our hand, not at God's. By the way we live we can destroy ourselves morally, personally, spiritually. And we also know that by God's enablement there are other patterns of behavior that bring life, that vitalize our ability to go out unselfishly in love to serve others, and build up our strength and gumption.

What the believing community—and consequently its enlightened scriveners who have given scriptural expression to the community's past—had done was to sense the life-or-death importance of human behavior, but in doing so they projected onto God what is all too human: alienation. Sin does not incur divine wrath, but it does cause us to wither, to sicken, to be estranged, to die, to reject that wrathless love. Sin can be mortal, not because it will interdict God's love for me, but because it will disable me from taking it in and responding with a like heart. Grace empowers me to recover and surmount my self-stunting sin by emerging from selfishness into love: indeed, by assimilating myself to the Lord. By the Lord's empowerment I can come to cherish those who do not cherish me, in hope of being such a grace to them (as others are to me) that I might prevail over their egotism as God through Jesus wears down mine.

On this view of things, the Law of Israel must be both rhetorically and ethically obsolete for the Christian. For one thing, it is grounded on the assumption that God will surely abominate those who violate it. But even if one reconstrues the ancient code as an inspired warning about what sorts of behavior lead humans to be alienated from one another and from their Lord, and what behavior enhances human ability to cleave to the Lord and one another, it is still obsolete, for it represents only a very early stage of reflection by the community. In this latter sense, the insights of the first Christians, memorialized in the New Testament, are also obsolete, for the community's reflection has already moved farther forward along the track they first marked out.

It should be obvious that by "obsolete" I do not characterize the canonical texts as abrogated or extinct. They belong to another time, a privileged and classical time for the believing community. Their force consists in their anchoring and sustaining the tradition. They are not an account of the community's faith, for that must always be a contemporary composition. The scriptures are of a different genre of discourse. They are ancient, even primitive; they represent the tradition as it was first being formed. They are "obsolete" as every past text of the tradition is now obsolete. But they are valuable differently from every other past text of the tradition, because it is with them that we must be in communion in order to be the heirs of the faith of the prophets and apostles. No single element of the canon is identical with the faith as it has thus far developed. Each belongs to its time and author. But assembled purposefully into a canonical collection all these components acquire a new clarity, for they resolve into a trajectory that points to where we now believe, and beyond.

But that directs us to the aspect of incalculable value which the Commandments, though obsolete, have for the Christian believer. The Law expresses the first cumulative wisdom of the community of faith about what various behaviors do to those who avoid or perform them.

The church believes herself to be an inspired community, endowed by a prophetic vision to help her see what she would otherwise have neither the mind nor the will to see. Her genre of ethical discourse is therefore highly experiential. The community has observed what gives life and what depletes it.

Thou shalt not steal. In Saudi Arabia the government may chop off your hand if you do. More enlightened governments like our own will imprison you if you are a poor robber, fine you if you are middle-class, and give you a suspended sentence if your stealing has been massive. But the cumulative lesson in scripture is a warning that the thief is robbed by his own hand. By violating his neighbor to steal her goods, he has incapacitated his ability to be her neighbor, and also his ability to receive the clasp of the everlasting arms drawing him into embrace.

Thou shalt not bear false witness against thy neighbor. For the understanding reader this becomes, not a warning of a judicial God, but an alert to the relentless lethal nature of lying. Those who lie lose the truth. They cannot look God in the eye because they can't look themselves or anyone else in the eye.

Do not commit adultery. You will be disenabled to cleave fast to anyone. Do not pass up the refugee, the handicapped, the humiliated. You will be victimizing yourself. Your eternity is at stake in how you deal with others.

Obviously this was not the understanding of the original authors of the *mitzvoth*. Their prohibition against false witness, of course, forbade perjured testimony in a society where tort and crime were settled on the word of reliable witnesses. In its original meaning it did not suggest a global command against all fraud. And the canonical author and primary audience believed that it was a divine imperative with a divine sanction.

For the believing reader who takes those as early expressions of a communal inquiry for which God has provided both the receptivity and the nourishment, those commands, exegeted in their original apodictic simplicity, convey the beginning convictions about how we are to wend our way to God. For the original addressees they were definitive on their author's terms. For us, the latter-day readership, they present the first prophetic insights in our tradition. The tradition continues on, and there is much in it which has enhanced our insight into stealing from the poor and truth-telling and life-giving. The fact that there are outright prohibitions in the scriptures against sodomy or crustacea or unveiled women or murder does not conclude our search for moral truth in these matters. It grounds the search. It is not enough to locate the *logia* in the text; we must account to ourselves why our ancestors in faith saw those things to be evil, and how that judgment was in partnership with their understanding of God, and the human community, and family, and neighborhood, and property, and child-bearing, and fidelity, and the rest. With the sextant of faith we must get an accurate historical sighting on the past in order to find a true bearing on the present. We cite the ancient command as a moral authority, not insofar as it lays down a certain course of action, but insofar as that imperative has been reconsidered, reiterated and reinforced while the tradition was gaining momentum and resolve. If, on the other hand, the ancient command has been marginalized or vacated or refined as the faith-community has clarified its vision, then the commandment's authority is accordingly altered.

Recall the early Christian injunctions presented in the previous chapter: the fourfold injunction to provide for the widow, the orphan, the pauper, and the foreigner, and then to provide further for the wife, the unborn or newborn child, the slave, and the enemy. Only one of those four new beneficiaries is not spoken for in the New Testament. Here is one of the most entrenched and resolute convictions in the Christian moral tradition, with no direct textual authorization in scripture. But neither the mere absence of explicit biblical warrant nor the mere presence of explicit patristic warrants is decisive. The contemporary moralist must study the documents in context to see that a clutch of moral injunctions of mercy that arise with a clamor in the Jewish scriptures, and are given a consistently wider application in the Christian scriptures, congruously give birth to a stringent prohibition that telescopes with utter authenticity out of its biblical antecedents, and was begotten by the biblical commitments to the helpless. To ratify this as binding today requires that one verify how rooted it is in those elements of our moral tradition which have been reinforced, not marginalized. The fact that this particular injunction is at odds with much modern social thought is but an echo of the invective it first encountered nineteen centuries ago.

Walter Harrelson has argued that the commandment not to kill cast its wider concern over such matters as armed warfare, capital punishment, abortion, euthanasia, and the slaying of the very ill or disabled. "In my judgment, all these matters do relate to the intention of the sixth commandment, especially as that commandment is developed through the centuries in Judaism and Christianity."[10] It seems clear that these are matters repeatedly addressed by the moral wisdom of the believing community—indeed several are very actively debated today. The *mitzvah* itself, I would say, took no notice of them, but its sharp note of command provided the key motif in an inaugural passage of the long fugue which both exceeds and ratifies its ancient ancestor, the law of Moses.

NOTES

1. *The Ten Commandments and Human Rights* (Philadelphia: Fortress, 1980), 6.

2. Reinhold Niebuhr, *An Interpretation of Christian Ethics* (New York: Harper & Brothers, 1935), 31.

3. Ibid., 51.

4. Dietrich Bonhöffer, *The Cost of Discipleship*, trans. R. H. Fuller and Irmgard Booth (New York: Macmillan, 1963), 157.

5. *Ten Commandments*, 12–13. Harrelson goes on eloquently to argue that the Commandments foreshadow the 1948 Universal Declaration of Human Rights.

6. See Solomon Zeitlin, "An Historical Study of the Canonization of the Hebrew Scriptures," in *Studies in the Early History of Judaism*, 2 (New York: KTAV, 1974): 1–42; Roger Beckwith, *The Old Testament Canon of the New Testament Church and its Background in Early Judaism* (Grand Rapids: Eerdmans, 1985).

7. Jacob Neusner comes at this same point from a slightly different direction, but his conclusion is harmonious with mine. "The system comes before the texts and defines the canon. No universally shared traits or characteristics, topical, logical, rhetorical, within the diverse texts can account by themselves for the selection of those texts for places in the canon. . . . The canon (so to speak) does not just happen after the fact, in the aftermath of the texts that make it up. *The canon is the event that creates of documents holy texts before the fact: the canon is the fact*. The documents do not (naturally, as a matter of fact) *coalesce* into a canon. They (supernaturally, as a gesture of faith) are *constructed* into a canon. . . . *The system does not recapitulate the canon. The canon recapitulates the system*." (original emphasis) *Canon*

and Connection: Intertextuality in Judaism (New York: University Press of America, 1987), 157–159. See also his *First Principles of Systemic Analysis: The Case of Judaism within the History of Religion* (New York: University Press of America, 1987), 131–153.

8. *The Merchant of Venice*, 5.1, 92–93.

9. Paul Bryan Crowe, quoted by John Flynn, (Louisville) *Courier-Journal*, 21 January 1977, B1.

10. *Ten Commandments*, 116.

*Moral Wisdom and the
Giving of Life*

4

"Human Life" and Human Love

THE PROPER MORAL RELATIONSHIP between sex and childbearing has been at the center of one of the most intractable contemporary debates about the giving and taking of life. *Humanae Vitae*, the encyclical letter of Pope Paul VI (Giovanni Battista Montini), dated 25 June 1968, stands as an emphatic attempt to offer a consistent Christian statement about sex and procreation. In the public mind, the pope is remembered for having excluded "any action which either before, at the moment of, or after intercourse, is specifically intended to prevent procreation."[1]

There are grounds for treating that document and the controversy it aggravated as a very intramural Catholic affair. If it seemed to be an unsuccessful resort to power by the bishop of Rome, that could be taken as one more episode in the history of papal authority which, by definition, is nothing anyone but Catholics need make their concern. As for the teaching itself, it appears to be a continuation of a nay-saying sexual ethic most other communions have been anxious to leave behind.

I want to propose, on the contrary, that the *Humanae Vitae* controversy raises issues of authority and sexuality that are germane to any community of moral inquiry today.

For some time now the commonplace has no longer been true: that Catholics must act out of obedience, and Protestants leave each person's conscience free. There is no sizeable church—no matter how congregational its polity or individualist its ethic or feisty its style—that does not maintain an office in Washington and/or New York with a staff issuing public policy advisories, and national task forces presenting moral resolutions on the great social, economic, and political issues of the day (or the week), asking for vehement and binding endorsement by synods and conventions, which then elect presidents to root out any dissidents in the seminaries. Intrepid magisterium presently abides in many ecclesiastical homes that had been swept and garnished for its arrival.

Since the publication of John Noonan's historical study *Contraception* in 1965, it has been clear that the original insight which roused the ancient church against anti-natal ideologies was precisely her defense of sex and childbearing as wholesome and sanctifiable enterprises of God-given flesh. Thus, however poorly one considers Paul VI to have done it, it was a Christian tradition he was managing and it was both originally anti-Manichee and Augustinian: accepting of carnal ecstasy but very wary of it.

In retrospect, then, the *Humanae Vitae* event may be instructive for any community of faith, especially Christian faith, that aspires to elaborate a moral wisdom about the sexual embrace.

The pope easily accepted from his recent predecessors the doctrine (not known to their predecessors) that sexual relations are compatible with some purposeful restriction on reproductive capacity. The question then arose: What made for right or wrong birth control? He rested the entire weight of his reply on a distinction between "natural" and "artificial" measures. "Artificial" was wrong, and it was anything that impeded the reproductive potential of a single act of intercourse. This load-bearing distinction proved to be too crude and fragile to sustain his argument. But worse still was his focus upon method rather than motive as the ethical issue. In doing that the pope forwent the opportunity to launch a telling and timely attack on the Western world's reluctance to welcome children into our lives. It was a moment for the chief shepherd to play the prophet, but he functioned instead as a technician. What happened in 1968, ironically, was that the pope backed away from speaking with robust authority. Instead, he spoke as the scribes do. Also ironic was his failure to speak out on behalf of sex—as an adult commitment rather than an immature pastime. *Humanae Vitae* was botched because the pope dared to say too little, not because he said too much.

AUTHORITY AT ISSUE

There are four distinct authority-related issues discernible in the affair. The first was the very fact that some people involved considered that it was primarily a test case for the right of the church to govern the behavior of its communicants. For these participants, the issues of sex and childbearing were but the occasion for the struggle.

Reaction to the encyclical was immediate and hostile. The criticism, unusually bitter among Catholics, seemed somehow to have depressed the pope's spirit and caused him to withdraw. During the first third of his pontificate he had associated himself with the publicly popular enactments of the Second Vatican Council. As the *papa viaggiante* (or Pilgrim Pope, as he liked to be known) he had broken all precedent by journeying far from the Vatican, to rally enormous crowds in Jerusalem and Bombay, New York and Fatima and Istanbul. But in the rancor that followed 1968 he went forth less and less and then no more. His demeanor and doctrine became more grieving, more hand-wringing, more explicitly resentful of resistance to his rightful authority. He never published another major encyclical.

Some say today that this one Roman pronouncement is what has eviscerated the traditional reverence of lay Catholics towards the authority of the Holy See.[2] I had occasion to learn how significant *Humanae Vitae* was when I crossed the wake of Peter's launch and was thrown about in its backwash. The academic world had been adjourned for summer vacations when the letter appeared. When we returned for the fall term in all that turbulence of 1968, I had just become chairman of the theology department. My first public appearance, only one month into the semester, was at the invitation of the student academic commission, to comment on the encyclical. Word of the lecture carried farther, and at a higher pitch, than I had expected or wished. The three Chicago headlines the next morning read: "Theologian Rips Ban on Pill," "Notre Dame U. Priest Hits at Birth Control: Calls Pope Encyclical 'Unfortunate Mistake'," "Notre Dame Priest Denounces Pill Ban." In order to circulate what I had said instead of what news editors extracted from my text, I published it a few weeks later. The phrase that stuck in some readers' memory was my description of the encyclical as "grossly inadequate and largely fallacious."[3]

I received mail: abundant, articulate mail expressive of strong convictions. Some months later, when it was no longer in every way burdensome to empty my postal box, I stacked the mail in two piles: pro and con. Then I reread them all and discovered that every single letter which took me to task spoke of the matter as an issue of authority: a failure in the deference which we all owed to papal teaching. Every correspondent who wrote in support of my statement was concerned instead about marriage and childbearing and family commitment.

This all came back with added clarity recently when I read Robert Blair Kaiser's account of the papal birth control commission that served under John XXIII and Paul VI and finally presented the latter with a recommendation that would, if followed, have produced a papal letter that came down on the other side of the controversy. The small minority of members that rejected this consensus and was to prevail upon the pope to let them write his encyclical, admitted openly that the struggle was over authority. Since they could not "bring forward arguments which are clear and cogent based on reason alone," they had to take their stand on the reputation of the church. "The Catholic Church could not have furnished in the name of Jesus Christ to so many of the faithful everywhere in the world, through so many centuries, the occasion for formal sin and spiritual ruin. . . . If the church could err in such a way . . . the faithful could not put their trust in the magisterium's (i.e., the clergy's) presentations of moral teaching, especially in sexual matters."[4]

Insofar as they spoke their minds, those who feared any deviation from the conventional Catholic doctrine on contraception were so alarmed by the threat of discredit to what they knew of the church's past that they could not allow themselves to look at the issue on its own merits.

The second symptomatic notion about authority is traceable to the Holy Father himself. In the days immediately following publication his frequent references to the encyclical in public contain telltale phrases. After confessing that his "grave responsibility" and "the weight of Our office" imposed "no small measure of mental anguish," he explained why he had to speak as he did. "We had to give an answer to the church, to the whole of mankind. . . . We felt Our own humble inadequacy in the face of the formidable apostolic task of having to speak out on this matter." "We had to give Our answer as shepherd of the whole church to questions posed by individuals." Even more significant is the pope's description of what he did. Repeatedly he calls it a "decision," "a ruling."[5]

It is well enough known that Paul VI, in this and several other public issues, was thoroughly dependent upon professional advice. And in this matter, unlike those treated in the very prophetic *Populorum Progressio*, he turned for the answer to an especially conservative group. What is perhaps more interesting, however, is his sense of burden: there must be no quandary faced by Christians to which he should not be able to supply the solution. More significant still is his way of describing it as a "decision," rather than a discernment. It is the language of moral theology to discern what is right; it is the vocabulary of law to decide what people must be told to do. And Paul, by his training and his intellectual grasp on this moral matter, confused his task as one of giving orders to people's wills instead of giving enlightenment to their intellects. Authority of command displaced the authority of conviction. The pope is daunted, not by the possibility that he will deliver a teaching that is wrong and therefore damaging, but by "the dilemma of giving in easily to current opinions, or of making a decision that would be hard for society to accept, or that might be arbitrarily too burdensome for married life."[6] His burden and his fear are the same: that he must decide what is right, and that others need not be convinced but only obey.

Another confusion about authority is the source of that

self-understanding of the pope. In any society authority tends to rise by a sort of capillary action and accumulate in high office. A variety of pressures—constant appeals to intervene in disputes, the need to assist local churches against state aggrandizement, or just plain zest for power—will tempt the pope and those who rely on him to feel that there are practically no limits to his competence. As pastoral need calls his warrant farther and farther—often for the service and with the eventual acquiescence of successive generations—it becomes more difficult to define any constitutional sense of limit to his capacity.

Many had been led to believe that Vatican II resolved the problem of power-accumulation. Not entirely. By asserting their own collegiality the bishops did insist that the papacy enjoyed no exclusive franchise on churchwide governance. They accepted and imposed a restored and improved arrangement of who should exercise global authority within the church. But they left largely unresolved the much more basic issue: How much authority does the church claim or possess, no matter who wields it?

Professor Bernhard Häring, the distinguished Roman moralist, took offense at the pope's statement because it was made unilaterally, not in concert with the worldwide episcopate. But this is perhaps an unfair complaint, to judge by the vocal support arising from bishops in all directions. Despite the testimony that there were many bishops whose convictions ran clean athwart the encyclical, they were entirely discreet and indirect in expressing their reservations or dissent. The point to pursue, then, is not whether the pope has spoken too much in isolation, but whether any or all Christians in united chorus could rightly say what he said. What poses publicly, then, as a dispute over papal power is often really an issue about the competence of the church itself.

Surely the most outright claim made about ecclesiastical empowerment, in the time of Pius IX, was the declaration made in 1870 by Vatican I. It has aroused bitter controversy about church polity, but few have troubled to read the text closely:

> When the Roman Pontiff speaks *ex cathedra*, i.e., when he
> acts as shepherd and teacher of all Christians, and defines with

his supreme apostolic authority a teaching on faith or morals to be accepted by the universal church, then through the divine assistance promised to him in blessed Peter he enjoys that infallibility which the divine Redeemer wished his church to possess in defining teaching about faith or morals; therefore the Roman Pontiff's definitions are irreformable in their own right, and not through the consensus of the church.[7]

What the nimble fathers of Vatican I were asserting was this: under certain conditions the pope is the spokesman and instrument of whatever infallibility the church possesses. But that only poses the greater question: What infallibility did God wish his church to possess? Infallibility has been a working presumption. In its more solemn and circumspect moments the Catholic Church has been cautious and wary when professing infallibility. But the more widespread, day-to-day claims have been reckless and unrestrained. We have, indeed, promises and hope that the church will endure; there are no promises that it must necessarily avoid serious error, despite abusive attempts to force the New Testament into saying so. We have simply presumed that in issues deemed at the time to be essential the church had to be preserved from making mistakes. Might it not be an equally warranted—or less unwarranted—presumption that whatever its mistakes, the church will outlive and correct them?

Twenty years after *Humanae Vitae* it appears even clearer that it was indeed a major event in the evolution of authority. It stands to *Quanta Cura* and the *Syllabus of Errors* of Pius IX (1864) as Boniface VIII's bull *Unam Sanctam* (1302) related to Gregory VII's *Dictatus Papae* (1075). In both cases the earlier pope had advanced a vigorous new claim to authority. Gregory claimed he could depose emperors as easily as bishops, that all princes owed the pope the courtesy of kissing his feet, and that the see of Rome "has never erred, nor ever, by the witness of scripture, shall err to all eternity." Boniface carried the claim farther by asserting that all temporal rulers are answerable to the pope as the holder of highest spiritual authority. "We declare, state, define and pronounce that it is altogether necessary to salvation for every human creature to be subject to the Roman Pontiff."[8] By then the papal assertion had begun to buckle under the weight of its own extravagance. Each time the claims were repeated with less and less plausibility, the papal authority was that much more diminished. Likewise, Pius IX had condemned those persuaded that the papacy had anything to learn from modern developments. Paul VI's doctrine on birth control, it seems now, was an exercise of this authority that no longer seemed credible, and raised fresh questions about the entire custom of relying upon the Holy See as an oracle.[9]

In each of these two eras the Catholic Church had been roughed up by military and intellectual forces without, and stressed by controversy and failure of nerve within. The bishops of Rome stood forth, in default of any other champion, and announced themselves possessed of every competence and charism the church needed to survive. It was only with time that their actual competence seemed to fail their valor. The church did survive—indeed, it was reinvigorated—despite papal shortcomings and errors. And other agents of strength and initiative emerged: some called forth by the papacy and others unwelcomed, as possible rivals or critics.

A fourth anomaly in this struggle over authority regarding birth control is the fact that it gives only passing respect to history. Paul offers as the reason why the encyclical dismissed and contradicted the report of the papal study commission that "certain criteria of solutions had emerged which departed from the moral teaching on marriage proposed with constant firmness by the teaching authority of the Church."[10] Astonishingly, the footnotes do not document this constant firmness back any farther than 1930. One gathers that this "teaching authority" refers to the previous three popes. The fear of departing from a divinely guided tradition, a fear that was paralyzing for Alfredo Ottaviani and John C. Ford and, it would seem, for Giovanni Battista Montini, emerges as little more than a compulsive need to defend Arthur Vermeersch, the Flemish Jesuit who drafted most of *Casti Connubii* for Pius XI.

The office of teacher in the ancient Christian establishment was entrusted to those who also served as pastors. This, I believe, was due to the fact the reflection in faith on the community's experiences and outcomes has from the first been a major source of moral wisdom for the Christian church. Paul VI, at a time when the conventional teaching was in turmoil, turned for advice to a mixed group of bishops, theologians, social scientists, medical specialists, demographers, and lay activists. They offered him exactly what was needed: a disciplined reflection on pastoral experience that was perceptive and articulate enough to see where the tradition had gone up a blind alley. For most of them this was a recent insight. There is reason to believe that one reason their advice was discredited by him was that virtually every leading voice in the group belonged to someone who had abandoned the old view only a year or two earlier.

The pope whose authority needed this support turned away from it to a small knot of technicians who quoted to him the conventional formulae. He and they were intimidated by their supposition that God could never allow so long a leash to folly that their predecessors would have led them astray.

The Catholic experience in all this has been the very reverse of the experience of the mainline Protestant churches, which is why this story may be of wider than Catholic interest. It has been the Protestants who have warmed to the Enlightenment, allied themselves in modern times with revolutionary and popular government, admired the methods and accomplishments of empirical science, smiled at the industrial revolution and the achievements of capitalism, and blessed the Lord for the modern advances that freed them from much of the backwardness of their past.

For the Catholics it has been so very different. They found the Enlightenment godless, they grappled with the nation-states and the new civil liberties, they condemned the hubris of the scientists and the employment practices of modern business. They, along with several other countercultural Christian communities, have been nay-sayers every step of the way. Now we witness the great reversal of roles, as the Protestant intellectuals begin to worry about the uncritical zest their preaching has shown for the secular agenda. These misgivings arise just as the Catholics are beginning to get downright cozy with modern culture. One might have expected that Pope Paul VI, who is clearly in lineal descent from forebears who distrusted the devices and applications of modern technology, could have directed his sobering gaze to the sterile agenda of the birth control movement. What a loss that he chose to offer a technical analysis of the philosophical nature of sexual intercourse instead.

The contraception issue is very crucial for Christians, comparable perhaps to the identity of Jesus or the value of a sacrament. For it deals with a massive cluster of issues: marital fidelity, and the human need to bear children, and the moral need for commitment to the uncontrollable needs of certain other persons. In a word, at stake is the radical Christian conviction that we cannot survive personally, morally, spiritually, if our service to others is left to our personal choice. Here was a matter on which an authoritative voice was needed. But *Humanae Vitae* was, as regards prophetic authority, a mumble.

What Is "Natural"?

Moving now from the issues of authority to the merits of the matter, let us examine *Humanae Vitae*'s doctrine on sex and childbearing.

It is clear that Paul VI already accepted "responsible parenthood," or "birth regulation." But this was, as papal doctrine, a modern innovation. In 1951 Pius XII executed a remarkable swerve in the course of ethical tradition when he accepted birth control in principle, in his famous allocution to the Italian Midwives' Society:

> There are serious motives, such as those often mentioned in the so-called medical, eugenic, economic and social "indications," that can exempt for a long time, perhaps even for the whole duration of the marriage, from the positive and obligatory carrying out of the act. From this it follows that observing the non-fertile periods alone can be lawful only under a moral aspect. Under the conditions mentioned it really is so.[11]

Once the pope admitted in principle that married couples might have good and wholesome reasons for controlling their fertility, discussion narrowed to the single question of method. Pius approved only two methods of contraception: total abstinence and periodic abstinence (unfortunately called "rhythm" in popular parlance). All other methods he unflinchingly proscribed.

One need only be a disciple of the Christian tradition that calls sexual intercourse the "marriage act," the exchange that must itself form the consummation of the ritual celebration of a wedding, the tradition which acknowledges sex to be a grave obligation that spouses owe to one another, to regard total abstinence between husband and wife as dysfunctional and alienating. There would, one reckons, be few instances when the denial—even by mutual consent—of one of the most appropriate embodiments of marital commitment and affection would not be judged immoral. As for all other means of contraception—withdrawal, rhythm, barrier devices, anovulant pills, implants, temporary or permanent sterilization—it is difficult to see any imposing, intrinsic ethical difference between them. All are obviously artificial. Some require cultural sophistication (rhythm, pills), some involve risk to health (chemical means), others are unpleasant (withdrawal, condoms, spermicide), and still others seem irreversible (sterilization). Catholic moralists conventionally had condemned all of them, and one ventures to suggest that much of their writing on the subject reads like treatises on sexual plumbing, with devastatingly equivocal use of the term "unnatural."

Of all these methods one is tempted to think of rhythm as the most unnatural of all, since it inhibits not only conception, but the expression of affection. It is an inadequate theology that would want intercourse to harmonize with the involuntary endocrine rhythm of ovulation and menstruation, while forsaking the spiritual and emotional ebbs and flows which should also govern sexual union. In the human species, especially, where coitus is freed from the oestrous cycle, it is obviously open to personal meaning and depth quite independent of fertility. Different methods of contraception will be employed by couples in different circumstances. Medical advice and cost and convenience will lead them to favor the surest and easiest means, although in certain instances they may have recourse to otherwise less preferable methods. All are artificial, of course, and artificiality in the biology of sexual intercourse need be no more loathsome than it is in synthetic fibers, vascular surgery, or musical composition.

Those who have benefitted from "natural family planning," an improved method of periodic continence, rightly recommend it over the more hazardous forms of contraception. But that it is more "natural" does not mean that it is less "artificial." Indeed, it is *more* artificial in that it benefits from technologically more sophisticated signals of the menstrual cycle.

The encyclical strains plausibility when it sees artifice in the use of contraceptives by a married couple in order to make love, but denies that it is artificial for them to forgo the sexual embrace altogether.

The second major tenet of the encyclical was that one must assign moral value to methods of contraception within the isolated context of a single event of coitus, rather than within the full sequence and story of love and childbearing throughout the course of a marriage. The pope parts company here with his advisory commission, which reported:

> The morality of sexual acts between married people takes its meaning first of all and specifically from the ordering of their actions in a fruitful married life, that is, one which is practiced with responsible, generous and prudent parenthood. It does not then depend upon the direct fecundity of each and every particular act.[12]

The pope rejects this view by simply stating that a single intercourse made intentionally infecund is intrinsically dishonest. But this only begs the question. It would seem apparent that the integrity of marital intercourse derives, not just from the individual act, but from the whole orientation of the marriage. Indeed, that differentiates marital from extramarital intercourse. There are certain features of intercourse which would always have to be present, like fidelity and gentleness. Other features need to derive from the total sequence of sexual union, but are in no way requisite to each event. Childbearing would be one of these features. Indeed, reproduction may attend less than one marital encounter among many thousands.

Conventional Catholic theology had claimed that the primary end of marriage and of sex is the begetting and rearing of children. Listed as secondary ends: the satisfaction of desire and mutual support. Contraception—so the argument ran—violates this primary purpose by frustrating procreation. So does sterility, said the unconvinced. The reply: contraception willfully interferes with that part of intercourse which is the "work of humans" (the transmission of the sperm into the unimpeded female genital tract), while sterility hampers the "work of nature" that lies beyond (gonad function, genital structure, etc.). It has been further objected that the approved "rhythm" method likewise frustrates procreation, but here, too, an answer is ready: to abstain is natural, to interfere is not.

Few non-Catholics accepted this outline. Fewer Catholics were anxious to defend it publicly. One feature that seems to repel the contemporary mind is the intricate casuistry of the argument, and indeed of much of the older Catholic sexual moralizing. John Howard wrote before *Humanae Vitae* in the Australian quarterly, *Prospect:*

> When I was at school, certain practices of the Pharisees aroused my curiosity and amazement. Years later I read a serious contribution by a Jesuit to the Transactions of the Guild of St. Luke, stating that AIH [artificial insemination by a husband] was acceptable if semen deposited in the wife's vagina by normal intercourse were drawn into a syringe and injected into, or near, the os of the cervix. To withdraw the syringe from the vagina in the process would, however, be gravely sinful.[13]

The argument's greatest weakness is that it bespeaks a stud-farm theology. It does little to set man and wife off from stallion and mare. What does "primary end" mean? If it is supposed to mean that the act of intercourse is basically a biological act whose immediate orientation is aimed at procreation, all would agree. But the preponderance of Catholic writers seem to take "primary end" to mean "principal purpose," "most important goal," "chief finality." This is quite absurd.

We could as well say that the "primary end" of the Nobel Prize Awards Banquet is nutrition, that the "primary end" of the Olympic Games is exercise, and that the "primary end" of baptism is hygiene.

There are plenty of indications that a broader view exists in the wisdom of the Catholic tradition. Pius XI, in his encyclical letter on marriage in 1930, cites the traditional Augustinian "reproductive" formula. Later in the letter, however, he goes beyond that:

> This inward moulding of spouse to spouse, this eager striving to draw each other to fulfillment, can in the truest sense be called the primary purpose and explanation of marriage, as the *Roman Catechism* teaches. Marriage would thus be considered, not in the narrow sense as created for the procreation and education of offspring, but in the broad sense as the sharing, the familiarity, and the companionship of life in its fullness.[14]

Pius XII laid similarly heavy emphasis on the personal dimension of sex when he spoke out sharply in 1951 against artificial insemination:

> To reduce the cohabitation of married persons and the conjugal act to a mere organic function for the transmission of the germ of life would be to convert the domestic hearth, sanctuary of the family, into nothing more than a biological laboratory. . . . The conjugal act in its natural structure is a personal act, a simultaneous and immediate cooperation of the spouses which, by the very nature of the participants and the special character of the act, is the expression of that mutual self-giving which, in the words of Holy Scripture, effects the union "in one flesh."[15]

Four years before *Humanae Vitae* Msgr. J. D. Conway, past president of the Canon Law Society of America, had called for the old Augustinian formula to be dropped from the books:

> Canon 1013, which defines the purposes—the philosophical ends—of marriage, should be worded with greater delicacy. The primary purpose, procreation and education of children, clearly relegates to second rank the mutual love, happiness and welfare of the spouses. And these secondary purposes are further

slighted by defining them as "mutual aid and the remedy of concupiscence." Even though law is not romantic it should be able to recognize in marriage something more human, positive, spiritual and amorous.[16]

What is needed is a restatement which gives personal values their proper due. *Humanae Vitae* should have been that restatement. Conjugal love is a many-splendored thing. Christian theology has no choice but to confront it in the fullness of its sexual embodiment: what has been called "psychospiritual union and abandon, the total orgasm of the body and spirit."[17]

Another weak point in the older formula is the undefined and ambiguous way it uses the notion "natural."

The encyclical depicts nature in a remarkably fatalistic way. It is as if there were some divine inviolability about the cycle of female ovulation. Bishop Carlo Colombo, a minority member of the birth control commission, wrote in defense of this point: "If in the 'nature' of the generative processes there are inscribed periods and rhythms of fecundity and infecundity, that means that God does not want each single act and each single moment of married life to be fertile." Contraception is therefore offensive but abstinence is not, "for in the latter case man holds himself in readiness to discharge his duty, which will be determined by God the Creator through man's organic make-up, whereas in the other cases man puts his own will and his own designs in place of God's."[18]

Detecting the all-purposeful hand of God in such natural events as ovulation would, one supposes, lead to the conclusion that barren women have been struck sterile by the Lord. Theologians are generally aware that God's ways are not our ways, and are hesitant to presume a particular, rational intention (as if God were human) behind specific natural phenomena. If female infertility displays God's rational plan, then what of crop failure in India, bountiful oil resources under Kuwait, and the Johnstown Flood? Are these all to be taken as rational displays of divine anger or favor? In attempting to inhibit hurricanes by sowing clouds with dry ice crystals, is the local government putting its own designs in place of God's? Is vaccination *contra naturam*? And if the ovulation cycle is part of a rational divine plan to be left undisturbed, then surely sterility and stillbirth must be features of some perverse divine scheme of planned parenthood.

Everyone agrees that it is good to be natural; no one agrees on what that might mean. The average European will think it natural to smoke, live gregariously in cities, and discuss politics and religion in the pub; the Peruvian Indian may do none of these, yet not think himself unnatural. The Carthusian menu of stone-ground whole wheat bread, boiled vegetables, and raw fruit is thought by some to be the last word in natural foods; but those who follow the *Guide Michelin* stick by their paté, lobster, steak, and Camembert. A child of three may feel it natural to suck his thumb, as he may feel it natural at fifteen to masturbate; his parents may think both activities are unnatural and immature, though perhaps not at those ages. Anthropologists have told us it is natural for all peoples to worship a deity; theologians find this suggestive of the supernatural. One group of social workers thinks it would be natural to cut the throats of Indian cows; another group insists it is natural to cut the sperm ducts of Indian men. Manuals of medical ethics teach that progestational steroids (the Pill) are unnatural because they inhibit ovulation; Dr. Rock replied that they are as natural as vitamins: if the body provides progesterone at times when conception is undesirable, why cannot humans provide it for the same purpose? Catholic moralists had claimed it unnatural to misplace, trap, kill, or block the seed in intercourse, but have labeled the rhythm method natural. Not all Catholic parents could agree:

> Our second child had shown us that the calendar approach to rhythm was ineffective in our case, and so my wife moved on to the more sophisticated paraphernalia of the rhythm system—thermometers, tapes, tubes and the like. . . . We read and re-read the Catholic teaching on the natural law as it applied to marriage in general and to the Church's position of birth control in particular. Again and again the emphasis was found to be placed on what is "natural." And then we thought of the tapes and tubes and thermometers. This was natural?[19]

It seems hopeless to disentangle from this thicket of cross-purposes a working notion of "natural" that could serve the discussion of conjugal morality. Let another be proposed.

Marriage the Measure of Sex

Moral decisions in statecraft, economics, and jurisprudence are in constant flux, since the state, the economy, and the law are artificial institutions always on the move. There is something more perennial about the family. Marriage, it seems, has certain inbuilt requirements for success: requirements as complex as the intricate, constant makeup of man and woman. Though they have often failed to take the total view of marriage, Catholics have rightly insisted that it has its own ineluctable rules. Says French layman John Guitton:

> No doubt the partisans of chance reckon it an unforgivable sin to seek the purpose of nature, the ends of creation. But since the human intellect cannot comprehend a reality without knowing its function, destination and use, those who deny finality utilize the concept of an end no less than their opponents. The difference is that they do not confess it, or at least only consent to utilize it in a restricted area. They accept enquiry into the function of the eyelid or the liver, but they refuse to put the same question concerning man and life.[20]

Marital life is not involuntarily controlled as are the eyelid and the liver; a life of love must be a life of free choice. Any appropriate notion of "natural" will have to be correspondingly supple. There is perhaps no other human activity which so completely draws on the full range of forces in our nature: the will, the passions and affections, and the body. A restored vision of the "natural" would view the way in which these components of human nature are intrinsically meant to respond to the conjugal situation: *what brings the personality of the spouses to full bloom, what promotes their growth to maturity, what brings husband, wife, and children to the highest pitch of happiness.*

It is unfortunate, not so much that the pope chose to repeat negative and unconvincing judgments on contraception, but that he continued to dwell almost exclusively upon the problem of method, without adequate attention to the more crucial issue of outcome. Catholics have offered too little insight into this more sensitive moral problem. Except for Pius XII's rather terse outline of reasonable causes, the conventional breeding theology has been about all we have had to give. On the other hand, the equally shrill and superficial sort of propaganda devised by those who promote contraception is frighteningly deprived of any rich vision of marital growth in love. In any Dantesque view of the future, surely the canonist-moralists of the narrow tradition and the evangelists of the Planned Parenthood Federation will be consigned to each other's company.

The distress is that all this picayune quibbling over method fails to challenge the illusory purposes that lead so many families to adopt contraception. That appears to be the case with individual couples, as also with entire peoples. In this country, for example, millions of families are most likely pressed by high fertility potential or medical urgency or financial crisis or similarly serious burdens that contraception can rightly relieve. But I would estimate that far more couples avoid or curtail children because they share the grudging national attitude that resents children as so many more drains on their generosity and budget. Bluntly: selfishness is perhaps the most frequent excuse for contraception in this rich country.

Recall that when Paul VI decided to address and resolve this issue of contraception the Catholic Church had already been isolated by its official position on the subject. Many other Christian churches had come out in favor of it: the Lutherans, the Church of Christ, the Episcopalians, the Methodists, the Presbyterians. The general consensus among Protestant bodies agreed that, given unselfish motives, contraception was an acceptable means of family limitation. The other churches had heard the signs of the times, it was widely said, while the Catholic Church had stopped its ears.

The records of the Lambeth Conferences of the Anglican communion can serve as a fairly typical example of how other churches had shifted their viewpoint. The Conference of 1908 resolved thus:

The Conference regards with alarm the growing practice of the artificial restriction of the family, and earnestly calls upon all Christian people to discountenance the use of all artificial means of restriction as demoralizing to character and hostile to national welfare.[21]

In 1920 a resolution spelled out the same message in greater detail:

We utter an emphatic warning against the use of unnatural means for the avoidance of conception, together with the grave dangers—physical, moral, and religious—thereby incurred, and against the evils with which the extension of each use threatens the race. In opposition to the teaching which, under the name of science and religion, encourages married people in the deliberate cultivation of sexual union as an end in itself, we steadfastly uphold what must always be regarded as the governing considerations of Christian marriage. One is the primary purpose for which marriage exists, namely the continuation of the race through the gift and heritage of children; the other is the paramount importance in married life of deliberate and thoughtful self-control.[22]

By 1930 this was no longer being "steadfastly upheld"; there was no longer any objection to the method itself (it was this letter that provoked Pius XI to publish his counterstatement, *Casti Connubii*):

Where there is a clearly felt moral obligation to limit or avoid parenthood, the method must be decided on Christian principles. . . . where there is a morally sound reason for avoiding complete abstinence, the Conference agrees that other methods may be used, provided that this is done in the light of the same Christian principles. The Conference records its strong condemnation of the use of any methods of conception-control from motives of selfishness, luxury, or mere convenience.[23]

The last Conference before *Humanae Vitae*, in 1958, was not content to be permissive, but approved quite positively:

The Conference believes that the responsibility for deciding upon the number and frequency of children has been laid by

God upon the consciences of parents everywhere: that this planning, in such ways as are mutually acceptable to husband and wife in Christian conscience, is a right and important factor in Christian family life and should be the result of positive choice before God.[24]

Lambeth had moved gracefully along with the findings and sensibilities of the age. If anything were missing, it might have been a suspicion of that *Zeitgeist*, an unwillingness to presume or even to allude to the possibilities of selfish misapplication of this new technology. If Rome held back from this trajectory of thought, it should not have been to protect its own reputation for consistency, but to exhibit consistency by reminding its communicants that we cannot be saved unless we open our lives to children and commit ourselves to others' needs that lie beyond control of our free choice. The issue would not have been the moral possibility of contraception, but the moral requirements for it to be employed without hardening the heart.

In this regard, one would fault the pope for having said too little, rather than too much. If a critic may be permitted to point out a passage in the encyclical which seems particularly well put, I would draw attention to the disappointingly brief remarks made in paragraph 9 about the characteristics of conjugal love:

> This love is above all fully human, a compound of sense and spirit. . . . It is a love which is total—that very special form of personal friendship in which husband and wife generously share everything, allowing no unreasonable exceptions and not thinking solely of their own convenience. . . . Married love is also faithful and exclusive, and this until death.[25]

Here was the vein of thought that could have been worked so much more. It is here, in throwing up to his readers the awesome challenges of marriage, that the pontiff could have confronted the world with its increasingly contraceptive mentality. This is a point which needed making, needed shouting from the rooftops.

Welcome for Children: An Affront to Western Culture

Someone is responsible for persuading our world of the extraordinary idea that marriage is easy. The Catholic Church has tended to think it frighteningly difficult. For a priest it is always moving to face a young couple before the altar and guide them through the awesome oaths of total abandonment. Like six-year-olds promising in their prayers to "love God with my whole heart," the bride and groom speak in hyperbole. They could hardly be expected to imagine what are the deeps of "for better, for worse, for richer, for poorer, in sickness and in health, until death do us part." Their parents in the front pew may have a good idea (provided that they are together in the pew); the church knows, and prays that the young man and woman will find the generosity to learn, and will learn the generosity.

Real love, to men and women born as we all are with a selfish streak, does not come naturally at all. When Paul tells husbands to love their wives as Christ loved the church and gave himself up for her, he is haunted by the symbol and measure of that cherishing: the crucifixion. Love, says the Song of Songs, is as strenuous as death. It is a struggle to the death to give self away. It has to be learned so very resolutely. Marriage is that great adventure in adult education, wherein parents have far more to learn and longer strides to take toward maturity than do the children.

Growth in love—like all human growth—means stress and sacrifice. The church has never tried to conceal this. She simply says that marriage is glorious if you accept the stress and sacrifice. It is hell if you try shortcuts. And there are all sorts of shortcuts offered these days.

Barbara Cadbury, for instance, returned from a good-cheer tour in Asia for the British Planned Parenthood Federation, wrote enthusiastically of the "courageous sense of realism" with which Japanese were eliminating their offspring. But the government, she said, had come to feel "that abortion is, as a regular method of birth control, harmful to the individual despite its benefit to the nation." The individual harmed was presumably the individual doing the abortion, not the individual being extirpated. (I was reminded of the complaint made by the commandant of a Nazi camp, that the excessive shipments of prisoners to be gassed and cremated worked unreasonable stress on the prison guards.) But Mrs. Cadbury's most telling remark was this: "No other country in the world has so rapidly passed from fertility-motivated habits to producing only desired and cherished children." The two million or so children each year who were not desired and cherished were eliminated. The Christian church should see it just the other way around from Mrs. Cadbury. If a man and woman have brought to life in the womb a child who is not desired or cherished, their problem is not how to eliminate the child but how to learn to desire and cherish him or her. One does not need the church to know it is often easier to kill your child than to love your child. But to the Japanese parents and to Mrs. Cadbury she recommends the latter.

A young woman at whose marriage I had officiated came to me several months later to tell me that every night during intercourse she was seized with fear that she might conceive. They couldn't possibly, she cried, afford a baby yet. Knowing that her parents had given them a house and land, and that both husband and wife were working for good wages, I was rather surprised. As it turned out, they had gone heavily into debt to buy an oak living-room suite, a maple bedroom set, a complete dining room ensemble, a roomful of kitchen appliances, and all their laundry equipment. The unfortunate couple had been sold a bill of goods—not by the furniture salesman, but by the culture that had so persuaded a man and his wife that a child came just below laundry equipment on their list of needs. Before the year was out they would come to feel the oaken and maple boredom.

There are plenty of other examples which betray the radical disagreement between Christianity and our culture regarding marriage. We are chided by the realists of the day for our intransigent stand against divorce. Once the marriage relationship is dead—especially when it is violently traumatized by adultery—it is false to pretend otherwise. The church replies that the marriage bond is grounded, not on the love of the moment, but on oaths made in view of love. Obviously the oath without the love is misery. But it is the very function of forgiveness to restore that love and breathe into it an even steadier life than before. The church never ignored the cold fact that adultery kills love; but she recommends resurrection instead of cremation. The church should know something of forgiveness and its power. The only love-bond she has as Christ's bride is one of her repentance and his forgiveness. Says Jean Guitton: "The remedy for the ills caused by love is a summons to progress in love. In other terms, love can cure the wounds it inflicts, on condition that it rises to greater heights."[26]

The source which has oriented me to learn much about marriage is the nineteenth chapter of the Gospel according to Matthew. This chapter records two interviews with Jesus. In the second, he is asked by a young man what he must do to possess eternal life. This was a standard question that any Jew would ask a sage and Jesus' answer at first is a very standard one: "You must keep the commandments." And he lists several of the very familiar laws. The young man is pleased and says, "I've done that ever since I was very young," but then Jesus says, "That's not enough. If you want to go all the way, then you have to sell everything, give it away, and come follow me." At this the young man is not so pleased because, as the evangelist points out, he has a great deal to sell. Somewhat disillusioned, he turns around and goes away. The point of the story is that he does not have eternal life even though he has kept the commandments from his youth. Jesus is opposing to the religion of his day another type of faith which has no terms or prior conditions. When a Jew purposely undertook the life of a member of God's people, he knew what he was undertaking. He was told in advance what were the terms of faith and he accepted them with eyes open. When a man accepted to follow Jesus, he had no idea what the terms were. Nothing specific was told him in advance except that he must surrender to whatever claims Jesus, through all of his neighbors, would put on him. The young man rightly recognized that this was far more frightening since there was no way of calculating how much he was giving away. And so . . . he walked away from

eternal life. After he leaves the scene, the disciples are somewhat nervous and they say, "Well, if this is the way it is, who
on earth could get into the Kingdom of Heaven?" and Jesus
says, "It is not just a matter of money, but of laying everything
aside for generous love; and that is done only by God's empowerment."

In the earlier part of the chapter, a very similar interview
takes place. Jesus is asked what are the terms for divorce. In
the religion of his day, people entered marriage knowing in
advance what were the limits of endurance: what things a man
could be expected to tolerate and what things he need not
accept. Jesus once again says: "In marriage, as I propose it,
there are no terms; there is no divorce." The people go away
shaking their heads. Once again the disciples are upset and
they ask Jesus, "But if this is the way it is, who on earth could
get married?" and he says, "It is not the normal way; it is God's
gift."

What I perceive from this chapter is that the unlimited
surrender which a person makes to Jesus Christ in baptism has
as perhaps its closest imitation among humans Christian marriage, wherein a man and woman surrender to one another
without terms. Just as Jesus can say to a fellow in the crowd,
"You! Follow me," and the person has no idea where that will
lead, so a man can say to a woman, "Follow me, and you have
no idea where that will lead or what I will become." And the
woman in her turn says to him, "And you follow me, not
knowing where that will lead." Marriage, like baptism, derives
from faith. It is a move based simply upon trust in a person—
not a policy, a religion, a moral code, a set of requirements. It
is a determined abandonment to an unpredictable person, who
is known and cherished enough that one can make the surrender.

If this be so, then Christian marriage is not like all other
marriages. Marriage is what you make of it and Christian marriage is one particular voluntary form which Christians have
fashioned out of their own inspiration. There are many other
forms of marriage and we should not imagine that they are not
legitimate. If in a certain culture it is accepted that a man has
six wives, it is none of our business to point to the man and

say, "Five of those are not really your wives—get rid of them." If a man says to six women, "You are my wife," then they are indeed his wives. If in another culture it is understood that a man may exchange wives at whim, then it is none of our business to say, "You must marry for life."

In fact, it is unfortunate that in our civil marriage ceremonies, words are put into the mouths of men and women whereby they promise to one another things that they in no way intend to promise. In our society it is not understood that a man and a woman give themselves away for better or for worse until death. They do not give themselves away unconditionally, they give themselves away indefinitely and with many implicit conditions. Yet because our civil marriage form is descended from the Christian sacramental forms, couples are constrained to say more than they mean.

Now if Christian marriage is a particular, extraordinary, peculiar way for a man and a woman to join together, then we must realize that it has particular obligations. The most important one is similar to the obligation to follow Jesus. When you tie yourself to a person, you cannot control your future. Every one of us has within an unbelievable potential for love and for generosity but we do not bring it out very willingly. It has to be required of us. And the thing about Christian marriage is that the surprises encountered demand a love and generosity from us that we can in no way calculate or control.

If that be so, then the incalculability of the demands of children fits very closely into the generosity that a man and a woman share in marriage. If a man and a woman can and do calculate and control the major claims made upon their generosity in the course of their marriage, then it is not a marriage of faith, and it will not blossom into a marriage of love such as Christians can enjoy.

The objection is made that regulating birth exclusively through sexual abstinence (periodic or total) is morally acceptable because the spouses must forgo a large measure of willful choice, whereas contraception leaves much of the choice to them. But one might similarly have thought it an immoral change when men (and later, women) first began to be allowed to select their spouses rather than acquiescing in the choices of their parents. The possibilities for self-indulgence seem no more alarming in the one innovation than in the other.

Therefore I would much have preferred that the pope challenge Christian men and women, Catholic husbands and wives, to feel differently about children than anyone else in the world, and to reject the resistance to children into which so many of us, at least in the affluent North, have been unwittingly brainwashed. I wish he had called people, not to breed, but to abandon themselves to their own children. This is not to deny that there are occasionally good motives for practicing contraception, but I would so have wished that the pope would have transferred the discussion from the issue of method, to the issue of purpose. He failed to confront us and say "What do you believe about children?"

The church should not be interested in breeding. A thoughtless priest said in the United States some years ago that Catholics would put an end to religious discrimination in a generation or two by outproducing their contracepting opponents. Preachers have occasionally been heard to suggest that the obligation to crowd heaven should stimulate Christian parents to optimum production. Both statements breathe nonsense. Yet the church has always had a smile for children, not because she is interested in population but because she is interested in love. And besides, she was once told that of such is the kingdom of heaven. A first child, especially a boy-child, can easily be a threat to his father, for he seems to be a competitor for the wife's love that had been all his before. Similarly, each new child that swells the brood can seem a burden: the loaf must now be sliced just that much thinner. The church sees another side to it. Bread may be sliced thinner, but love is sliced larger, and greater love sets about winning more bread. Every person, every parent is a fathomless well of love-potential.

Children are not threats to love or competitors for it—they are new claims upon it, new tugs on the ungenerous heart to force it open further than it felt it could go. Children do not divide parents' love, they multiply it. Enormous resources of parent-love are left to stagnate in the heart's reservoirs for lack of children to make it gush and flow. Now obviously physical resources are not fathomless, and children must have bread.

But in our age and culture, when parents feed their children cake and live in fear of a bread shortage, the church has reason to weep that the children are starving in a famine of love.

NOTES

1. Pope Paul VI, *Encyclical Letter on the Moral Principles Governing Human Procreation ("Humanae Vitae")*, par. 14. Translation in *The Pope Speaks* 13 (1968): 337.

2. Professor Andrew Greeley has been a most persistent advocate of this view. *Humanae Vitae* was in large part responsible, he believes, even for the 50 percent reduction over the last twenty-five years in the proportion of their income that U.S. Catholics contribute to their church. See Andrew M. Greeley and William McManus, *Catholic Contributions: Sociology and Politics* (Chicago: Thomas More, 1987). That the ability of the Holy Father to command obedience has suffered in recent years might also be traced to the restoration of uncensored public discourse in the Catholic Church, which occured several years earlier during during Vatican II, and exposes quite ordinary laypeople to articulate criticism of the pope that had previously circulated only within an intellectual elite.

3. A Catholic journal in Italy noted that this "unconventional statement" occurred at the same time Msgr. Ferdinando Lambruschini was appointed archbishop of Perugia. Lambruschini, a professor of moral theology at the Lateran seminary in Rome, and a majoritarian member of the papal commission (1962–1966) that had advised the pope to accept contraception, later set aside his convictions, participated as a drafter of the encyclical and provided the public relations support at its first-day press conference. Said the journal: "If Father Burtchaell is a professor (*un professore*), the new archbishop Lambruschini is a great big professor (*un professorone*)."

4. "The Minority Working Paper" (said to be the work of John C. Ford, S.J., with Germain Grisez, both American moralists). Text from Peter Harris et al., *On Human Life: An Examination of "Humanae Vitae"* (London: Burns & Oates, 1968), 178,181–182.

5. See various post-publication statements in *The Pope Speaks* 13 (1968): 206,210,257,309–310. Also see an interview the pope gave to Alberto Cavallari in Robert Blair Kaiser, *The Politics of Sex and Reli-*

gion: A Case History in the Development of Doctrine, 1962–1984 (Kansas City, Mo.: Leaven, 1985), 107–109.

6. *The Pope Speaks* 13 (1968): 207.

7. H. Denzinger, *Enchiridion Symbolorum*, #1839.

8. See Brian Tierney, *The Crisis of Church & State, 1050–1300* (Englewood Cliffs, N.J.: Prentice-Hall, 1964).

9. It is instructive to compare the respectful tone of those who called for a reform in the church's doctrine on sexuality and reproduction before the encyclical with the stridency of those who wrote in the aftermath.

See Ambrogio Valsecchi, *Regolazione delle nascite* (Brescia: Queriniana, 1967); William Birmingham, ed., *What Modern Catholics Think About Birth Control: A New Symposium* (New York: New American Library, 1964); Donald Barrett et al., eds., *The Problem of Population*, 3 vols, (Notre Dame, Ind.: University of Notre Dame Press, 1964–65); Daniel Callahan, ed., *The Catholic Case for Contraception* (New York: Macmillan, 1969) [including older documents].

Surveys quickly showed that Catholic opinion and behavior, both lay and clerical, did not follow papal injunctions: Oscar Perez Maldonado, *Los católicos y la planeación familiar: Resultados de una encuesta nacional* (Mexico City: Instituto Mexicano de Estudios Sociales, 1969); Maurice J. Moore, *Death of a Dogma? The American Clergy's Views of Contraception* (Chicago: Community & Family Study Center, 1973); J. Mayone Stycos, *Ideology, faith and family planning in Latin America: Studies in public and private opinion on fertility control* (New York: McGraw-Hill, 1971); Osmund Schreuder and Jan Hutjes, *Priester zur Geburtenregelung; Eine empirische Erhebung* (Munich & Mainz: Kaiser & Grunewald, 1972).

The aftermath: Claudia Carlen, ed., *The Papal Encyclicals 1958–1981* ([Wilmington, N.C.]: McGrath, 1981), 233–236; John Horgan, ed., *Humanae Vitae and the Bishops: The Encyclical and the Statements of the National Hierarchies* (Shannon: Irish University Press, 1972); Fernando Vittorino Joannes, *The Bitter Pill: Worldwide Reaction to the Encyclical Humanae Vitae* ([IDO-C] Philadelphia: Pilgrim, 1970); Charles E. Curran, ed., *Contraception: Authority and Dissent* (New York: Herder & Herder, 1969); Franz Böckle and Carl Holenstein, eds., *Die Enzyklika in der Diskussion: Eine orientierende Dokumentation zu "Humanae vitae"* (Zurich: Benziger, 1968); *Humanae Vitae: sí y no; antología de estudios doctrinales* (Buenos Aires: Paidos, 1970); William Shannon, *The Lively Debate: Response to Humanae Vitae* (New York: Sheed & Ward, 1970); Leo Pyle, ed., *Pope and Pill: More Documentation on the Birth Regulation Debate* (London: Darton, Longman & Todd, 1968);

Norman St. John-Stevas, *The Agonizing Choice: Birth Control, Religion and the Law* (Bloomington, Ind.: Indiana University Press, 1971).

10. *Humanae Vitae*, par. 6, p.332. On the work of the commission, see Kaiser, *The Politics of Sex and Religion.*

11. Address to the Italian Catholic Union of Midwives, 29 October 1951. Translation in *Catholic Mind* 50 (1952): 57.

12. Quoted in Kaiser, 252.

13. "Sex ex Machina," *Prospect* 7 (1964): 14.

14. Pius XI, encyclical letter *Casti Connubii,* par. 24, *Acta Apostolici Sedis* 22 (1930): 548–549. This important paragraph was omitted from the English version of the encyclical for nine years; it appeared in a revised translation as of 1939. Earlier, pars. 10ff, the encyclical discourses upon the three ordered goods, or blessings of marriage according to Augustine: offspring, conjugal fidelity, and sacramental indissolubility.

15. Quoted by Gerald Kelly, S.J., *Medico-Moral Problems* (St. Louis: Catholic Hospital Association, 1958): 230.

16. "Revising Canon Law," *Commonweal* 80 (1964): 145. The 1918 *Code of Canon Law* stated:

> Canon 1013,1. The primary end of marriage is the procreation and education of children; its secondary end is mutual help and the allaying of concupiscence. (T. Lincoln Bouscaren, S.J. and Adam C. Ellis, S.J., *Canon Law: A Text & Commentary* [Milwaukee: Bruce, 1951])

The revised *Code* of 1983 now states:

> Canon 1055,1. The matrimonial covenant, by which a man and a woman establish between themselves a partnership of the whole of life, is by its nature ordered toward the good of the spouses and the procreation and education of offspring; this covenant between baptized persons has been raised by Christ to the dignity of a sacrament. (*Code of Canon Law,* Latin-English Edition [Washington: Canon Law Society of America, 1983])

17. Daniel Sullivan, letter, *Commonweal* 80 (1964): 52.

18. This perspective was defended in a series of articles entitled "The Vatican Speaks Out," commissioned and syndicated by Publishers-Hall Syndicate and appearing in forty newspapers in the United States in the fall of 1969, just before the meeting of the synod of bishops in Rome. Eight dissenters, representative of the minority that eventually prevailed over the birth control commission, wrote to defend *Humanae Vitae:* Cardinals John Wright and Pericle Felici of

the Vatican and Karol Wojtyla of Krakow, Bishop Carlo Colombo and Msgr. Giovanni Guzzetti of Milan, Revs. Michel Riquet, and Gustave Martelet, S.J., of France, and Professor Colin Clark of Oxford. The "argument from nature" was repeated in the series, though for the most part the authors grounded the value of the encyclical on papal authority rather than on intrinsic cogency.

19. William G. Keane, letter, *Commonweal* 79 (1964): 752–753.

20. Jean Guitton, *Essay on Human Love* (London: Rockcliff, 1951), 154–155.

21. *The Lambeth Conferences, 1867–1948* (London: SPCK, 1948), 295. The encyclical letter of that 1908 conference offered a sharp if somewhat daintily expressed condemnation: "No one who values the purity of home life can contemplate without grave misgivings the existence of an evil which jeopardizes that purity; no one who treasures the Christian ideal of marriage can condone the existence of habits which subvert some of the essential elements of that ideal." *The Six Lambeth Conferences 1867–1920* (London: SPCK, 1929), 310.

22. Resolution 68, ibid., appendix, 44.

23. Resolution 15, *The Lambeth Conference 1930* (London: SPCK, n.d.), 43–44.

24. Resolution 115, *The Lambeth Conference 1958* (London: SPCK, 1958), 1.57.

25. *Humanae Vitae*, par. 9, pp.333–334.

26. Guitton, 106.

5

The Child as Chattel

THE VATICAN'S CONGREGATION FOR the Doctrine of the Faith (CDF) aroused a firestorm of criticism with its 1987 "Instruction on Respect for Human Life in Its Origin and on the Dignity of Procreation: Replies to Certain Questions of the Day."[1] U.S. theologians promptly began to call the Instruction "unpersuasive."[2] Various Catholic university hospitals in Europe announced that they were going to ignore it and continue their fertility services.[3] The *New York Times* found it an occasion to reiterate its doctrine concerning official Catholic authorities: like the earlier bans on abortion and contraception, this condemnation was an act of resistance against enlightenment, against a technology the editors regarded as "an enormous step into the future."[4]

The document was heavily discounted because it dealt with procreation and had presumably been written by male celibates who must lack an insider's knowledge.[5] Lay dismay was widely cited as well. An American woman, 40, who had adopted one child and with her husband was trying to conceive through *in vitro* fertilization (IVF), said: "Parenting is such a strong urge. I don't think the church can stop it."[6] An Australian wife who hoped for her second child via the same technology, complained, "All we're asking for is to allow a man and wife to have a family."[7]

The document, which was published over the signature of Joseph Cardinal Ratzinger, prefect of the Congregation (with the annotation that Pope John Paul had personally authorized it), does set forth a rationale for its ethical conclusions. CDF, the legatee of a terse and cautionary prose style developed in the curia to deal with doctrine-on-the-stray, is charged with expounding and clarifying Christian faith. It must beat the bounds of the church, and tend the fences that mark the borders of sound belief.

If this recent publication, despite its efforts to give out the whys and wherefores, should fail to be persuasive even among many thoughtful Catholics, that may be due to certain systemic handicaps within the Congregation itself. Among the twenty cardinals and bishops listed as official members at the time the document appeared, less than a handful were known to have been professionally trained and experienced as practicing theologians. The in-house staff, numbering hardly a dozen persons, listed no one known as a leader among scholars. There is a board of academic consultants, among whom faculty members at local Roman seminaries traditionally predominate.

The task of scrutinizing new attempts to interpret and apply the doctrine of a community scattered across all the cultures of the world, with an intellectual lineage back to the apostles, indeed back to Abraham and Sarah, is surely a work for skilled intellectuals. It would seem that an agency charged with that scrutiny ought not be denied the resources needed to produce perceptive and cogent teaching on complex and crucial issues. Full many a theologian is born to blush in Vatican offices unseen, but such an accumulation of anonymity as this virtually guarantees that the CDF never will have the capacity to reply effectively to Certain Questions of the Day.

I want to argue, nevertheless, that the insight which the Instruction so stiffly represents and unpersuasively defends is both true and timely.

TECHNOLOGY AND THE "CONTROL OF NATURE"

The Vatican is well aware that its adversary in this matter of human procreation is modern technology. Now the technologist is a "can do" person, whose success is usually proportionate to his ability to fix total attention upon a given problem, to isolate it from all extrinsic factors, and resolutely to manipulate the variables in order to produce the client's satisfaction. The technologist tends to see into a problem by squinting, by narrowing the gaze.

Only a few days after the Instruction appeared I had occasion to admire the pluck and pertinacity of modern technology near Boston where I was visiting friends. The affluent townships encircling that city lodge the executives of the corporate world which assembles each morning in the downtown business district. The problem presented to Boston technology was how to get those suburban executives to work and back with a minimum of inconvenience. The solution was to build the Massachusetts Turnpike straight out and through Weston. And, so that the commuters would not have to slow their pace during the snow and ice of winter, hundreds of tons of industrial salts have been strewn upon the turnpike's surface each year. The result is—as specified—that the good residents of Weston can be at their desks after a brisk and direct journey in the morning, and back out amid the leafy wonderland of ponds and copses and meadows in the evening.

But there have been additional results. The gracefully contoured countryside of the area, which is one of the most moneyed neighborhoods in the United States, has had the settled life of its wetlands deranged, and its water run-off is now disturbed. The town reservoir has been rendered saltier than the Atlantic Ocean and is undrinkable.

The vulnerability of contemporary technology consists in its readiness to view tasks no more largely than the desires they are asked to satisfy. George Parkin Grant has written: "Thought is steadfast attention to the whole."[8] I would take that to be a pretty good description of classical Christian morality as well. The fellows who built the turnpike did just what the burgesses beyond Boston wanted. And they ignored the fact that nature cannot be refashioned on demand. They steadfastly ignored the whole to serve the interests of a segment of the whole. And that is what sin often is.

Look southward for another moral tale. The Ogallala Aquifer is possibly the largest underground freshwater source in the world. Eight Great Plains states depend upon it for their water. The aquifer was created of sand and gravel deposits more than a million years ago. It fills slowly; about 700 years of rainwater seepage is needed to replenish it.

When farmers in the Southwest recently decided to augment their agricultural output and financial income, they began drawing on that water supply more thirstily. They now extract nearly ten times as much water as the aquifer can recapture each year. The water table sinks lower each month. The subsoil is consequently collapsing and becoming too compacted to take in the water needed to recharge the reservoir below. As in Weston, there is a twofold result. Increased irrigation has increased agricultural production and profit, exactly as desired. But by failing to defer to nature the users have guaranteed that virtually all farmland from Kansas to Texas, from Arizona to Arkansas, will be wasteland in thirty or forty years. It is not that they act in ignorance: they know the facts. But they avert their gaze. There is no steadfast attention to the whole. In its willful and impetuous determination to fit nature to its will, technology is irreversibly violating the earth. The present dwellers have impoverished their offspring. That is a sin.[9]

Twenty-five years ago the *New Yorker* first published Rachel Carson's *Silent Spring*, an exposé of pesticides, which she called the "elixirs of death." The sophisticated and very modern chemicals which technology had produced on request to control insects and other crop predators were irreversibly poisoning the earth and the air and the water and the living organisms with whom humans must abide in respectful partnership. Carson inscribed her book with Albert Schweitzer's complaint: "Man has lost the capacity to foresee and to forestall. He will end by destroying the earth."

We must cultivate, Carson argued,

> the awareness that we are dealing with life—with living populations and all their pressures and counter-pressures, their surges and recessions. Only by taking account of such life forces and by cautiously seeking to guide them into channels favorable to ourselves can we hope to achieve a reasonable accommodation between the insect hordes and ourselves.

The current vogue for poisons has failed utterly to take into account these most fundamental considerations. As crude a weapon as the cave man's club, the chemical barrage has been hurled against the fabric of life—a fabric on the one hand delicate and destructible, on the other miraculously tough and resilient, and capable of striking back in unexpected ways. These extraordinary capacities of life have been ignored by the practitioners of chemical control who have brought to their task no "high-minded orientation," no humility before the vast forces with which they tamper.

The "control of nature" is a phrase conceived in arrogance, born of the Neanderthal age of biology and philosophy, when it was supposed that nature exists for the convenience of man. The concepts and practices of applied entomology for the most part date from that Stone Age of science. It is our alarming misfortune that so primitive a science has armed itself with the most modern and terrible weapons, and that in turning them against the insects it has also turned them against the earth.[10]

The technologists were not amused to be told they were using modern methods but primitive attitudes. They denounced Carson as shrill, hysterical, romantic. The most cutting denunciation was that she was backward, that she was flailing at technological progress.[11] But the tides eventually pulled with Miss Carson, and her book was one of the inaugural works of the environmental movement, born of her "anger at the senseless, brutish things that were being done."[12]

It is not technology itself that is sinister, nor even its method, which is to restrict its gaze to the problem at hand. The damage comes when a technologist (or any professional) acts only on the competence of his or her discipline, while blind to any wider view of the fuller human agenda. The technologist goes berserk and becomes the sorcerer's apprentice when she devises tactics in ignorance of what strategy or policy or ethic they are going to serve.

The ecological movement, now well underway, is the first effectively persuasive rebuke to a belief that had grown apace with modern science and technology since the Enlightenment. The doctrine held that human purpose and choice would encounter no limits in its dominion over nature. Or, to put a finer point on the doctrine: it held that there was no nature, no creation with an ingiven character and requirements quite beyond what we could choose to infuse in things or bleach out of them.

But the environmental disillusionment was all to do with the elements and with plants and animals. We have yet to be persuaded that there are given, natural forces and needs in humanity ourselves that may be as aloof from our willful preferences and choices as are the tides of the ocean that make sport of our retaining walls and waterways.

We are more conscious now that a healthy diet of bread and pulse and fish and fresh vegetables and fruits is naturally good, and is hardly enhanced by lashings of sodium hexametaphosphate, FD & C Yellow No. 5, monosodium glutamate, or potassium sorbate. And we sense that a sedentary pace coupled with gluttony at table must not be facilitated by stapling the stomach or excising half of the bowel or surgically stripping off a girdle of excess fat. And there is enough alarm at the readiness of some physicians to overmedicate that some nurses now will not take even an aspirin tablet to fight a headache.

This reticence towards technological intrusion for the "control of nature" is really a later application of ecological conscience to our own bodies. But if we go deeper, if our steadfast pursuit of the whole draws us beyond our physical selves to our distinctively human and personal makeup, are we prepared to doubt that we can be whoever or whatever we choose, unconstrained by what we were created and fashioned to be?

PROCREATIONAL TECHNOLOGY

The movement to assist sexual intercourse with technology was begun by two valiant women: Marie Stopes in Great Britain and Margaret Sanger in the United States. The prescribed purposes of this movement were clear and cogent. Inferior members of the race were to be prevented from breeding, and worthwhile persons were to be spared the burden of begetting more children than they cared to care for.

The eugenic agenda was explained by Dr. Stopes:

> It is perhaps only to be expected that the more conscientious, the more thrifty, and the more lovingly desirous to do the best for their children people are, the more do they restrict their families, in the interests both of the children they have and of the community which would otherwise be burdened by their offspring did they not themselves adequately provide for them. Those who are less conscientious, less full of forethought, and less able to provide for the children they bear, and more willing to accept public aid directly and indirectly, are more reckless in the production of large families. . . .
>
> The thriftless who breed so rapidly tend by that very fact to bring forth children who are weakened and handicapped by physical as well as mental warping and disease, and at the same time to demand their support from the sound and thrifty.[13]

For the very reason that worthwhile people were conscientious and the undesirables were not, contraception was the technology proposed for the "fit." Something less voluntary was appropriate for the unfit. "It seems easy enough to supply the intelligent and careful woman with physiological help; and for the careless, stupid or feeble-minded who persist in producing infants of no value to the State and often only a charge upon it, the right course seems to be sterilization."[14]

Mrs. Sanger advocated an even more vigorous application of remedies:

> to apply a stern and rigid policy of sterilization to that grade of population whose progeny is already tainted [feebleminded, idiots, morons, insane, syphilitic, epileptic, criminal, professional prostitutes, etc.], or whose inheritance is such that objectionable traits may be transmitted to offspring . . . also, to give certain dysgenic groups in our population their choice of sterilization or segregation.
>
> The second step would be to take an inventory of the secondary group such as illiterates, paupers, unemployables, criminals, prostitutes, dope-fiends; classify them in special departments under government medical protection, and segregate

them on farms and open spaces as long as necessary for the strengthening and development of moral conduct.[15] [She expected that the first group might comprise five million people; the second, possibly twenty million.]

Historian Daniel J. Kevles recounts the early orientation of their movement:

> Before the war, Sanger had linked birth control with feminism. Now, like her British counterpart Marie Stopes, she tied contraception increasingly to the eugenic cause. "More children from the fit, less from the unfit: that is the chief issue of birth control," said Sanger.[16]

Once the defective and morally objectionable people were prevented by sterilization from further tainting the future citizenry, good people of modest means could be provided with safe and healthy contraceptives. This dual program of fertility control would obviate two great horrors: abortion and war.

There was an early recognition that this progressive undertaking would go down badly with Catholic officials. Stopes wrote:

> The Roman Catholic Church in particular is the most unyielding in its total condemnation of the use of scientific aid in controlling the production of children, although it—like the other Churches—concedes the *principle* of the justifiability of control in some circumstances. To concede the principle, even while condemning the best methods of effecting such control, is to deny the uses of intellectual progress.[17]

There would be others disposed to stand in the way of such a plucky, "can do" venture:

> To those who protest that we have no right to interfere with the course of Nature, one must point out that the whole of civilization, everything which separates men from animals, is an interference with what such people commonly call Nature.[18]

The venture succeeded. Sterilization and contraception are now legal throughout the land, endorsed by virtually all religious bodies, advertised openly and urged with subsidy upon the poor. There are, in fact, more sterilizations performed annually upon Americans today than there were American marriages being performed when Stopes and Sanger began their work of enlightenment.

But the venture of technology overshot its original goals in several unforeseen ways. America now has the highest rate of teenage pregnancy in what we like to call the developed world. The incidence of sexual promiscuity, venereal disease, abortion, marital collapse, fatherless children, child abuse and abandonment, and wanton breeding by the thriftless (and dusky) poor is probably higher than at any time in our national history.

The founders did concede that their program might not immediately achieve its desired results. But that was because of the lack, in their time, of an "ideal" contraceptive. Its development was to be expected from further assiduous scientific research. Seventy years and much assiduous research later, the same message is still bravely recited. With more technology— more instruction in contraception, more availability of contraceptives, and more access to abortion as a failsafe backup—all of these problems can be licked. There is nothing that enlightenment and scientific progress cannot overcome.

Planned Parenthood and its research organ, the Alan Guttmacher Institute (AGI), are aware that their accomplishments still fall short of their hopes. Yet an enormous breakthrough has recently put success within their reach at last. The problem had previously been viewed too narrowly, in terms too exclusively biological.

> Some researchers have begun to attack the problem of teenage pregnancy from a sociological perspective. Their studies suggest that if the problem arises mainly out of cultural and socio-economic conditions, the longer-term solutions may also have to address those same conditions.
>
> The evolution of Joy Dryfoos' own thinking in this regard is instructive. Dryfoos, one of the country's leading experts on the issue of school-age pregnancy and former planning director of the AGI, says: "One of the last things I did at the Guttmacher Institute was to help prepare *Teenage Pregnancy: The Problem That*

Hasn't Gone Away. It was a statistical pamphlet that documented
the need for sex education, access to contraception and abortion
services, and services for adolescent parents and their children.
And yet I knew that, even doing all those things, the issue of
teenage pregnancy would not go away. And it wouldn't go
away because there are young people who do not perceive that
there is any reason to use contraceptives and avoid parenthood."[19]

The problem, then, is motivation: not motivation regarding sex or friendship or love or childbearing, but motivation to
use technology when one refuses to think of those other—less
simple and more troubling—matters. So new programs to encourage the use of contraceptives are now underway.

On other fronts, where motivation is less sluggish, biotechnology has been producing admirable results. For those
who beget children but do not desire them, pharmaceutical
preparations so safe that one can keep them in a medicine
cabinet and dose oneself at home will regularly expel the product of conception. For those who beget children but want to
verify whether or not they are desirable, amniocentesis or
chorionic villi sampling can examine the unborn for defects
before it is too late. For those who beget undesirable children
but fail to determine that and destroy them before birth, compassionate doctors have devised an acceptable medical way to
minister to their chagrin by orders to withhold all nourishment
and liquids until parental desires have been assured of satisfaction. For those who desire children but fail to beget them, *in
vitro* fertilization (IVF) occasionally gives them their heart's desire. For those who desire children but not pregnancy, other
women have been put at their disposition to breed for them:
your egg or hers, as specified.

In the face of such awesome, versatile, abundantly funded
accomplishment, it appears never to have occurred to the
authors of the technical assistance that their very program
might, for all its proficiency of method, be "senseless and brutish" in its imagination and results. The naïveté of the technicians seems never to have been jolted by any suspicion that
their massive scheme of helpful contrivances might itself have

been one of the surest stimulants of irresponsible sexual activity. It has escaped them that their efforts might have been to sex and childbearing what the turnpike and salt have been to the Weston groundwaters and reservoir.

One is reminded somewhat of the editorial amazement expressed in our land when the voters in Ireland were presented recently with a measure that would finally legalize divorce and remarriage. Stories were told of Irish couples whose second or third unions were suffering for want of legal recognition. It was, we were told, such a backward thing for Ireland to deprive these good folks of a remedy for their problems. Here were the literati of America, with our runaway rates of adultery, divorce, unsuccessful second and subsequent marriages all at plague level compared with Ireland, lecturing the Irish on how they would improve their domestic relations if only they would adopt our custom of divorce as the remedy for marital breakdown.

To have addressed the problems of undesired pregnancy without ever considering that it is the sexual irresponsibility itself which needs to be confronted; to remedy the chronic failure of a program composed entirely of contraception, sterilization, and abortion by providing nothing but more contraception, sterilization, and abortion—this can only remind one of the claim by American military commanders in Vietnam that if only they could have a few hundred thousand more troops, and more cluster bombs and fragmentation bombs and Agent Orange and all that other good stuff which wins wars, then the campaign could be won.

THE DIGNITY OF THE PERSON

Meanwhile, back at the Vatican, the pope and his theological subalterns have borne high annoyance, frustrated because they have been so unsuccessful in rousing us all to alarm. Among his scriveners, Cardinal Ratzinger obviously employs no one like Rachel Carson. They all write with a grace and a clarity that are not user-friendly.

An attentive reader of the "Instruction on Respect for Human Life in Its Origin and on the Dignity of Procreation: Replies to Certain Questions of the Day" in its official English version, however, encounters some lively new vocabulary. One expects mention of natural law, and it does make an appearance here. Eight times the text speaks of the natural moral law, a divine law that is unwritten in any sacred text but inscribed in the very being of men and women and their orientation to sexual union. But this is a minor motif. Much more prominent in the argument is an insistence on "dignity," on "rights," and on "respect" for human dignity and rights. Together these terms appear twelve times more frequently than all references to moral law.

From the first paragraph on, the Instruction repeatedly asserts the dignity of the human person, of spouses, of parents, of children. The origin of humankind, procreation through marital union, is also possessed of dignity. When the talk shifts to rights, the document reaches for emphatic adjectives. It speaks of fundamental rights, inviolable and inalienable rights. The right of every innocent human to life itself is primary. Next comes the right of every person to be respected for oneself, and also to be assured in marriage of exclusive sexual intimacy with one's spouse, and the right to beget any children with that spouse alone. Several times the document speaks of a right that is not familiar from previous Vatican statements: the right to be conceived, carried in the womb, welcomed into the world, and brought up within marriage.[20] "It is through the secure and recognized relationship to his own parents that the child can discover his own identity and achieve his own proper human development."[21] Near the center of its argument, however, there is one very fundamental right which the Instruction denies: the right to possess a child.

> A true and proper right to a child would be contrary to the child's dignity and nature. The child is not an object to which one has a right nor can he [or she] be considered as an object of ownership. Rather, a child is a gift, "the supreme gift" and the most gratuitous gift of marriage, and is a living testimony of the mutual giving of his [or her] parents.[22]

All humans are called to a respect for each other that is unconditional and absolute. The child, no matter how young, must be respected as one's equal in human dignity from the moment of conception. In his conclusion Cardinal Ratzinger characterizes the entire Instruction as an appeal for respect, in family and in society, for human life and human love. The dark opposite of such a respect is contempt for both. "The Congregation ... hopes that all will understand the incompatibility between recognition of the dignity of the human person and contempt for life and love, between faith in the living God and the claim to decide arbitrarily the origin and fate of a human being."[23]

Pope John Paul II himself is responsible for this newly preferred vocabulary. It goes some way towards talking the language of contemporary social advocacy movements. Despite the soothing sound of "rights" and "dignity" to the establishment liberals that direct most of those movements, their dogmas do not bend sufficiently to allow many of them much sympathy with this part of his agenda. The words are the words of Voltaire and Tom Paine, but the thoughts are the thoughts of Jesus.

Even with this venture into contemporary idiom, the Roman text labors. This must be due in part to the Vatican's abhorrence of rhetorical flair or eloquence. Still, one asks why the prose is so curt, why it states its most contentious and confrontational and prophetic insights so flatly that they have little chance to engage the reader's mind or imagination. When two parties have shared considerable experience and long conversation to the point where they possess a common recollection and interpretation, they can evoke that common understanding later by a brief word or phrase ... even a glance across a crowded room. But to any outsider who has never participated in the exploring or the resolving of the same matter, that word or phrase would have no ring or sense to it. The allusions would be missing.

Here we are listening to the man assigned the most venerable rostrum in the Catholic Church in order to address some of the most profound life-and-death issues over which the vision of faith is at war with the public culture. It simply will not do for him to state those convictions tersely as if most readers—indeed, even most Catholic readers—had cared, and thought them through, and concurred. He must plead his points, and illustrate his convictions, and win our minds and imaginations to his commitment.

Consider one of the themes most central to the Instruction: that biology and medicine can heal, but the powers they deploy can as easily be used to injure or to destroy people. The point is stated, but it is never offered enough chance to gather strength:

> Medicine which seeks to be ordered to the integral good of the person must respect the specifically human values of sexuality. The doctor is at the service of persons and of human procreation. He does not have the authority to dispose of them or to decide their fate. . . . The humanization of medicine, which is insisted upon today by everyone, requires respect for the integral dignity of the human person first of all in the act and at the moment in which the spouses transmit life to a new person.[24]

> If the legislator responsible for the common good were not watchful, he could be deprived of his prerogatives by researchers claiming to govern humanity in the name of the biological discoveries and the alleged "improvement" processes which they would draw from those discoveries. "Eugenism" and forms of discrimination between human beings could come to be legitimized: This would constitute an act of violence and a serious offense to the equality, dignity and fundamental rights of the human person.[25]

These are potent ideas, strenuous worries. Rome sees herself defending humanity from the excesses of our own power,[26] yet she speaks with a rhetoric that could keep only a philosopher awake. The point is stated, but it is not propounded.

The legitimate role of technology to assist in human procreation must be vigilantly supervised, for it is as ready to overpower humans as it is to be of help to them.

Thanks to the progress of the biological and medical sciences, man has at his disposal ever more effective therapeutic resources; but he can also acquire new powers, with unforeseeable consequences, over human life at its very beginning and in its first stages. Various procedures now make it possible to intervene not only in order to assist, but also to dominate the processes of procreation. These techniques can enable man to "take in hand his own destiny," but they also expose him "to the temptation to go beyond the limits of a reasonable dominion over nature."[27]

Through these procedures [IVF which creates new human persons and then discards some of them], with apparently contrary purposes, life and death are subjected to the decision of man, who thus sets himself up as the giver of life and death by decree. This dynamic of violence and domination may remain unnoticed by those very individuals who, in wishing to utilize this procedure, become subject to it themselves. The facts recorded and the cold logic which links them must be taken into consideration for a moral judgment on *in vitro* fertilization and embryo transfer: The abortion mentality which has made this procedure possible thus leads, whether one wants it or not, to man's domination over the life and death of his fellow human beings and can lead to a system of radical eugenics.[28]

Technology *macht frei*! This is Rachel Carson stuff, only escalated from sedge and bracken, plovers and thrushes to men and women and girls and boys. The same themes are here. Technology is invited in to alleviate some of the ills of life and it can, if given its own head, seize control of the very lives it was asked to assist, with no one the wiser about what had happened.

Another scenario portrays those who are involved in technology, not as its victims, but as its users: to exploit others. The Instruction pursues this latter point when it warns parents of their temptation and ability to treat their own offspring without the respect due them as human equals.

The human person must be accepted in his [or her] parents' act of union and love; the generation of a child must therefore be the fruit of that mutual giving which is realized in the conjugal act wherein the spouses cooperate as servants and not as masters in the work of the Creator, who is love. . . . He [or she] cannot be desired or conceived as the product of medical or biological techniques; that would be equivalent to reducing [the child] to an object of scientific technology.[29]

The Vatican is too technical, or perhaps too dainty, to state graphically enough that we have been turning procreation into science fiction, and that we become monsters as a result. A society which venerates Drs. Masters and Johnson and their lab-coat lore of orgasm as advisors on the fullness of human sexuality, or that hearkens to Dr. Ruth as a *sage femme* of how men and women give themselves to one another, or that orders up children the same way it uses the Land's End catalogue: this is a creature-feature that ought not appear even on late Saturday television. Or so I take the Vatican to be telling us.

Turn now to the second central tenet of the "Instruction on Respect for Human Life in Its Origin and on the Dignity of Procreation: Replies to Certain Questions of the Day": the demand within human nature that sexual intercourse be a vital and intrinsic link not only between spouses but also between parents and children. The Catholic understanding of human procreation is bewilderingly compact, and it begins something like this. It is in a committed and steadfast community that we find the vision and the gumption to emerge from our infantile selfishness into mature love. The two closest bonds which sustain us through life are the enduring devotion we receive from our parents and then give to our children, and the enduring devotion we give and receive by pledge with our spouses: the bonds of blood and the bonds of promise. These commitments are lifegiving, Catholics observe, only if both of them are unconditional and lifelong: for better or for worse, until death. And the two bonds find their ligature in sexual intercourse, wherein the embrace of two in one life gives flesh-fruit in children. This is what lies behind the document's statement:

> The church's teaching on marriage and human procreation affirms the "inseparable connection, willed by God and unable to be broken by [humans] on [their] own initiative, between the

two meanings of the conjugal act: the unitive meaning and the procreative meaning. Indeed, by its intimate structure the conjugal act, while most closely uniting husband and wife, capacitates them for the generation of new lives according to laws inscribed in the very being of man and of woman." [*Humanae Vitae*] This principle, which is based upon the nature of marriage and the intimate connection of the goods of marriage, has well-known consequences on the level of responsible fatherhood and motherhood.[30]

COMMITMENT TO SPOUSE, COMMITMENT TO CHILDREN

The insight that the Vatican has been honoring more obstinately than persuasively through the years is that it is both naturally needful and, by God's grace, possible for human persons to celebrate *both* of their most loyal commitments in sex. That is where a husband and wife are most vividly and revealingly summoned into fidelity, which is one of our better ventures at imitating the love God has for us. He loves and embraces us, regardless of what we have done or could do ourselves, out of the constancy of his benevolence. It is very difficult for us to grow into such an unconditional love. The marital union is a unique schooling in that love, in that a woman or a man can clasp close a partner, not merely because of that other person's qualities or accomplishments. And in accepting one another on those terms, they accept their children on those same terms, children who quite literally issue forth from that union.

From the Christian reflection on experience, this is how we have to live. To others who find it too demanding and call it an ideal, the church replies that it is an ideal like drinkable water is an ideal, and like noncarcinogenic food is an ideal, and like cars that are not unsafe-at-any-speed are an ideal, and like telling the truth is an ideal.

From such a perspective, it is no surprise that contempt for marital fidelity would provoke a disintegration of the sexual experience, and that this in turn would threaten the children both in their welfare and in their very existence. The erotic is divorced from the relational, and both are estranged from the procreative. All aspects alike will wither by their separation.

If man and woman do not pledge themselves for better or for worse until death, then their relationship is wary and hedged and revocable. Choice becomes the predator of commitment. Children then cannot be welcomed into an assured acceptance for they too are now subjected to scrutiny and conditional loyalty. They are similarly victims to the defeat of commitment by unlimited freedom of choice. Their security is hedged because the fidelity from their parents is also revocable. What person could grow in that sterile a setting?

Rome, who is haunted by the conviction that commitment entails the forfeiture of some future free choices, and that without fidelity we must wither, wails to the world that we cannot—we dare not, we must not—have the arrogance to make every relationship in our lives revocable, and still expect to survive.

Rome is invoking the old argument from nature. We are simply not made to survive under certain conditions, and it is up to a perceptive community of faith to draw upon its cumulative experience and to formulate its observations of what such conditions usually are. When the Instruction does invoke the old expression, "natural law," it means what Rachel Carson meant: that we cannot manipulate our cosmos or our society or our persons or our bodies at will, and still survive.

An era so appreciative of bran and ozone and Lamaze cannot be all that offended by insistence upon what is "natural." Perhaps it is the word "law" that most offends us. What law connotes is somebody else's will coercing mine. For a generation whose velocity on the highways and whose creativity in drawing up tax returns implies that the law has bite to it only if we are apprehended and punished, "law" may be a very deceptive metaphor for nature. For when you cheat on nature in a serious and chronic way, you are enfeebled, you sicken, you die. It makes no essential difference whether you are caught in the act or not. You suffer. Whether or not your doctor finds out you haven't quit chain-smoking, the emphysema is likely to ensue. And if your deviance is more moral than physical, you can die spiritually yet still keep getting out of bed physically every morning.

Technology is art: complex and purposeful artifice. And art, as Burke has said, is itself what human nature is all about. But art, as we need no Burke to tell us, has the capacity either to enhance our natural lives or to afflict them.

Technology has been misunderstood because nature and art have been misunderstood. Nature has been considered to be what is determinate within a human being, what can be studied by physics, chemistry, biology or, as some would have it, by psychology. Artifice, on this same view, was what is not determined but free in us: choice. It is the subject of economics, politics, and ethics. Once those two elements had been divvied up and allotted to their respective experts, a major task assigned to technology would be to humanize the physical, animal aspects of our experience by subjecting them to our free preferences and choices.

This seemed at first to correct the naïve, materialist way our "lower" and "higher" elements were being studied independently of one another. Human nutrition, coupling, reproduction, exertion, locomotion, recreation, combat and death could never be rightly understood or undertaken if they were treated as merely animal events. Lactation, to take one example, is not something we share with other mammals. For humans it needs to be invested with love and self-sacrifice that transcend and transfigure any lamb's or whale's experience at the breast. Mammalian suckling is not a specimen or a prototype of what human mothers and children do together; it is but a metaphor of human nursing. For many of our physical actions are inspirited by our intellectual purposes and needs and relations.

The technological mission, then, could be construed as uplifting human nature by making all physical aspects of human life responsive to free choice, our highest faculty. But what was being ignored, all along, was the counterpart truth: that our powers of judgment and decision are those of embodied creatures, and they may not work their whim or will with our physical selves by acting like foreign occupation forces.

This is manifest in our case in point, human reproduction, for the dual reason that it cannot be defined in narrowly physical terms, being an undertaking of body and spirit together, and that it has inherent purposes and vectors of its own quite resistant to some we might prefer. It requires the intense involvement of our spirit, but not merely by way of absolute mastery.

Our nature is mysteriously composite, in which the will is not quite a stranger, nor yet quite a sovereign; the gastrointestinal tract is not quite autonomous, but also not quite controlled. It is our nature to expectorate, to calculate, and to defecate, just as it is our nature to marry, to chew, and to owe loyalty to our own people and governors. All are physical acts and each is spiritual; all are subject to our governance, but it is that of a constitutional, not an absolute rule.

The inherent needs and fulfillment of our lower functions are typically less ambiguous than those more evolved. A healthy diet, for instance, allows of more exact science than a sound economy, though we naturally need them both. Vitality through exercise is easier to work out than stability in marriage—yet neither is merely physical and neither is merely relational. Each requires the satisfaction of our inherent nature and each, the pursuit of our chosen purposes. Thus any enterprise, like that of technology, which invites the control of our natural lives, must give steadfast attention to the whole.

And this is not easily done. My friends in engineering confess chronic impatience with legally required environmental impact studies. No matter how painstaking the work required, for example, to design a power plant to serve intricate residential and commercial markets, it proceeds on winged feet compared with the studies and licensures which assure that all the other interests and needs and resources of the community and the future community are being honored. That is because power plants have a way of doing some things beyond what was originally intended. It takes so much less time to produce a part than to accommodate it to the whole.

In her doctrine of nature and artifice, and the resulting criticism of technology that is reckless and improvident, Rome is speaking with the cautionary voice of tradition, issuing, as it were, an interior environmental impact statement. In the other large matter at hand, the relationship between intention and action, Rome and her adversaries may both be pulling the classic tradition off its course, in opposite directions.

A DIALECTIC BETWEEN ACTS AND MORAL MEANING

The ancient conviction was that individual acts could, by divine enablement and through determination and discipline, form virtues. Likewise, by wastage of divine grace and by neglect and self-indulgence, individual acts form vices. The amalgam of habituated good or evil was seen to give shape to a person's character, to one's fundamental commitment: either to oneself or to others. Acts have an inherent, structured dynamic that tends to shape character, as telling lies tends to make one dishonest: not by withholding the truth from others, but more by losing the nerve to face it oneself. Conversely, habits of character tend to invest individual acts with meaning. Thus, the difference between child abuse and a salutary swat resides, not in the dynamics of force, but in the disposition and purpose of the batterer.

Catholic moral theology in the Middle Ages had lost sight of this dialectic whereby human behavior natively embodied both habits of character and the moral force of actions, each affecting the other. A shift to legalism gave sovereignty to acts abstracted from their habits. On this view a single event, no matter how uncharacteristic of a person's development and character, might be morally lethal because grievously forbidden.

The Reformation and the Enlightenment retaliated, not just by withdrawing definitive moral meaning from actions, but by ignoring an ability in acts to create and reinforce, or to enfeeble and destroy, character. The Reformers did this by belittling human agency in good acts. The Enlightenment did it by denying any inherent, repercussive power of acts upon the self, and by replacing habitual character with free choice.

Here, then, was the perfect standoff. The conservatives (if I may so characterize them) were arguing that a single action stood in its total significance without reference to the person's dispositions or habitual behavior. The liberals were arguing that every act received its total significance from the disposition of the agent—only that disposition was not the (traditionally conceived) character forged by long and reinforced behavior, but the momentary whim or wish known as free choice.

Bring those two opponents to the issue of reproductive technology, and their respective doctrines will be predictable. Rome has said that a single sexual act of intercourse without openness to conception, or a single act of reproduction without sexual intercourse, is wrong by its very nature. The folks in white lab coats are saying that the entitlement to pleasure and the right to children of choice authorizes us to pursue our preferences by any variation upon sex and reproduction, in the confidence that our freedom of choice will invest that sex, however conceivable or inconceivable, with our good intentions.

I am arguing here that the forces inherent in human actions embody and enact human habits, just as human character directs and informs human behavior. The Vatican is standing on the higher ground in this skirmish by insisting that humans need fidelity for the begetting of their children, and the random fortunes of fertility to make their marriages generous. One appreciates the wisdom that led Roman teaching to allow for birth control, but one regrets the failure of nerve which led it to condemn contraception as an intrinsically denatured act, rather than as a tactic available to selfish habit.

A church which professes that acts are good or evil insofar as they enhance or damage character must rely heavily on its cumulative experience of what happens to people who perform certain actions. The abundant testimony of credible believers has been suggesting that self-sacrificing Christians who have made themselves generously open to spouses and children, neighbors and strangers, appear to moderate fertility contraceptively, and yet to thrive morally. This implies something about the act itself and about the full claims of sexual responsibility and about the greatness of character it both requires and fosters. I would anticipate that consultation with the faithful will suggest as well that in the context of a self-sacrificing marriage, recourse to assisted fertility (AIH or IVF), if available without destruction of offspring, may also be a morally good act.

Assisting the Marital Embrace

What the Vatican actually said is this:

By comparison with the transmission of other forms of life in the universe, the transmission of human life has a special character of its own, which derives from the special nature of the human person. "The transmission of human life is entrusted by nature to a personal and conscious act and as such is subject to the all-holy laws of God: immutable and inviolable laws which must be recognized and observed. For this reason one cannot use means and follow methods which could be licit in the transmission of the life of plants and animals [*Mater et Magistra*]."[31]

Much as most people admire Pope John XXIII from whom that quotation was taken, we get nervous at talk about immutable and inviolate laws. The agrochemical industry felt the same way about Rachel Carson's talk of the inexorable.

What the Vatican might have written could go something like this:

The procreation of a person is unlike any productive activity possible to human beings. Human production is an act of mastery. Whether it be in manufacture or in artistry or in agriculture or in animal husbandry, we produce objects, artifacts, and organisms that belong to us as the fruit of our handiwork. But with the yield of our bodies it is starkly different. All children are begotten, not made. We receive them; we dare not make them; we must not possess them. As our companions, children are given into our care and nurture but not into our dominion.

Our very survival, as parents and as a race, depends on the generosity with which we make room in our world for every newcoming child, with deference and fellowship. All the advantage and power we enjoy because of our seniority must be restrained from exploiting the young. It must be turned instead to the work of guardianship.

Now what is it about this recent program of technical assistance to people in their parenting that seems so perverse to us?

It makes little difference whether a given individual will actually resort to any particular procedure, but across the world today men and women (proportionately to their affluence) are commonly invited:

- to embrace one another sexually without leaving themselves open to children;
- to conceive without any sexual union between the parents;
- to examine children once conceived and once born, and decide whether to shelter them;
- to destroy undesirable children by expulsion or dismemberment or poisoning, or by "putting them to sleep";
- to purchase children from poor women when unable to bear them oneself;
- to pay others to rear them when neither parent will agree to nurture and nourish them.

What is wrong with that? The child has become a chattel, a commodity, a pet, a possession. Under the equivocal pretext of "producing only wanted children" men and women have denatured their awesome faculty of procreation into one of manufacture and possession.

What we behold is an entire generation of adults poisoning its own capacity to parent. Marriage and the marriage embrace are no longer a single promise and a single acceptance of both spouse and children. People imagine that commitment to a beloved spouse can be made fast without enclosing within it a commitment to beloved children. It is our observation that they are doing violence to themselves and to their children.[32]

To the extent that biotechnology can truly facilitate the marital union—which is a single but twofold bond between spouse and spouse and between spouses and children—then we value it as art enhancing nature. But where it overrides our natural human makeup and relationships and fulfillment, it is an intrusion. Technology is proposed as the instrument of human self-determination, freedom, and choice, but if it is used to subvert our inherent needs and obligations, it will surely handicap and even destroy us.

Yet this only leads us to the gaping question which Rome has not yet resolved: How *do* we discern when technology is enhancing nature? How do we differentiate what is appropriately from what is inappropriately artificial?

The Instruction tells us that artificial interventions into procreation and gestation must be morally evaluated insofar as they serve the dignity of the human person. According to Rome this requires that procreation occur within marriage and that it follow from sexual intercourse that honors its two linked aspects: unitive and procreative.

Here one can look more closely at the document's treatment of artificial fertilization involving husband and wife (through either IVF or artificial insemination [AIH]). IVF is disallowed as it is presently performed, because a number of eggs are extracted and fertilized, and then some are discarded when conception succeeds. But even if and when the procedure is perfected so that such destruction of human beings be avoided, the Instruction stands by three moral requirements for rightful conception:

1: It must respect the inseparability of the unitive and procreative meanings of the sexual act. Contraception is rejected because it involves sex that is intended to be unitive but not procreative. IVF and AIH are rejected because they involve separate sexual acts that are procreative but not unitive.

2: It must be an act that is embodied as human beings are, with harmonious involvement of both body and soul. Fertilization outside the human body is therefore not acceptable.

3: Conception may be assisted but never dominated by outside assistance. Neither IVF nor most AIH makes possible procreation in conformity with the dignity of the person. The child must be respected and recognized as equal in personal dignity to those who give him or her life. "The human person must be accepted in his parents' act of union and love; the generation of a child must therefore be the fruit of that mutual giving which is realized in the conjugal act wherein the spouses cooperate as servants and not as masters in the work of the Creator, who is love.

In reality, the origin of a human person is the result of an act of giving. The one conceived must be the fruit of his parents' love. He cannot be desired or conceived as the product of an intervention of medical or biological techniques; that would be equivalent to reducing him to an object of scientific technology. No one may subject the coming of a child into the world to conditions of technical efficiency which are to be evaluated according to standards of control or dominion.[33]

A SINGLE EMBRACE OR A LIFE TOGETHER

The Instruction is arguing that technical assistance to a husband and wife is damaging when it offers a generative act that does not involve the marital embrace. And because technical skill is so essential, that skill is said to dominate the couple, or to assist them in dominating their offspring.

Here, I suspect, some good principles may be getting a careless application. The generative act is being viewed as an isolated event, separate from the sequence of sexual union that the married couple have enacted all along. And we are not given a principle adequate to discern when technology is assisting and when it is intruding.

The Instruction argues repeatedly that the only context for moral evaluation is the individual sexual act, not the totality of a couple's conjugal life. Biomedical intervention which might be considered an assistance to the long sequence of sexual union is accused of being an intrusion when judged within the single event. The very same point was argued in 1968, in Pope Paul VI's encyclical on birth control, *Humanae Vitae*.[34]

Oliver O'Donovan, professor at Oxford, has addressed this subject:

> What upset so many in the teaching of Paul VI's encyclical *Humanae Vitae* was that it seemed not to perceive the difference of structure between sexual relations in marriage and simple fornication. Chastity in marriage was analyzed into a series of particular acts of sexual union, a proceeding which carried with it an unwitting but unmistakable hint of the pornographic. A

married couple do not know each other in isolated moments or one-night stands. Their moments of sexual union are points of focus for a physical relationship which must properly be predicated of the whole extent of their life together. Thus the virtue of chastity as openness to procreation cannot be accounted for in terms of a repeated sequence of chaste acts each of which is open to procreation. The chastity of a couple is more than the chastity of their acts, though it is not irrespective of it either.[35]

The very same issue is raised by the Vatican rejection of IVF and AIH. And on this O'Donovan has made a like observation that

> there are *distinct* acts of choice, which may involve persons other than the couple, in any form of aided conception, including those forms of which [Catholic official opinion] approves. Whether they are *independent* acts of choice is precisely the question which requires moral insight. If they are indeed independent (and not subordinate to the couple's quest for fruitfulness in their sexual embrace) then they are certainly offensive. But that point cannot be settled simply by asserting they are distinct. The question remains: is there a moral unity which holds together what happens at the hospital with what happens at home in bed? Can these procedures be understood appropriately as the couple's search for help within their sexual union (the total life-union of their bodies, that is, not a single sexual act)? And I have to confess that I do not see why not.[36]

There is, I would say, good reason to consider contraception, IVF, and AIH as capable of enhancing the natural course of a marital life in the same way that a caesarean section or carefully disciplined ("natural") birth or bottle-feeding with special supplements do. There can be artifice and technology that enhance nature. But that needs to be evaluated within the full continuity and integrity of a couple's sexual life. The moral worth of technical intervention would derive from whether or not the union itself was generous between the spouses and towards offspring. It is, after all, a union with many encounters. The Instruction points out early in its argument that since humans are persons, our sex is quite different from the sex of

other animals, and its biological aspects must be viewed in the
light of its personal aspects.[37] And the fact that individual acts
of sexual intercourse are, for a human couple, incidents within
a continuing story, obliges us to assess biomedical interventions insofar as they serve the saga, not just the episode. Steadfast attention to the whole . . .

No one will accuse Rome of not having been steadfast.
Indeed, in the longer run of history it may emerge that Rome's
disdain for most modern efforts to govern the procreative
power of sex was the earliest campaign of resistance to the
dogma that human choice need encounter no limits to its dominion over nature. More is the pity that this resistance movement has been a stammering effort, blessed with little of the
convincing rhetoric of its younger sister, the ecological movement.

Morality Beyond Motives

Journalists reporting immediate reactions by Catholic couples to the Vatican Instruction sympathetically presented those
involved in the new reproductive technologies as outraged that
their well-intentioned desire for children should be called into
question.

> Two Catholic couples turned on their TVs last Tuesday night
> and learned that they were sinners. . . .
> "It [IVF] was just a little helping hand," Doug says of the
> procedure.
> "Pronouncing this a sin is almost unbelievable," says Mi-
> chael, 31, who was educated in parochial schools. "When I
> think of sinning, I think of murder and lying and cheating—not
> of all the happiness I get from Lindsay. I just don't think it's
> morally wrong. I guess you have to have your own standards
> about this.[38]
> John Pieklo, 40, of Perrine, and his wife who is 35, just had
> a healthy baby in December. Although they are Catholic, his
> wife had amniocentesis with the idea that she would have had
> an abortion if there had been a severe problem with the baby.

"I do realize this is against our church principles, but I also feel it is very important that we raise a healthy child," said Pieklo. "If it had a brain problem or handicap problem before birth and could have been aborted, I'm sure we would have aborted. . . . Raising a child is hard enough without putting yourself in the position of raising a handicapped or brain-damaged child."[39]

In reading these remarks I was reminded of correspondence I had had with a civil engineer about the depletion of the Ogallala Aquifer. I had oversimplified the groundwater crisis in the Southwest, he told me.

These farmers are not, as a whole, greedily consuming water with total disregard for the present and future good of the world. . . . Through enhanced understanding of the limitations of man, technology and nature, the farmers of the desert Southwest hope to be able to provide grain, cotton and cattle to an ever increasing world population.

To say that the role of the farmer in drawing water from the Ogallala is a sin is, I believe, a mistake. Many of these farmers are deeply religious people.

This is a pervasive modern moral argument: that the moral worth of our actions derives not at all from their inherent direction and force, but is infused into them by our wishes. The tradition, of course, has doggedly pointed out that there is as well a reverse movement: our actions have a power within them to transform our attitudes, by enhancing them or by enfeebling them.

Perceptive critics within and without the Catholic Church, though dissenting from what they consider an indiscriminate application of principles by the Instruction, commend the Vatican for insisting that much more is at stake than a good-natured wish to have one's own, healthy child. Columnist Charles Krauthammer sees Rome as resistant to three scientific innovations: synthetic families (surrogate parenting), synthetic children (test-tube babies), and synthetic sex (artificial insemination). In general, they pose a threat to the integrity of the family, the dignity of the individual, and the personal bonds of sex.[40] Sidney Callahan writes:

> In the case of reproductive technology, ethical positions best emerge from the question: What will further the good of the potential child, the family, and the general social conditions of childrearing, while strengthening our moral norms of individual responsibility in reproduction? We should move beyond a narrow focus upon either biology or individual desires for children.[41]

Rome in this Instruction is addressing the issue of procreation on wider terms than most other parties to the conversation. Yet something is still missing. The See of Peter, which ought to be drawing on the wisdom from its network of compassionate and insightful pastoral interchange across the world and down the centuries, is not speaking out of the most reliable source of insight it possesses: an inspired and imaginative and attentive reflection on experience. Instead, Vatican theologians may have had their eyes too close to their task, and their task has been on paper. And that, ironically, is the failing endemic to technology.

A MATTER FOR LAW?

The Roman Instruction has also been berated for having urged that civil laws protect both individuals and families from the clumsy hands of irresponsible technology. Much outcry about clericalism and coercion has been heard.[42] Yet the very moral questions raised by the Vatican have been echoed by others whose call for legislative regulation has never been criticized. Listen to one psychiatrist writing about the famous Baby M case in the *New York Times*:

> When the child learns, as she inevitably will, that she was conceived to be sold, what will she feel and think about herself and her natural mother, Mary Beth Whitehead? The child will understand that the bottom line—which cannot be erased or

rewritten—is that the natural mother, her own mother, sold her. What is the fair price of this merchandise? . . .

Mrs. Whitehead's children saw their mother carry and deliver a child like themselves—a half sister—whom the mother then gave or sold to another family. All children fear that if they are bad they will be sent away or abandoned. Won't these children fear that their mother might sell them, too? . . .

Another issue, obviously undemocratic in a democratic society, is the exploitation by a middle-class well-to-do couple of a woman of a lower socio-economic class. The implication clearly is that the richer, better educated couple—Dr. Elizabeth Stern and her husband William—can offer more (at least materially) and that the child's "best interests" thus would be served by awarding the child to that couple. This slippery slope can lead only to racist and supremacist rewriting of laws and controlling of human rights. . . .

But what of a man's desire to have a child who will carry his own genes? While the feeling is understandable, it has elements of narcissism and ego that have more to do with the man's needs than the child's best interests. . . .

Society is faced with a situation in which biotechnology and commerce conspire to invent a complicated transaction that leaves little room for ethical or moral values. The fact that something can be done does not mean that it must be done. "Surrogate mothering" should be outlawed. . . .

Morality, ethics and values are not a religious matter alone. They determine how we live and how far we go in reaching our full potential as humans.[43]

This is plain talk, by a citizen, arguing that an immoral form of widespread personal abuse ought be curbed by the law of the state. Surely the same suggestion is not any less allowable if the leaders of a church are making it.

Rachel Carson defended her work in these words:

Now to these people, apparently the balance of nature was something that was repealed as soon as man came on the scene. Well, you might just as well assume that you could repeal the law of gravity. The balance of nature is built of a series of interrelationships between living things, and between living things and their environment. You can't just step in with some brute force and change one thing without changing a good many others. Now this doesn't mean, of course, that we must never interfere, that we must not attempt to tilt that balance of nature in our favor. But when we do make this attempt, we must know what we're doing, we must know the consequences.[44]

One cannot put words into Cardinal Ratzinger's mouth, even elegant words like Carson's. But one hopes that this is what he also would have to say.

The curial Instruction, like the encyclical *Humanae Vitae* of two decades earlier, seems to stumble by locating the pivot of moral meaning in the invariable linkage of procreativity with each individual act of intercourse. Neither document allows the single sexual act to be significantly coupled into the long train of sexual union between spouses. That has been and will continue to be a vulnerable point at issue among Christians who share the Vatican's overall moral imperatives. It is those prophetic imperatives, insisting that the personal dignity and bonds and loyalties which differentiate human mating and begetting from those of unspirited animals, which will survive their fumbled applications here.

One is sometimes led to think that such divine guidance as Rome enjoys comes more in the form of stubborn intuition than as articulate insight. But in this matter of the love between husband and wife, and the love between parents and children, and the natural needs men and women and children have to be bound together through sexual intercourse ... though she sees through a glass darkly, Rome on this occasion did strive to attend steadfastly to the whole.

NOTES

1. *Origins*, 16, 40 (19 March 1987). For response, see *New York Times*, 10 March 1987, Y10.

2. *New York Times*, 11 March 1987, 1.

3. Ibid., 18 March 1987, A1.

4. Ibid., 12 March 1987, A30.

5. Daniel C. Maguire, "Vatican birth decree casts a long shadow," *Boston Globe*, 15 March 1987, A21–24.

6. *New York Times*, 12 March 1987, B11.

7. Ibid., 19 March 1987, Y6.

8. George Parkin Grant, *English Speaking Justice* (Notre Dame, Ind.: University of Notre Dame Press, 1985), 87.

9. See "The Browning of America," *Newsweek*, 23 February 1981, 26–37; "Water: The Nation's Next Resource Crisis," *U.S. News and World Report*, 18 March 1985, 64–68.

10. Rachel Carson, *Silent Spring* (Boston: Houghton Mifflin, 1962), 296–297.

11. Norman Boucher, "The Legacy of *Silent Spring*," *Boston Globe Magazine*, 15 March 1987, 17ff.

12. Paul Brooks, *Speaking for Nature* (Boston: Houghton Mifflin, 1980), 286.

13. Marie Stopes, *Wise Parenthood*, 9th ed. (London: Putnam, 1922), 17–19.

14. Ibid., 44.

15. Margaret Sanger, "A Plan for Peace," *Birth Control Review* 16,4 (April 1932): 107–108.

16. Daniel J. Kevles, *In the Name of Eugenics: Genetics and the Uses of Human Heredity* (New York: Knopf, 1985), 90.

17. *Wise Parenthood*, 13.

18. Ibid., 24–25.

19. "Adolescent Pregnancy: Testing Prevention Strategies," *Carnegie Quarterly*, 31,3–4 (Summer/Fall 1986): 4.

20. II,6,a.

21. II,1,c.

22. II,8,c; gender inclusion added.

23. Conclusion,2.

24. II,7,b.d.

25. III,2.

26. Conclusion,3.

27. Introduction,1,2.

28. II,3.

29. II,4,c,1–2; gender inclusion added.

30. II,4,a,1; gender inclusion added.

31. Introduction,4.

32. See, on a similar note, Richard Stith, "Thinking About Ecology," *The Cresset*, November 1981, 7–10.

33. II,4,c,2–3.

34. See chapter four.

35. Oliver O'Donovan, *Resurrection and the Moral Order* (Grand Rapids: Eerdmans, 1986), 210.

36. Idem, *Begotten or Made?* (London: Oxford University Press, 1984), 77–78.

37. Introduction,3,2.

38. Sandra Rubin Tessler, "Little bundles from heaven are theological nightmares," *Detroit News,* 15 March 1987.

39. Cathy Lynn Grossman, "Many Catholics dispute Vatican edict," *Miami Herald,* 13 March 1987.

40. Charles Krauthammer, "The Ethics of Human Manufacture," *New Republic,* 4 May 1987, 17–21. Krauthammer had observed earlier that the decision of the trial court to uphold the Whitehead-Stern surrogacy contract and to award Baby M to her father and his wife had ironically honored two of the very principles cherished by Mary Beth Whitehead's feminist supporters. The decision to consider the surrogacy contract valid was harmonious with the doctrine that women should have control of their own bodies. "If they should have the right to terminate the life of a fetus, how can they be denied the right to grow one for a fee?" The ruling that the child's father was the fitter parent (against the older presumption that the maternal bond made her the more nurturing parent) was at peace with the feminist claim that biology is not destiny, and fathers can and should be as much nurturers of children as mothers. "Feminists helped make rules, 'lost' by them," *Chicago Sun-Times,* 6 April 1987, 25.

41. Sidney Callahan, "Lovemaking & Babymaking," *Commonweal,* 114,9 (14 April 1987): 233–239.

42. See Maguire, note 5 above.

43. Robert E. Gould, "And What About Baby M's Ruined Life?" *New York Times,* 26 March 1987, Y27.

44. Carol B. Gartner, *Rachel Carson* (New York: Frederick Ungar, 1983), 107.

Moral Wisdom and the Taking of Life

6

The Use of Aborted Fetal Tissue in Research and Therapy

HUMAN TISSUE HAS BECOME an effective medium for medical therapy. One recalls the transfusion of blood and its derivatives, the transplanting of organs such as kidneys, eye parts, hearts, and lungs, and immunization by pathogens, antigens, or antibodies. New therapies are now being proposed through the implantation of fetal tissues, which appear to have especially potent regenerative effects upon some neural and endocrine systems. The therapeutic use of tissue from human bodies has aroused a series of ethical concerns. May one put parts of someone's body to alien use? Need consent be obtained and, if so, from whom and under what conditions? May human tissue be bought or sold? The recent proposal to use fetal tissue—typically obtained from aborted subjects—now puts a new spin on those questions.

The issue raised here, however, concerns the use of human fetal tissue for research and experimentation, even before therapy.

Animal studies suggest possible relief from Parkinson's disease, juvenile diabetes, congenital absence of the thymus, various blood disorders, Alzheimer's and Huntington's diseases, and other disabling and lethal afflictions, through transplantation of human fetal tissue. There are distinct advantages in the laboratory use of fetal remains. This is notably so, for instance, in studying neural tissue. In comparison with tissues obtained from mature bodies, those of the unborn or very young adapt more readily to *in vitro* environments, proliferate more abundantly, are less differentiated and therefore more versatile for experimental uses. In a word, they perform much more naturally and normally and responsively *in vitro*.

Thus the advantages. Are there countervailing moral realities that would dissuade or interdict the use of human fetal tissue for transplantation? One considers with repugnance the prospect of women hired to conceive and nurture offspring intended for abortion and marketing as a prime supply of tissue for research and therapy. But the basic moral issue is, in its substance, not all that new. One must decide at the outset not to exploit any human individuals to obtain prospective benefits for others. The scientific result from such exploitation might be good but the undertaking could not be. That principle has always been at the heart of the need to protect the human subjects of research.

INFORMED CONSENT

A first consideration is that of informed consent. Who can grant consent for the use of electively aborted fetal remains? One might propose that the mother can do so, because the tissue is from her body. The flaw in this claim is that the tissue is from within her body but it is the body of another, with distinct genotype, blood, gender, etc. Thus she cannot assign rights to its use in her own name. She would have to be acting as the parent/protector of her offspring.

In that role she could give consent, as mother, at the time she signs the consent form for the abortion. But when a parent resolves to destroy her unborn she has abdicated her office and duty as the guardian of her offspring, and thereby forfeits her tutelary powers. She abandons her parental capacity to authorize research on that offspring or on his or her remains.

The late Paul Ramsey considered the plausibility of an aborting mother giving consent to have her unborn offspring's body used for research.

The fundamental model for legitimate parental consent in place of a child's is ... proxy consent that is medically *on behalf of the child.* .... American research policy and practice and the NIH guidelines deem parental proxy consent to be valid in carefully circumscribed instances of non-beneficial research.... In these cases parental consent is sought and is believed valid because parents are presumed to be "caretakers" for their infant children. Care is the attribute or virtue that qualifies parents as proxies, not strong or weak feelings, or strong or mild "interest" .... It would be odd if we do not rescue from the deputyship of parents abortuses who have been abandoned by them as we would children abandoned in institutions.[1]

He concludes that it is "morally outrageous," "a charade," to give to an aborting woman any legitimate standing to act as a protective proxy for that child's body. Though Ramsey was speaking of research on a still-living fetus, the moral force of his comments applies as well to permission to use aborted fetal remains.

This same point was made clearly by the President of the United States in his letter to the spokesman for the group of more than 800 signatories of an appeal not to permit fetal transplantation research with aborted remains:

The use of any aborted child for these purposes raises the most profound ethical issues, especially because the person who would ordinarily authorize such use—the parent—deliberately renounces parenthood by choosing an abortion.[2]

A third alternative might be that the right to dispose of the remains devolves upon the abortionist, as the physician in possession. But there is no ground for claiming that medical professionals incur rights over the bodies or the corpses of their patients. Still less is that so when death has resulted from nontherapeutic intervention by the practitioner, most especially when the victim has not consented to that activity.

The prerogative and right of the father to release the remains of his aborted offspring for medical research is rarely considered, yet in comparable instances of significant parental guardianship neither parent is considered to act rightfully when he or she avoids consultation or consensus with the other parent. Fathers are by design almost never involved in consent procedures prior to abortion. The absence of their consent, unless the right to give it could credibly be assumed to have been waived, would further encumber any others' claim to dispose of the remains.

When the natural protectors of the immature have either deserted or abused or absented themselves from their wards, guardianship usually devolves upon the state as *parens patriae*. But if the state agrees—as some have suggested—to consign to research the remains of only those fetuses who have perished under the ultimate abuse, that inevitably places the state in a position of patronage towards their destruction. The state would, like the aborting mother, also be implicitly derelict in its protective powers.

Thus no guardian emerges whose consent would rightfully suffice to release the remains of the deceased fetus for research.

Yet how prohibitive is that? Physicians and surgeons since Vesalius have sought cadavers to study anatomy. Their first obstacle was the conviction that the human body, live or dead, was inviolable. Their way round that resistance was to appeal to free consent (of the decedent or a guardian). But since, until recently, their usual supply had to be the corpses of derelicts, what really counted was the absence of anyone to object, more than the presence of anyone to consent. Thus consent has been interpreted as removing an obstacle, not as a positive and necessary warrant. But there may be more at stake here than this suggests.

Ours is an ancient obligation to treat human remains— body and property—with deference. The body may be a mere corpse and the estate mere chattels, but our treatment of them—insofar as they are identifiable with the person who left them behind—takes on the color of our relationship to that person. "If the body is indivisible from that which makes up personhood, the same respect is due the body that is due persons."[3]

How we treat human remains is both a function and a cause of our bond with human persons. No one who remembers Mussolini's body hanging by the heels from a Milan lamppost could doubt it. The partisans were dishonoring his person, and enacting defiance against any future tyrant. Creon's insistence that Polyneice's corpse lie exposed and Antigone's determination to bury her brother at peril of her own life are both quite personal actions: towards the dead youth, and towards all whose spirits crave rest. John Kennedy's funeral and the disposal of Adolph Eichmann's remains both illustrate how our treatment of bodies is, in a powerful way, our definitive treatment of those they embodied.

If we honor a fellow human while she is living we have no choice but to honor her body after death. To confiscate it discredits all ostensible dignity we accorded that person *in vivo* and orients us to treat still other persons with contempt. Stephen Toulmin mentions the importance and the moral relevance of the "fear that any relaxation in the general feelings of reverence towards the tissues and remains of the dead and dying could give the color of extenuation to other forms of callousness, violence and human indifference."[4] If my property is the extension of my person, then my body is my surrogate. Especially if one has had an ambiguous association with someone's death, to appropriate the dead person's remains for one's own purposes is the act that dissolves all ambiguity. When we forcibly requisition someone's body we are treating that person—not just that person's corpse—as of negligible dignity, or none.

Professor John Robertson proposes to sidestep this difficulty of abrogated parenthood by interpreting maternal consent in an entirely different way:

> But the disposer of cadaveric remains is not the guardian or proxy of the deceased, who no longer has interests to be guarded. A more accurate account of their role is to guard their own feelings and interests in assuring that the remains of kin are treated respectfully, rather than assure that wishes of the deceased expressed while alive will be fulfilled.[5]

In like vein, Dr. Benjamin Freedman claims that consent by an aborting mother is not a grant of authorization but merely an expression of sentiment that must be respected because she is one of "those who should have a say in this decision."[6] In a word, it is her interests, not those of the decedent, which are at stake.

As is well known, the disposition of bodily remains may be made in one of two ways: by someone in anticipation of death, or by the next-of-kin after death. These are two very different proceedings. During one's lifetime the decision can be made only by the person himself or herself, or by someone who has protective custody of that person: the parent of a minor child, a person who has been appointed as guardian by a court, or someone to whom the power-of-attorney has been ceded. The only legitimate reason for any person to hold such power over another is some incapacity of the child/ward/client to provide for his or her own welfare. Such authority is characterized entirely as protective, as a guardianship wholly obligated to the ward's welfare. My contention has been that the decision to abort, made by the mother, is an act of such violent abandonment of the maternal trust that no further exercise of such responsibility is admissible.

The claim Robertson advances is that the pregnant woman would not be not acting as mother on her child's behalf, but as the child's surviving next-of-kin looking out for her own "interests." This relationship, as he sees it, does not oblige one to act on the decedent's behalf but leaves a person free to act on one's own.

This claim labors under several difficulties. The scientific requirements of tissue preservation impose the practical necessity of arranging for fetal tissue donation before an abortion, so that sterility can be maintained and the tissue swiftly preserved or used. Thus the practice of securing maternal consent after she has signed the consent to the abortion but before the abortion itself.

Kinship, however, as distinct from guardianship, does not authorize anyone to dispose of another's body except *post mortem*. No one can make that decision *ante mortem* except the decedent or the decedent's guardian. By his innovative suggestion Robertson is essentially proposing that during his or her lifetime one human being might legally and ethically be put at the disposal of another person, not at all for the safeguarding of the ward's welfare, but exclusively for the pursuit of the "interests" (or "sentiments," as Freedman puts it) of the one in power. This is a ruthless proposal and an ominous innovation.

The second defect of this proposal is that it implicitly treats the remains of the aborted offspring, not really as a human body to be respected, but as an impersonal object to be owned and used at will.

The Uniform Anatomical Gift Act implies otherwise when it designates human cadavers, organs, and tissues to be treated as human subjects—not objects—of research, protected from arbitrary intrusion or seizure by the essential requirement of voluntary consent by the person (or that person's protector).

It has been a longstanding moral conviction that a human body cannot be a chattel or a property. It cannot be owned; it can only be held in trust.[7] It no more belongs to the next-of-kin than an estate belongs to an executor. The reason why bodily remains are capable of honor and reverence, or profanation and outrage, is that even in death a body continues to claim and to receive consideration on behalf of the person whom it embodied. My body is always and only mine; it will remain so even when those who have cared for me continue that kind service by taking it into their possession in order to give my remains their sepulture.

The claim that a person's interests are extinguished by death is too narrow even for the law, which protects our property, our literary creations, and even our reputations as powerful posthumous "interests." But I would carry the argument beyond the confines of law out into the wider concerns of ethics, and press the point that our actions upon a body are directed to the person who once gave it life, not to the survivor who has the right and duty of caring for it. And when the only reason there is a lifeless body to be disposed of is that it was violently destroyed at the choice of his or her next-of-kin, that survivor surely forfeits her right *post mortem*, just as she violated her duty *ante mortem*, to provide the services of posthumous kinship.

There is nothing inherently unethical in experimentation upon the remains of humans who are victims of homicide, provided that consent is given, as is normally required, by the surviving guardian or next-of-kin. But the very agents of someone's death would surely be disqualified to act on the behalf or in the stead of the victim—disqualified as a man who has killed his wife is morally disqualified from acting as her executor. And in the case of a human abortus, it is the very guardians of the unborn who have collaborated in his or her destruction.

Freedman and Robertson also misconstrue what is meant by the argument that to expropriate a body without rightful consent is an act of disrespect, of indignity. Freedman writes:

> The cadaver of the derelict, should it not be autopsied, is destined to burial in Potter's field. The fetal tissue, on the other hand, will alternatively be disposed of as organic trash, a destiny substantially less respectful towards it and its claims to human attention, in my eyes, than its use as a source of transplanted material.[8]

Robertson makes a similar point: "If [the mother's] consent is given, otherwise dignified experimental use of fetal remains would not be any less dignified."[9]

The human meaning of human acts is vested in their full complexity. A man hurls himself at a woman and flings her violently to the ground. From that fact alone you cannot assess what happened. If you are to discern the character of the act you must know further that it was an assault with intent to kill, or that it was a rescue from the path of a speeding vehicle. To disinter a body for evidence of foul play is one thing; to dig it up in search of its valuable wedding ring is quite another. The indignity is not in the sheer physical action but in the full human event.

The insult involved in research upon aborted fetal remains does not arise from dissection or maceration or clinical use or the like. It comes from the fact that the unborn has been destroyed at the will of those entrusted with his or her safety, and that this infidelity can only be aggravated were one of them to presume, in virtue of that violated office of protective care, to hand over the remains for the advantage of others. Use of those remains for research or therapy—in itself beyond reproach—

turns into abuse when it is sanctioned by the same hands that extirpated the unborn in the first place.

One might well object that if our society yields to any woman the right to destroy her unborn offspring on demand, it is surely a lesser thing for her to assign the remains as she wishes. It may indeed be a lesser thing, but it is a very similar thing, and that similarity renders the second act morally continuous with the first. It is an act whereby a human being is put at another's disposal, an act of unrestricted and self-interested domination. Our ethical convictions have allowed such domination only for the welfare of the ward. Freedman and Robertson are essentially saying that the unborn is there to serve the "interests" of those who have him or her in their power. I do not understand how anyone could morally survive the exercise of such ruthless interests.

This moral continuity between the decision to abort and the expropriation of the aborted remains leads us to examine how participation in the second act makes one a colleague of those who perform the first.

Moral Complicity

There is an additional ethical question, quite beyond the absence of rightful consent. The researcher would become a party, after the fact, to the destruction of the unborn.

One encounters four distinct ethical defenses of the use of tissue obtained through abortion. Firstly, objections to scientific use of abortion-supplied body parts have repeatedly been characterized as strongly felt sentiment, "deeply charged with emotion."

"Emotivism" is the name for this kind of moral reflection, if it can be called that at all, which "understands" the warrants for serious moral judgments to rest ultimately upon rationally undiscussible and irreconcilable desires, or feelings. Thus the measure of rightness for any moral claim is not its coherence with a rationally defensible set of practical principles or their position relative to some objective "good," but the degree of emotional vehemence behind it. "Good will" replaces the good; "sincerity," or personal authenticity, displaces rational argument. In the discussion of fetal transplantation research, determined and disciplined moral discourse has been so regularly confused with emotion that one may fairly ask whether some advocates of this research believe that all ethical conviction is nothing more than passionate and irrational feeling.

Another vindication of fetal research with aborted tissue was grounded on the assumption that our inward dispositions alone determine the ethical value of our behavior. Research scholars express their indignation that the work to which they have dedicated years of goodwill could be considered exploitative. They resented having their integrity impugned by reference to anything but their good intentions.

A third ethical stance dealt with the abortion-transplantation matter as one to be adjudged by weighing health benefits against moral deficits. Its advocates behold the prospect of relieving handicap and affliction as so incomparably beneficial that acquiescence in abortion seems an acceptable price to pay. As the director of the American Parkinson Association has been quoted as saying: "The majority of people with the disease couldn't care less about the ethical questions—they just want something that works."[10]

But the history of the abuse of human research subjects, from Tuskegee to Dachau to Willowbrook to Helsinki, cries out unambiguously that neither the goodwill of the researcher nor the prospective yield in beneficial knowledge has the slightest fingerhold on any moral right to relieve one human's affliction by exploiting another. That same abuse-marked history shows well that when scientists or therapists set out to exploit one group to benefit another, it is invariably the disadvantaged who suffer for the powerful.

It is the fourth defense of transplantation research that one finds most thoughtfully argued. Its advocates are alert to the issue of moral complicity, as shown by the numerous ways they propose to dissociate the research from the abortion: informed consent for the research must be distinct from and subsequent to consent for the abortion; different medical personnel must perform the two procedures; no financial incentive may offer inducements to parents or providers of aborted remains; parents must not be permitted to designate the beneficiaries of their aborted childrens' tissue; no abortion and donation should be permitted if the child was conceived for this purpose; abortion procedures may not be altered to accommodate the transplantation; no added "risk" to the unborn is allowed, even though he or she is already consigned to abortion.

Those who take this position attempt to evade the ethical issue by sequestering fetal tissue research from the broader debate concerning abortion. They attempt to dissociate the two issues so as to avoid the difficulties besetting the abortion question. By doing so the research problem is reduced to a legal or scientific one, and the only moral problems left are procedural ones.[11]

Advocates of this use of fetal tissue have acknowledged that induced abortion is a "tragedy," that they regret or even deplore it, but that the use of human flesh supplied by abortion implies no moral agency in that abortion. Research can draw some benefit for medical science from what might otherwise have been an unrelieved tragedy. Death was not the scientists' doing. Indeed it was they who turned one victim's death into another victim's recovery. And by establishing various barriers between abortion and tissue use, they imply that a sort of moral autoclave will sterilize the tissue ethically so that it can be used without contamination by association with its method of supply.

It is the assumption of such an argument that transplantation research with fetal tissue supplied from induced abortions neither implies nor fortifies a moral acquiescence in or complicity with the prerequisite abortions. But as Peter McCullagh points out:

> For a scientist to claim that the ethical status of any experiment can be assessed in splendid isolation from its antecedents is as myopic as to maintain that its consequences are irrelevant.[12]

In its drift and its dimensions that claim yields instructive comparisons with the War Crimes Trial in Nuremberg known as "The Medical Case." There is a special irony in this for it was that Tribunal's "medical" trial which produced the Nuremberg Code of 1946, the great charter that initiated formal protection for human subjects of research. It inspired the Declarations of Helsinki in 1964 and 1975 that in turn begot virtually all of our present ethical norms for protecting human subjects in experimentation. Without Nuremberg and its judgment the world's conscience might never have gazed head-on at the intrinsic depravity of the doctors' defense.

One lawyer who had taken part in prosecuting Nazis for war crimes explained how the German nation could have acted so savagely: "There is only one step to take. You may not think it possible to take it; but I assure you that men I thought decent men did take it. You have only to decide that one group of human beings have lost human rights."[13]

The insight of Nuremberg taught us that when we take possession of others, when their bodies are forcibly delivered up to be used as we wish, then no antecedent goodwill and no subsequent scientific yield will absolve us from having been confederates in their oppression.

The device of conscience whereby the Nazi physicians absolved themselves from moral association with the torment and abuse of their human subjects was a belief that they had had no say in how those subjects were delivered into their hands. The Nazi doctors had learned the ethic of their profession: that a physician may not relieve one human being's affliction at the cost of another fellow human's suffering. But they contrived to believe that if an associate had already done the subjugating and they then did the healing-oriented research, they could divide the responsibility down the middle. The Tribunal and the world judged otherwise—and condemned the researchers for it all.[14]

The arguments of the physicians in defense of their experiments upon prisoners and patients are exemplified by the chief defendant, Dr. Karl Brandt. It was in the "interests of the community" confronted with "hard necessity," when many lives had to be protected from death and epidemics, that he and his colleagues were given leave by the state to experiment on human subjects put at their disposal. "There is no prohibition against daring to progress."

The traditional restrictions that protected human subjects from harm had to yield to this urgent community need. "In all countries experiments on human beings have been performed by doctors, certainly not because they took pleasure in killing or tormenting, but only at the instigation and under the protection of the state, and in accordance with their own conviction of the necessity of these experiments in the struggle for the existence of the people." This apparently inhumane treatment of their helpless fellow humans for the sake of research was admittedly brutalizing, but as Brandt's lawyer Dr. Robert Servatius (who would later appear as attorney for Adolph Eichmann) explained: "a measure may be as unavoidable as war and yet be abhorred in the same way."[15]

Most of the Nazi research subjects, of course, were still living, though their lives were forfeit, when they fell into the doctors' hands.[16] But there were many experiments that employed organs and tissue from cadavers: human muscle for culture media at the Hygienic Institute in Auschwitz; livers, spleens and pancreata for Dr. Kremer's experiments on site; hearts, brains, and other organs provided by Dr. Mengele for research in Berlin; testicles and heads sent to Dr. Hirt in Strassburg for study, and brains for the work of Dr. Hallervorden.[17]

One sees, however, instructive similarities in the ways the Nazi researchers dealt with both live subjects and cadaverous remains:

> There was also a scramble for bodies and bones. When anatomy professor August Hirt set about assembling a collection of body casts for his institute, he requested that captured Russian Jews, both men and women, be brought to Strassburg alive so that he might arrange for a "subsequently induced death" in such fashion "that the heads not be damaged." They were not; the U.S. Army arrived unexpectedly to find 150 bodies still floating in formaldehyde.
>
> Some German laboratory people also harbored a scientific curiosity about the Polish intelligentsia. When Dr. Witasek of Poznan and a group of his comrades in the resistance movement were executed, their heads were removed and sent in

gunnysacks to Germany for study. Professor Julius Hallervorden, who was shipped six hundred preserved brains of "mercy
death" victims for his research in neuropathology, testified after
the war: "There was wonderful material among those brains:
beautiful mental defectives, malformations and early infantile
diseases. I accepted these brains, of course [he had requested
them]. Where they came from and how they came to me was
really none of my business." [One American professor commented that Hallervorden "merely took advantage of an opportunity."][18]

For both research groups, what lies within their grasp is
anonymous "tissue," brains, pancreata, spleens. To an unblin-
ded world those are the remains of Jews, Gypsies, mentally
handicapped or unborn children sent nameless to destruction.
It is the flesh of victims.

The carry-over in the analogy is the naïve but vain belief
that both groups of researchers and those they benefit are not
pulled into the gravity field of responsibility for the violent act
which supplies them with vanquished human bodies for study.
The Nazi physicians were generally careful to keep the medical
personnel involved in research separate from those responsible
for killing.[19] They were much more explicit in their insistence
that their experiments were going to bring some good out of
tragedy. Dr. Hallervorden explained: "If you are going to kill
all these people, at least take the brains out so that the material
could be utilized." Dr. Hirt was of a similar mind: "These condemned men will at least make themselves useful. Wouldn't it
be ridiculous to execute them and send their bodies to the
crematory oven without giving them an opportunity to contribute to the progress of the society?" Likewise Dr. Rose: "The
victims of this Buchenwald typhus test did not suffer in vain
and did not die in vain." Countless numbers of people "were
saved by these experiments."[20]

One perceives this same justification at work among researchers who derive their materials from abortion. Dr. Martti
Kekomäki, whose experiments on the severed heads of late-
abortion fetuses is widely known, has said: "An aborted baby
is just garbage and that's where it ends up. Why not make use

of it for society?"[21] Dr. Lawrence Lawn, of Cambridge University: "We are simply using something which is destined for the incinerator to benefit mankind."[22] And Drs. Willard Gaylin and Marc Lappé, associated with the Hastings Center, believe that the death of the "doomed fetus" "can be ennobled" through experimentation because the scientific results can be used for "the saving of the lives (or the reduction of defects) of other, wanted, fetuses."[23]

"Abortion is a tragedy," says one transplant researcher. "But as long as it occurs, I believe it is immoral to let tissue and materials go to waste if it can cure people who are suffering and dying."[24] To compensate for the obvious lack of informed consent, both groups of doctors have supposed that those who gave their victims over to destruction should, by some grotesque contortion of human rights, be acknowledged as their protectors and empowered to hand over their remains. "All of us that work in fetal research feel that if someone has decided to have an abortion and gives permission, it is all right to use that tissue to help someone else."[25]

What this line of thinking does not wish to recognize is that we can associate ourselves with others' moral agency after the fact. Consider a Florida banker who judges narcotics use to be a tragedy, but agrees to accept the proceeds from the local drug network in order to make more capital available for homeowners and small businesses in the area. Who would or should believe that his readiness to accept those funds is not an act of acquiescent association—indeed, of partnership—in the human wastage and abuse that those moneys have already purchased? The banker has become a party to destruction even though it was complete before his subsequent involvement.

Freedman writes:

> Causes (on the macro level at any rate) must precede effects, and so one cannot be complicit in some misbehavior by approving it, or failing to sanction it, or failing to dissociate oneself from it, after the fact. . . .
>
> We must of course keep in mind the necessity to take care to avoid any direct or indirect causal contribution. . . . In using fetal tissue, for example, a researcher or physician would be

complicit in the elective abortion by altering its conduct in some way, e.g., by recommending the woman prolong her pregnancy or have her abortion performed in some unusual manner (like hysterotomy) so as to optimize the tissue use. Failing any such causal connection, however, there is no complicity in the recovery and use of tissue obtained after an elective abortion.[26]

Robertson agrees. To be complicit in a murder, for example, requires that one have been responsible for it. In post-abortion fetal research this is not the case.

The researcher and patient will ordinarily be removed from the abortion process: they will not have requested it, and will have no knowledge of who performed it or where it occurred. The abortion will have occurred for reasons unrelated to tissue procurement, and the tissue procured by a third party. They may even be morally opposed to abortion for family planning reasons [sic], and should suffer no corruption or moral disintegration because of a willingness to then salvage some good from the abortion . . . Burtchaell's approach to the problem of complicity is to assume that researchers would necessarily applaud the underlying immoral act of abortion, thereby allying themselves with it, and being corrupted in the process.[27]

What neither critic seems to grasp is that we may become accessory to the actions of others after the fact, without having had any causal role in what they have done. Madame Defarge, *la tricoteuse* who sat knitting at the foot of the Paris scaffold throughout the Reign of Terror, neither prosecuted nor condemned those to be guillotined. Yet she was complicit in every death by her public endorsement: after the condemnation, after the fact. The citizens of two towns near my university, Cassopolis and Vandalia in Michigan, had no causal role in the abolition movement in the southern states, yet by functioning as the northern terminus of the underground railroad they became complicit in the freeing of every black slave who found the way to their doors: after the long escape was complete, after the fact. Likewise the banker who accepts the money from drug transactions that are already completed becomes complicit in the drug trade: after the sales, after the fact.

In the case of carnage-minded Madame Defarge and the freedom-minded Cassopolitans and Vandalians, they very clearly applauded the acts they sustained by their complicity. But explicit approval is not essential to complicity. In the case of the laundering banker, he may very well have told himself that he does not applaud the drug trade, and that he is simply trying to draw some good out of it (increased capitalization for local industry). I would say that he deceives himself, though probably only himself. If he is knowingly in an established relationship whereby he agreeably processes the ill-got gains of others, no mental maneuver will succeed in disentangling him from complicity, whatever he imagines his moral judgments to be. His institutionalized complicity subverts all of his moral disclaimers.

The ethical situation of the researcher and the beneficiary of research is comparable. Grant, if you will, Robertson's description: they had no hand in the abortion, they do not know who was involved, and they have even arranged for an intermediary to bring them its proceeds so as to avoid ever looking the abortionist in the face. Yet they are still accessory to the abortion.

Their complicity is not at all one of applause; it is one of disregard. It is like that of the banker who has no desire to acquaint himself with any details of the sordid enterprise which yielded his deposits. When we become accomplices in good we do applaud the deeds of others. When we become accomplices in evil we do the opposite: we avert our gaze, we fend off knowledge, we fancy that deeds done carry no taint for those who arrange to benefit from them. But the complicity remains. The alleged moral separation between researcher and abortionist is as effective a moral barrier as the fence between the I. G. Farben plant and Auschwitz.

Elie Wiesel has said: "If we forget, we are guilty, we are accomplices. . . . I swore never to be silent whenever and wherever human beings endure suffering and humiliation. We must always take sides. Neutrality helps the oppressor, never the victim."[28] Wiesel is saying that even by acquiescent silence after the fact we can sign on as parties to a deed already done. What we are considering here is no mere *post mortem* silence, no simple averting of the gaze after the fact. We are considering an institutional partnership, federally sponsored and financed, whereby the bodily remains of abortion victims become a regularly supplied medical commodity.

The validity of our concern was suggested in 1974 by bioethicist LeRoy Walters:

> Ought one to make experimental use of the products of an abortion system, when one would object on ethical grounds to many or most of the abortions performed within that system? . . . If a particular hospital became the beneficiary of an organized homicide-system which provided a regular supply of fresh cadavers, one would be justified in raising questions about the moral appropriateness of the hospital's continuing cooperation with the suppliers.[29]

This resonates with the concern of eighteen staff members at the EPA who called for a halt in the application of Nazi research data from experiments with phosgene gas on prisoners of war. Their moral misgiving was that "to use such data debases us all as a society, gives such experiments legitimacy, and implicitly encourages others, perhaps in less exacting societies, to perform unethical human experiments."[30] When Dr. Robert Pozos of the University of Minnesota, Duluth, proposed to use the findings of the Dachau experiments in freezing prisoners, it was because "it could advance my work in that it takes human subjects farther than we're willing." Reaction was prompt. Daniel Callahan said, "We should under no circumstances use the information. It was gained in an immoral way." Abraham Foxman, national director of the Anti-Defamation League, added, "I think it goes to legitimizing the evil done. I think the findings are tainted by the horror and misery."[31]

The Nazi atrocities are now nearly a half-century behind us, and they are universally condemned, yet any impression of nonchalance about them is taken still today to be morally alarming. When the affliction is still underway in our own time, and has received only ambivalent repudiation in our society, any act of association speaks with much louder significance.

The notion of complicity in mischief has been blurred and perhaps trivialized by its reduction in the popular mind to a legality. It is a much larger reality than that. It is the awesome moral fact that often we fancy ourselves as bystanders to injustice and injury—distressed and regretful bystanders, to be sure—when actually we are confederates in the very affliction we ostensibly deplore.

One can discern four types of moral complicity in evil: active collaboration in the deed; indirect association that implies approval; failure to prevent the evil when possible; and shielding the perpetrator from penalty.

The classic cooperator in evil is the driver of the getaway car. Without ever entering the bank, he or she is an active and causative member of the team. Every member of that team is the coauthor, *in solido*, of all the harm any one of them inflicts.

One way of disavowing the moral burden of complicity is the claim that "If I hadn't done it, they would simply have gotten someone else to do it." If we don't sell arms to General Stroessner to subdue the Paraguayans he will buy them from the Belgians or the Czechs. Medical personnel are asked to perform civil executions because with or without their participation the prisoners would meet the same doom. This proves to be only a rationalization, however, for the arms merchants soon lose all ethical restraint in purveying their merchandise of death, and the medics who kill are deformed in a way their recusant colleagues are not. There is, after all, a stark moral difference between beholding outrage and staffing it. It is not an indifferent matter whether I or another is the cooperator, since the cooperator is the one stunted personally and morally by his involvement.

There is a second mode of moral complicity, by association, when one is not actually joining in the work itself but somehow enters into a supportive alliance. The difference here between a neutral (or even an opponent) and an ally derives from the way in which one does or does not hold oneself apart from the enterprise and its purposes.

One may be an adverse observer, as when one consorts with an organized crime ring as a journalist or a researcher or a covert agent of law enforcement. This by itself would not necessarily make the observer a party to immoral activity. In a different mode, one might be associated with immoral activity in order to serve its victims, as when a chaplain or a physician agrees to serve the inmates of a genocidal concentration camp. Even in this close association, one can refrain from being party to the operation, for instance, by specifically refusing to be a staff member. The International Red Cross, in its services to war prisoners, must cooperate with belligerents but hold itself aloof from any partnership that would convert it into a partisan or a confederate.

As one enters into closer association, however, one eventually becomes party to the activity. Suppose that a sociologist struck an agreement with a child pornography operation in order to study the effects of such employment on the children. Or suppose an economist secured admission to the workings of a red-lining real estate operation in order to study the racial discrimination at work there. These researchers would undertake their studies, not with the informed consent of persons at risk, but with the informed consent of the victimizers. This would have the effect of drawing them into a sort of acquiescent partnership.

It is the sort of association which implies and engenders approbation that creates moral complicity. This situation is detectable when the associate's ability to condemn the activity atrophies.

There is no measurable way to determine such complicity. One must use sense and judgment, and one's assessments will be arguable. But they will be real. Imagine a pharmaceutical experiment carried out on an unsuspecting group of women in a Third World country: an experiment which leads to the death of several dozen subjects. If tissue from their cadavers were available from the experimenters for further research, it would seem that those who used the specimens could not avoid being complicit, albeit after the fact, with those who had destroyed those women. If the primary research, however, had led to the production of a new and powerfully therapeutic medication, a physician who prescribed that drug, even though sadly aware of its malicious origins, could reasonably be considered not to have entered into confederacy with the offense. This is a distinction arrived at by analogy, not by measurement. The moral realities it detects are no less objective.

A third sort of complicity arises from culpable negligence. When parents are derelict in supervising their children they become responsible for their children's vandalism. When an employer turns a blind eye upon careless safety compliance by workers, she is morally complicit in the injuries that result. Anyone with supervisory responsibility who defaults in that duty becomes morally engaged precisely by that inactivity. One is morally complicit, not only by involvement in another's actions but also by shirking an obligatory involvement.

To go still further, it is possible to be morally complicit in another's wrongful behavior by actions that purport to curb the ill effects of the behavior but actually legitimate it or even stimulate its continuance. The single-minded policy of many public agencies in this country to curb adolescent pregnancy simply by proffering contraceptives and abortions to teenagers has had a misplaced effect. By addressing only the consequences (pregnancy) and not the activity (inappropriate sex), the program tacitly approves of what its sponsors deplore, and in the eyes of the sexually active teenagers it seems not only to acquiesce in their promiscuity but even to facilitate it. Thus the puzzling research finding that the incidence of teenage sexual activity and pregnancy and abortion has resolutely increased in direct proportion to the benevolent availability of contraceptives. Any venture that prescinds from the ethical aspect of someone's behavior, to alleviate only its consequences, may become naïvely complicit in it.

One can discern, then, four modes of moral complicity: direct and active participation, association that fails to disentangle itself, dereliction of the duty to supervise, and protective assistance. The common reality which is steadily present throughout these different ways of sharing moral intentionality is approbation. However one aligns oneself with another's act, by collaboration or working alongside or looking the other way or shielding from aftereffects; whether by being active or by being passive; whether it furthers another's undertaking or merely endorses it: the complicity puts one person in the same moral stance that another person has assumed by direct action.

Naturally, all of these forms of association with harm vary

in degree. There is a difference between the driver of the getaway car and the mother who prepares breakfast on the day
of the crime with the faint intuition that mischief is afoot. It
must be a human estimate how close and operative complicity
actually is.

There is difficulty for some in identifying complicity after the
fact. One cannot cause a deed that is already done. But this is
to misconstrue the two elements in complicity. I am an accomplice in evil, first, insofar as I produce the harmful or immoral
event, and second, insofar as my association with the evil
causes me to be corrupted alongside the principal agent. Actually the chief effect of evil behavior is not the harm it inflicts
on another but the moral disintegration and compromise it
incurs in myself. This latter, more intrinsic, element of complicity is present even when actual causative harm is not.

Experimentation upon fetal tissue derived from elective
abortion places the scientist in moral complicity with the abortionist. The mode would be the second described above. The
researcher is a confederate by resorting to the abortionist as a
ready supplier of primary tissue obtained from unborn humans
who have been purposely destroyed.

Scholars anxious to perform research on such subjects
often plead that their involvement offers them no financial advantage, plays no causative role in the harmful activity because
it would have occurred with or without their presence, and at
least allows them to extract some beneficial result from an otherwise regrettable enterprise. The gist of this plea is that conspiracy in harm requires causative responsibility. But this argument from moral nonchalance, as we have stated, does not
succeed in disengaging one from complicity. A partnership
whereby one achieves direct benefit from another person's in-
jurious behavior, after the fact, can place the former in silent
but unmistakable alliance with what the latter is doing.

Is it possible to fend off moral complicity by some sort of
disclaimer, by asserting aloud that one's use of this tissue for
research implies no approbation of the antecedent abortion?
There is little to encourage such a hope. Consider that most
explicit of disclaimers composed by Mr. Justice Blackmun in

1970 on behalf of the U. S. Supreme Court. The Court acknowledged in *Roe* v. *Wade* that the entire ethical and legal reality of abortion pivots on whether the unborn is a live human being entitled to the protections promised to all persons by the Constitution.[32] It then proceeded to strip the unborn of those protections. "We need not resolve," Justice Blackmun wrote, "the difficult question of when life begins."[33] But they did. The public disallowed the Court's disclaimer and saw it had indeed resolved that, being disposable at the will of another, the unborn was no fellow human. That is the confident inference one hears from many advocates of this use of abortion-derived human remains: abortion is the law of the land, so it must be ethical. So much for disclaimers when actions prevail over words.

If, for the refining of his healing art, today's physician goes for his authorization to a mother who has abandoned her offspring to destruction, takes delivery of an insulted and mutilated body from the practitioner who dispatched the offspring, undertakes sponsored research upon those remains, publishes his results in professional journals and then turns those findings to the resulting benefit of patients in pain—all this being held together by a network of accounts payable and receivable—then he becomes party, even though after the fact, to all that it took to put that research subject's body at his disposal. He has effectively acquiesced in it all.

A MOTIVATION FOR MORE ABORTIONS[34]

I now proceed to a further ethical issue: that an institutionalized use of aborted human remains constitutes complicity with abortion, not only after the fact, but before the fact. In other words, this research endeavor can be expected to increase abortions.

Freedman is consistent enough to acknowledge that an institutionalized trade relationship with the abortion industry would indeed involve some responsibility for the future abortions for which it might provide enhanced incentive.

In a broader sense, however, one can indeed become complicit in an ongoing *series* of crimes. . . . In any given case, the user of the cadaver could claim that whatever wrong had been committed is already done, so that he cannot be an accomplice, morally speaking, to these nefarious deeds. By purchasing and using bodies, however, he is nonetheless complicit in a series, in a practice, of offenses. By subsidizing and legitimating the practice, he contributes to its perpetuation.[35]

The actions by the Supreme Court are generally believed to have increased abortions in this country by legalizing them. A reasonable reckoning is that there are perhaps about five times as many abortions annually after *Wade* and *Bolton* as before.[36] It is reasonable to conclude, however, that the Court unwittingly had as much ethical influence as it did legal. The action which decriminalized abortion also drew the cloak of powerful moral approbation over a practice that had been inhibited even more by shame than by criminal penalty.

Some nourish the belief that scientific sponsorship of this research and therapy will have a negligible effect upon the choices women will make in the future about whether to abort. The *New York Times* is more realistic: "Where an abortion is planned anyway, some doctors, lawyers, and ethicists say that donating the fetal tissue may help to relieve some of the sadness surrounding the abortion. 'Donating tissue to help someone else can be helpful in the process of grieving or bereavement,' said [Dr. Arthur] Caplan."[37] From what I have been given to know of women's hindsight on their abortions, many of them were beset with confusion at the time, and abiding self-reproach afterwards. The widespread depiction of abortion decisions as "deeply personal and complex" is at variance with so many recollections shared with me over the years, which recalled impulsive and conflictive judgments that had not been nearly complex enough, and were followed only later by an understanding of all that had been at stake.

It is willful fantasy to imagine that young pregnant women estranged from their families and their sexual partners and torn by the knowledge that they are with child but do not want that child, will not be affected by the new accolade of respectability publicly accepted fetal tissue transplantation proposes to confer on abortion.

The abortion industry, despite its efforts, has remained a furtive enterprise. Its practitioners are for the most part obstetricians who are marginalized in the professional esteem of their peers. Women who resort to them do so with shame and guilt. Will it then mean nothing that the nation's medical establishment will now reconcile itself with the abortionists it had disdained professionally? That the most enterprising and imaginative intellectuals in medical research and practice will have gone into partnership with the industry as the supplier of preference for one of their most venturesome endeavors? How can we estimate the dignity and patronage this confers upon a trade from which they had previously kept their distance?

And how can we persuade ourselves that the distressed young woman will not be powerfully relieved at the prospect that the sad act of violence she is reluctant to accept can now have redemptive value? Governmental sponsorship of research with tissue supplied by the abortion industry is likely to be the most persuasive, implicitly moral, accolade given to abortion since *Roe* v. *Wade*. This would mean that official sponsorship then becomes complicity before the fact, not just after the fact.

ALTERNATIVE SOURCES OF MATERIAL: CELL LINES

There are other possible sources of fetal materials for research. There is no moral objection to using the remains of unborn or newborn children who have perished from spontaneous abortion or trauma. The same would be true when surgery to save a pregnant mother's life has unavoidably aborted or destroyed her child. The parents would retain the right to release the bodies of the child for study. The drawbacks here are scientific, not ethical. Spontaneous abortion is often associated with genetic abnormalities that would compromise the physical remains as material for research, as would also be the case with many neonatal deaths. A second drawback arises from the difficulty in approaching emotionally traumatized parents to ask them to release portions of the bodies of their still-born or miscarried or deceased newborn children for research. While these are real obstacles, however, they make the acquisition of fetal or newborn tissue difficult, not impossible. There are enough fetal deaths with no genetic abnormality to yield considerable research material if there is a concerted effort to solicit it. And the emotional difficulty of asking parental consent in the wake of a wrenching loss is no more difficult than that faced by surgical teams doing heart transplants, who typically obtain the organs from young motorcyclists just killed in road accidents.

There is another possible source: cell lines cultured from fetal tissue. Some kinds of human tissue can be cultured *in vitro* and induced to reproduce and nourish and proliferate. Though there is great variation among the kinds of tissue and their respective susceptibilities to cultivation, when it is possible it can produce stable, controlled, and plentiful tissue that can last through as many as fifty cycles of replication. In a few cases a tissue culture will undergo "transformation" and become a quasi-permanent "cell line."

The proposal has been made to secure a modest amount of primary tissue from electively aborted abortuses (usually in their second-trimester) and culture that tissue to produce stable cell lines available for research. Is this any different ethically from using fresh aborted remains?

MORAL DISTANCE

There is a significant difference, one might suggest. A moral distance intervenes between the abortion that yielded the original tissue and the cultured cells that are many generations descended from that original flesh. But this is an assumption we must examine.

Let a parallel illustration serve to illustrate. If I defraud your mother of her life's savings and then launder the money by converting the dollars into pesos, there is no acceptable moral claim that those pesos need not be returned since they are not what was stolen. There is a moral identity between the money before and after the exchange. And if I use those pesos to buy a house for my own mother who is unaware of its source, the house would still revert by ethical right to your mother. My mother would incur the duty to restore it to your mother when she learned the truth. And if she refused, she would then become my partner in the fraud. No claim of moral distance through transaction would protect her.

But the legal and moral rule of prescription holds that wrongfully obtained property, if held long enough, should eventually be considered a rightful possession by the one who holds it. Thus a piece of land which B obtained from A by fraud a century or so earlier should now be left in quiet title to the innocent heirs of B and not subject to claim by the aggrieved descendants of A. In criminal law the statute of limitations serves a similar purpose: the people agree not to prosecute anyone for a crime committed so long ago that its reality has really faded from present human relations.

It would appear that the reality of moral distance which would enable an injustice or an injury to fade away is merely a matter of time. This purifying moral distance, however, is not absolute. It has exceptions. Prescription is usually not recognized, even after centuries have passed, if the beneficiaries were aware that their possession was wrongfully obtained, or if the aggrieved parties have in the intervening period been pressing their claim for justice. And certain crimes of greater enormity are exempted from most statutes of limitations. In fact the willingness to allow moral claims of justice to expire seems based entirely on society's need, for the common peace, to have limits put on the investigation and possible upheaval of present circumstances.

Stipulate that a laboratory—one of the National Institutes of Health, for instance—were to culture and make available on a non-profit basis certain cell lines derived years previously from aborted tissue. The technicians at the NIH had no participation in the events that yielded the primary tissue. Even less would the experimenter/user be associated with those events. Could it not be said that the tissue has been purged of the stigma of complicity in the original destruction? Can bygones be ethical bygones in this case?

The question is whether the generation of cells cultured *in vitro* creates a significant enough moral distance to neutralize the original lack of informed consent and complicity in abortion. There are grounds to propose that it might not.

Moral association in the activities of others allows of a more and a less, and therefore it can be attenuated to the point of insignificance. For instance, would it amount to a protest against war to picket or boycott a corporation because it manufactured cluster bombs with a fragmentation effect calculated to destroy civilian populations? If we grant that it would, then compare that to an identical demonstration against a corporation which supplies a large share of the nation's soap, on the grounds that the nation's troops at war bathed with that soap. Surely the latter demonstration would carry with it very little moral credibility by comparison with the former.

If it were known that an abundant supply of cadavers of persons in relative youth and sound health were available internationally for medical research, that would surely present to medical schools a better learning medium than the cadavers of aged people or derelicts that they receive now through donation arrangements. But suppose that those bodies were all black, and all from South Africa. Then would medical school deans think it an ethically neutral matter to avail themselves of this supply source?

Perhaps the most widely known human tissue supply in modern research is the "HeLa" cell-line derived from the body of Henrietta Lacks (generally known pseudonymously as Helen Lake), an American woman who died of cancer in 1951. That tissue has been cultured and manipulated in virtually all major teaching laboratories in this country. But suppose that it were the "EsDa" cell-line instead, derived from the body of a Polish woman named Esther Dawidowicz who died of typhus in 1944 . . . in Auschwitz. It is very doubtful that scientists would have considered themselves as free to retain and use that material, for a nonchalance about it would make a moral statement: a statement of neutrality about the Holocaust.

There are indeed limits to the persistence of moral taint. It can attenuate. But when, in human experience, its source is particularly odious, a casual willingness to ignore it would still constitute complicity even when separated by the passage of time. If an attentive world failed to see the moral taint of the Bitberg war cemetery bleached out after four quiet decades, or that of President Kurt Waldheim's wartime involvements neutralized after four decades of energetic public service to the world, can we believe that the casual experimental usage of abortion-derived tissue could fail to embody a moral indifference towards an intentional victimization whose death toll in this country alone now stands at nearly four times that of the genocide which provoked the first explicit moral norms about research on human subjects? It would be a nonchalance imbued with moral apathy.

In any case, the claim that moral distance has obliterated or attenuated all significant association of researchers with the original destruction may at least be argued when the offense has been publicly repudiated and terminated. The claim is hardly credible if the exploitation is still ongoing and enjoys a measure of public indifference which scientific collaboration could only legitimate.

It would seem that the moral reality of abortion resonates about as clearly and distinctly along the cell-line as it does in primary tissue taken directly from abortuses. Indeed, the readiness of researchers to accept such material must exercise a considerable moral influence in awarding to the abortion industry the quiet and complicit acquiescence of the scientific profession.

This inquiry arrives at the conviction that in respect both of primary tissue and of cultured cells and cell lines, it is difficult but not impossible to obtain human fetal materials, fresh or cultured, that derive from unintentional death instead of intentional destruction, and that are made available by authentic consent. This alternative renders moot the question of whether one need or ought, out of the urgent potentialities of research, resort to using aborted tissue. But even were that option to be considered, it ought be rejected as unethical, for want of informed consent and because it would place the researchers in complicity, before and after the fact, with the abortion.

I conclude with a recollection of François Truffaut's film

The Last Metro, which dramatized the conflict within the theatrical world of Paris during the Nazi occupation. The German military exhibit a cultivated interest in the arts and join the audiences in a theatre whose Jewish impresario has fled to avoid arrest. Several times in the film the leading male actor, played by Gérard Dépardieu, is presented socially to appreciative German officers, but he refuses to shake their hands. It is not that he insults them openly. He simply backs away physically; he cannot bring himself to touch one of them. He is surrounded, however, by stagefolk who are fraternizing in various degrees: some by craven imitation of their masters' anti-Semitism, others by simply going along with events. For most of them the fraternization was no more than a passive acquiescence in events that were none of their doing.

As the story progresses, those who symbolically and physically resist and dissociate themselves from the good-natured oppressors emerge heroically. Those who go out of their way to collaborate end up pathetically. But the third group—those who fraternized more by opportunism and inertia—are subtly but inexorably corrupted. Their moral disintegration is the more alarming because it involves no determined acts, only passivity in the face of events.

The oppression we grace with our respect, the abuse we behold without response, the injustice we let pass without declaring ourselves, can be awesomely important, for we declare ourselves by default. When evil walks the land and craves our courtesies, the onlooker is put under moral constraint, not free simply to stand back and watch. Complicity in destruction is fearful because so often it involves doing nothing at all. And that is what it makes of us in the end: nothing at all.

NOTES

1. Paul Ramsey, *The Ethics of Fetal Research* (New Haven: Yale University Press, 1975), 89–99.

2. President Ronald Reagan, in a letter to Joseph R. Stanton, M.D., Brighton, Massachusetts, of the Value of Life Committee.

3. U.S. Congress, Office of Technology Assessment, *New Developments in Biotechnology: Ownership of Human Tissues and Cells—Special Report*, OTA-BA-337 (Washington, DC: U.S. Government Printing Office, 1987), 130. This study stated that if the Congress were to be guided by the view quoted, it should incline to the policy that commercialized sale and purchase of body parts ought to be prohibited (ibid., 15). This did prove to be the choice of the Congress whose bill to that effect, the Organ Transplant Amendments Act of 1988, P.L. 100–607, was signed on 4 November; see also 42 U.S.C. sec. 274e.

4. Stephen Toulmin, "Fetal Experimentation: Moral Issues and Institutional Controls," *Research on the Fetus*, Report of the National Commission for the Protection of Human Subjects of Biomedical and Behavioral Research (Bethesda, Md.: DHEW, 1975), *Appendix*, 10–11.

5. John A. Robertson, "Fetal Tissue Transplant Research is Ethical," *IRB: A Review of Human Subjects Research* 10,6 (November-December 1988): 6.

6. Benjamin Freedman, "The Ethics of Using Human Fetal Tissue," ibid., 3.

7. P.E. Jackson, *The Law of Cadavers and of Burial and Burial Places*, 2d ed. (New York: Prentice-Hall, 1950), 51,132 ff.

8. Freedman, 3.

9. Robertson, 6.

10. In Richard John Neuhaus, "The Return of Eugenics," *Commentary* 85,4 (April 1988): 18.

11. See *Report of Human Fetal Tissue Transplantation Research Panel*, December 19, 1988 (National Institutes of Health) 1:1–2.

12. Peter J. McCullagh, *The Fetus as Transplant Donor: Scientific, Social, and Ethical Perspectives* (New York: Wiley-Liss, 1987).

13. R.J.V. Pulvertaft, "The Individual and the Group in Modern Medicine," *The Lancet* 2 (1952): 841; cited in Jay Katz, *Experimentation with Human Beings* (New York: Russell Sage Foundation, 1972), 292.

14. After elaborating its code of ethics for medical experiments the Tribunal proceeded to condemn defendants, not only for having acted as principals in criminal experiments, but even for having "taken a consenting part" in these and other atrocities. *Trials of War Criminals before the Nuernberg Military Tribunals under Control Council Law No. 10*, vols. 1&2 (Washington, D.C.: U.S. Government Printing Office, 1949). "Permissible Medical Experiments," 2:181–84.

15. See especially "Final Plea for Defendant Karl Brandt by Dr.

Servatius," ibid., 2:123–138; "Final Statement of Defendant Karl Brandt," 2:138–140.

16. This type of research on doomed, living subjects may be compared to the research project presented by Dr. Ezra Davidson of UCLA as a model for incorporating ethical concerns into research protocols. With Federal funding in 1979 Dr. Davidson tested a diagnostic procedure, fetoscopy, on the unborn offspring of a series of black and Hispanic women intending to undergo elective abortions, to see how often it would cause a miscarriage; his defense was that the fetuses were already slated for death. Congress regarded this experiment as so unethical that in 1985 it banned for three years any use by DHHS of the regulation that had allowed it, *Report of the Human Fetal Tissue Transplantation Research Panel* 2:D82–89. Lifton's remark is apposite: "If one felt Hippocratic twinges of conscience, one could usually reassure oneself that, since all of these people were condemned to death in any case, one was not really harming them. Ethics aside, and apart from a few other inconveniences, it would have been hard to find so ideal a surgical laboratory" Robert Jay Lifton, *The Nazi Doctors: Medical Killing and the Psychology of Genocide* (New York: Basic, 1986), 295.

17. Lifton, 285–295; William Brennan, *The Abortion Holocaust: Today's Final Solution* (St. Louis: Landmark, 1983), 58–61.

18. Leo Alexander, "Medical Science Under Dictatorship," *New England Journal of Medicine* 241(1949): 40; James Tunstead Burtchaell, C. S. C., *Rachel Weeping*, (Kansas City, Kan.: Andrews and McMeel, 1982) 182–183.

19. As Dr. Hallervorden noted, there was strict division of labor: "I gave them the fixatives, jars and boxes, and instructions for removing and fixing the brains, and then they came bringing them in like the delivery van from the furniture store," Bernhard Schreiber, *The Men Behind Hitler: A German Warning to the World*, trans. H. R. Martindale (Les Mureaux: La Haye-Mureaux, n.d.), 56. See also Lifton, 285,292.

20. Brennan, 62.

21. Naomi Wade, "Aborted Babies kept alive for Bizarre Experiments," *National Examiner*, 19 August 1980, 20–21.

22. J. & B. Willke, *Handbook on Abortion*, 2d ed. (Cincinnati: Hayes, 1975), 131.

23. Willard Gaylin and Marc Lappé, "Fetal Politics: The Debate on Experimenting with the Unborn," *Atlantic*, May 1975, 69–70.

24. Dr. D. Eugene Redmond, Jr., director of Yale Medical

School's neurobehavioral laboratory, in the *New York Times,* 15 March 1988.

25. Dr. Robert Gale of UCLA, in the *New York Times,* 16 August 1987.

26. Freedman, 3–4.

27. Robertson, 7.

28. Excerpted from his 1986 Nobel Prize acceptance speech.

29. LeRoy Walters, "Ethical Issues in Experimentation on the Human Fetus," *Journal of Religious Ethics* 2 (Spring 1974): 41,48.

30. Letter to Lee Thomas, Administrator of the Environmental Protection Agency, 15 March 1988. See also the letter to the *New York Times,* 19 April 1988, by Howard M. Spiro, M.D., of Yale.

31. Chicago *Sun-Times,* 12 May 1988.

32. *Roe* v. *Wade,* 410 U.S. 113 (1973) at 156–7.

33. Ibid., at 159.

34. See James Bopp, Jr., and James Tunstead Burtchaell, C.S.C., Statement of Dissent, *Report of the Human Fetal Tissue Transplantation Research Panel,* 1:52–63.

35. Freedman, 3.

36. Burtchaell, *Rachel Weeping,* 90–96.

37. 16 August 1987.

7

How Authentically Christian Is
Liberation Theology?

ALTHOUGH THE SCHOOL OF THOUGHT known as liberation theology has been elaborated by Latin Americans out of their local experience and for their own distinctive needs, it merits attention from scholars who live and work elsewhere. Much respectful curiosity and attention have come from North America, possibly even more than from the Third World churches in Asia and Africa. Since liberation theologians state that the United States has exercised the most repressive influence over its southern neighbors, our attentive respect for their theological work is both appropriate and ironic. If Latin America is to find its way to fuller freedom, we might be the audience with the most leverage to make that possible. But if our compatriots have been the source of so much misery and repression down south, we might have difficulties understanding this particular cry of the poor, especially when some of its most articulate spokesmen construe it as a cry raised to heaven for retribution.

The liberation school is gifted with intellectual vitality. In the decades since the theological disciplines of scripture studies, historical research, and, to some extent, systematic theology have moved into a new maturity, one has not seen all that much progress in theological method and fruitfulness. It is all the more interesting now to listen to this energetic new cluster of theologians become so articulate and present a distinctive new method for acceptance in the world market of theological discourse.

The substance of true liberation is claimed to be social, economic, political, and religious. Were that an apt portrayal, the goals of the movement might be attractively integrated. But as Michael Novak has observed, the liberationists are actually little interested in economics;[1] likewise for social theory. Their readiness to trust in a socialist government to abolish injustice and exploitative privilege leads them to dispense with much explicit description of the desired social or economic order. This fairly well conflates the social and economic agenda into the political. The fact that their religious aims are also converted into political relief suggests that the reduction is even more sweeping. As a religious movement whose purposes are constricted to a political revolution that is expected to wreak all further changes, no matter how transcendent, this is an ecclesiastical doctrine with more than ordinary political significance.

The leaders of this school are sophisticated scholars. One thinks particularly of Gustavo Gutiérrez in Peru, Juan Luis Segundo in Uruguay, Segundo Galilea in Chile, Leonardo Boff in Brazil, Jon Sobrino, the Basque working in El Salvador, and Enrique Dussel, the Argentinian working in Mexico. They are all the more interesting for being independent. It is true that much of their intellectual orientation is beholden to the work of European Christians such as Johann Baptist Metz and non-Christians like Dorothee Sölle. But the direction and development of the school is firmly in its own hands even though they borrow from others, as do we all. It is fair to say also that this is one of the movements created predominantly by Catholics which has attracted the most respectful attention today from an ecumenical audience.

There are, however, some difficulties that await anyone intent upon examining the liberation school. The first difficulty awaits any North American who must depend upon translations from the Spanish and Portuguese. Orbis Press has adopted liberation theology as its principal scholarly interest, and is producing capably translated versions of its theological output at a plentiful rate. One is reminded of the mission undertaken after World War II by Fides Publishers, who brought to our attention so much of the new and creative French theology. Nevertheless, only a small portion of the full corpus has been made available, and that must make our study and our judgments tentative.

This is a young school of thought. There is considerable interaction and discourse among its authors, but there has not been time enough for internal cohesion.[2]

Also, since the mood of these theologians is one of defensive solidarity against external critics, they have not yet reached the stage of maturity that would allow for a more strenuous and self-correcting internal critique. Leonardo Boff was quoted not long ago as saying that no one who has not lived in the midst of Latin America has the standing to criticize their theological work. One hopes that this was a remark born of understandable stress, not a thoughtful statement of principle. Gustavo Gutiérrez has said it better. Dealing as they do with a particular set of issues they are elaborating a theology with a local perspective, but with comment and contribution from the worldwide Christian community, and with the hope of offering back to the Great Church a theology that would speak to the needs of all. But in what they give and in what they receive, he sees the need for "a healthy and frank scrutiny."[3]

As a colleague who takes their work seriously and is persuaded that we must both offer and accept critical evaluation, I want to offer some misgivings about several themes which seem repeated often enough and located centrally enough to be of signifance in this new school of thought.

It has to be understood at the outset that liberation theology is not the only vital aspect of Christianity in Latin America. The basic Christian communities are another, and the two movements owe much to one another but they are not identical. They began about the same time. The *comunidades de base* were meant as cells of laypeople exploring their common situation and deciding how to act together to improve it in light of their faith. It was essential that their insights arise from below; no clerical or intellectual governance was to restrict their grassroots character. The liberation theologians themselves have attributed their formative experiences and insights to their membership in such base communities.[4]

Recently, however, the theologians have felt called to play a more directive role. Since the oppressed masses are unable by themselves to rise out of imperialist domination and take proper pride in their own culture, the intelligentsia must accept the responsibility to lead them. "After having tried to lose themselves within the people, to identify with the people, they come to understand that they must shake the people. Instead of favoring the people's lethargy they become the ones who awaken the people."[5] The base communities are now increasingly being supplied with formative ideas and agendas by the theologians. Indeed, the altered designation of the base communities as *comunidades eclesiales de base* may suggest a move towards clerical cooptation of the movement. That may eventually provoke a crisis. It is not clear how populist cells so dedicated to self-initiated deliberation can accept much ideological direction. In any case, the communities have yet to submit entirely to any theological bridle. Therefore any interested and critical study of liberation theology will not serve as an assessment of what is stirring among the base communities.

THE CANONIZATION OF POVERTY

One's first misgiving has to do with what has come to be known by the awkward but probably permanent translation: the preferential option for the poor. It is regularly stated by liberation theologians that the church must take sides, just as Jesus did. The liberation Jesus preached was the abolition of injustice and exploitation. It must be preached today, as it was in his time, within a society already rent by conflict, where one social class is degraded and humiliated by another. To accept the gospel proclamation it is not enough to believe: one must enter into the concrete tumult and strive to refashion society. Since society is already cleft by class struggle, every disciple is obliged to take sides in that struggle.

Hence, an option for the poor is an option for one social class against another. An option for the poor means a new awareness of class confrontation. It means taking sides with the dispossessed. It means entering into the world of the exploited social class, with its values, its cultural categories. It means entering into solidarity with its interests and its struggles.[6]

The poor are usually described in economic terms, but sometimes the category is enlarged to include other oppressed persons: "We shall be taking sides with the poor, with the populous classes, with the ethnic groups others scorn, with cultures that are marginalized."[7] This is because as a class, the poor are sometimes defined dialectically, and not just economically. They represent any group on the downside of oppression: exploited females, or laity in a clerically dominated church, or immigrants in a hostile country. Indeed, suffering is considered almost exclusively as a result of oppression. There is no consideration of disease, pain, depression, bereavement, mortality, or any impoverishment except what has been inflicted by others.[8]

Juan Luis Segundo has examined the New Testament texts and he claims that although Paul preached a gospel addressed universally to all classes and groups, the earliest versions of the Synoptic Gospels, which are presumably more primitive than Paul and thus of higher authority, express a clear preference and privilege for the poor and other marginalized groups. Whereas Paul's universal gospel embodies the faith as it developed after the Easter events, this partisan preference of the early Synoptics reflects the original and therefore the most reliable preaching of Jesus. Segundo chides theologians who see Jesus as transcending all enmity and conflict. Hans Küng, for instance, has claimed that Jesus stood above the divisions he encountered. Not so, says Segundo. He may have stood above the quarrel between Roman and Jew, but he was surely not indifferent to the respective merits of the Pharisee and the publican.[9] He took sides.

Indeed, Segundo argues that the good news is not even addressed to the oppressors.

> [Luke] redacts the Beatitudes . . . as addressed exclusively to
> *the poor*, the hungry, and the mournful. But he is especially
> anxious to indicate and stress the corresponding negative side:
> the kingdom of God is a piece of *bad news* for the concrete

groups that stand opposite the poor in the social spectrum. Its arrival sounds the death knell of the privileges that have so far been enjoyed by the rich, the satisfied, and all those who have been able to laugh in the world as it has actually been structured.[10]

The oppressors are waved away with contempt. They are not invited to conversion. It is too late; they are consigned to destruction. Christ's preaching is directed to them, not in order to convince and convert and rescue them, but to reproach them.

That this is not the only interpretation is shown by Chile's Segundo Galilea, who states that conversion is a universal call:

> All Christians, whatever their status, secular or ecclesiastical, are permanently called to the dynamism of their conversion in which there are no privileges or respect for persons, and which radically depends on our response to Christ.[11]

Leonardo Boff joins in this view:

> The first to benefit in that kingdom
> are the victims of injustice, oppression, and violence.
> The powerful, the rich, the proud
> will be toppled from their places.
> Thus they will be able to stop being inhuman.
> Freed from the schemes that made them oppressors,
> they too will have a chance to share in God's new order.[12]

The poor, however, in the view more generally expressed throughout the liberation school, are not addressed by the gospel either, in any classical sense of being called to repentance and discipleship. They are to be given preferential treatment and assurances without any regard for their moral status, either before or after the kingdom comes. The poor are favored for no other reason than that they are poor.

> God loves the poor with special love because they are poor and not necessarily because they are good. The Beatitudes tell us more about the goodness of God than about the goodness of the poor. They reveal a *Go'el* [avenger] God, defender and protector of the real-life poor, those deprived of what is necessary

to live as human beings. It is this condition that makes them the preferred people of God.[13]

The poor are not offered joy because they are morally qualified. Indeed, we are told that their deprivation has reduced them to a submoral state, for they have been dehumanized.

> This total struggle with a power that enslaves human beings and strips them of their humanity cannot be understood in a moralizing key: as an individual call to a free decision, to a conversion to faith, on the part of the "patient." Why? Because this person, precisely insofar as he is possessed, is suffering from a negative, inframoral quality. It is the political key that is operative here as elsewhere: Jesus makes *no* demands before curing and restoring the "spoils" of humanity to their legitimate, original owners. In so doing, he is carrying out his mission. He is announcing the proximity of the kingdom, which is addressed—without restrictions—to all the poor, all the victims of inhumanity. The difference between the kingdom of Satan and the kingdom of God is not that human beings sin more or sin less. It is that they *freely* can sin or not, when the kingdom of God restores their human condition to them.[14]

Deprivation, we must evidently conclude, reduces people to so low a state that they can engage in neither sin nor virtue. Nor can they be asked to embrace any very demanding standard of morality in the struggle to liberate them. So the gospel, as a call to conversion, is really not addressed to either the oppressors or the oppressed: it is addressed to the disciples.

Because the Christian disciple is so much more morally mature than the poor, revolutionary violence, being so profoundly contrary to love, is something that a sophisticated Christian must not allow himself or herself. But that is not a standard that one could expect of the poor.

> Love of God can require the Christian to accept one's own powerlessness and suffer injustice toward oneself. With regard to love of neighbor, however, one is not permitted to come to terms with the powerlessness and oppression of others, of the

"least of the brethren," nor to desire to love God, as it were, with one's back turned to these suffering people. In the language of the Sermon on the Mount, this means: the Christian is expected to turn the other cheek when he is struck on the right cheek, but he is not allowed to encourage someone else who is struck on the right cheek to turn the other cheek as well."[15]

The poor are therefore not called to serve the kingdom: they are invited to benefit by it. Their material misery is to be relieved, but they are not called to discipleship. The disciples, by contrast, are recruited into the kingdom and told to abide by an even more rigorous standard of righteousness than what had been required previously in Israel.

> To describe this "greater" righteousness, Matthew depicts Jesus using the same basic expression six times: "You have heard that it was said [in the law] . . . but I say to you" (Mt 5:21,27,31,33,38,43). And each time Jesus uses the latter phrase, he makes the moral obligation of the law even more demanding than it was. Thus he equates adultery of desire with actual adultery, and insult with homicide. Jesus' law, in other words, is even more demanding, an even "heavier" burden, than the law taught and interpreted by the scribes. Jesus could hardly be inviting those laboring under the weight of the burden placed on [the poor] by the scribes to take an even heavier burden on their shoulders![16]

According to this theological perspective Jesus makes no moral demands on the oppressed. No radical conversion is preached to them or required. The kingdom is theirs simply because they are suffering under the world's existing structures.

Now what might a respectful colleague, one not enrolled in this school of thought, think about this preferential and partisan patronage for the poor and oppressed? The foundational Christian documents disclose a Lord who distinguishes among us by our needs, but not by his love for us. Those who believe in Jesus are obligated in emphatic ways to care for the widow, the orphan, the poor, and other notably vulnerable categories of people. But that is not because those afflicted are dearer to God; it is because their needs make the strongest claims on our service as sisters and brothers.

The God of Abraham, Isaac, and Jacob was thought to have favorites. The Father of Jesus has none. A favorite class is as alien to the gospel as a favorite race or a most favored nation. It is an implausible task to square with the Christian revelation any doctrine that Jesus has disclosed a differential love towards humankind. Sinners are welcomed because they are the Lord's children ... as are the dutiful. In fact, Jesus speaks of a preferential option for the sinners, for their need is greater even than that of the oppressed. Moral degradation is hardly less ominous or less destructive than socioeconomic deprivation.[17]

There are serious difficulties in the notion that the gospel call to conversion is withheld from the poor, for the reason that their miseries have exempted them from the struggle between sin and grace. What could be more bourgeois than to declare the poor to be so subhuman that they live beyond the reach of the universal undertow of lust and jealousy and greed and anger and sloth and pride? Is one to imagine that they are therefore not offered forgiveness and transformation in Christ? Are the best tidings Christians can announce to the poor only that they will eventually be poor no longer, and that their opppressors have been marked down for destruction? Are they—and they alone—not to be summoned to forgive their oppressors as Jesus did his, or to appeal to those oppressors that they be converted and live? What could be more patronizing?

An exegetical argument used to justify this theological stance is the claim that it is found in the earliest recoverable layer of evidence in the Synoptic Gospels. By the time Paul was in full cry, the argument runs, there was another theology being noised around, a theology that did not take sides, and that theology addressed the gospel evenly to all.

But this exegesis makes the assumption that the earliest gospel materials derive in a more direct way from Jesus himself, and thus enjoy a higher authority than any later version which would have incorporated the compromising views of the developing church. There is little consideration of the likeli-hood that these earliest materials might represent, not Jesus' own mind, but the way Jesus was first heard by the Jewish disciples who understood him at first on their own terms. The later versions of the gospel materials, we are told, represent compromises which infected the new fellowship as it came to terms with all manner of alien influences. But why is it not as likely that the disciples were unprepared at the first to absorb the full brunt of what Jesus set forth to them, and that they came to digest and appreciate and submit to his fuller meaning only as the message had time to work its way into their hearts and minds?

The teaching of liberation theology, in the way it deals with oppressors and oppressed, moves off in a direction which the gospel cannot follow. By treating the oppressed as aliens to moral struggle, not needing to be called into the kingdom by faith, transformation, and service, and by promising them an inheritance primarily enclosed within socioeconomic and political terms, it seems to treat the poor in a condescending way. By its tendency to consider oppressors as adversaries rather than as fellow-sinners in dire need of rescue, it speaks more of secular class warfare than of the struggle for the Christian kingdom.

OLD TESTAMENT PARADIGMS FOR LIBERATION

A second concern I would raise is this: one of the struc-tural elements which reinforce the proclivity of liberation theol-ogy to identify allies and enemies is its manner of following the Old Testament. Even to a sympathetic observer there seems to be little concern to read those older texts from a Christian per-spective.

The Exodus, for instance, is often designated as the arche-typal event for true liberation.

> The Exodus experience is paradigmatic. It remains vital and contemporary due to similar historical experiences which the People of God undergo. . . . it is characterized "by the twofold

sign of the overriding will of God and the free and conscious consent of men." And it structures our faith in the gift of the Father's love. In Christ and through the Spirit, men are becoming one in the very heart of history, as they confront and struggle against all that divides and opposes them. But the true agents of this quest for unity are those who today are oppressed (economically, politically, culturally) and struggle to become free.[18]

To work, to transform this world, is to become a man and to build the human community; it is also to save. Likewise, to struggle against misery and exploitation and to build a just society is already to be part of the saving action, which is moving towards its complete fulfillment.[19]

Many Christians mistakenly suppose that the sarcastic tirades against the scribes and the Pharisees were retained in the New Testament as a record of Jesus' or the evangelists' contempt for Judaism. It is far more likely that by the time the gospels were being actively edited the same perversities that had outraged Jesus in Jewish sectaries and officials were already displaying themselves in the early Christian communities. The stories were retained, not simply to show the Christian way as liberated from the faults of the Jewish way, but to display how much inveterate human blight the new believers had in common with their ancestors. It was the same with the older narratives of the Hebrews and their adversaries. For the Christian reader of a story like the Exodus it would always be clear that the foreigners were not merely enemies nor the Hebrews merely heroes, for in their sinister moments they were all too similar. And the follies of the Hebrews were the more frightening.

For a Jew today, the Exodus might serve as the paradigm of his own people's continuing struggle to be free of oppression by gentile adversaries. But for a Christian, the Exodus cannot serve to call down the blessings of sacred legitimacy and purpose on any ethnic or civil or class struggle. For Christians the Egyptians in that story stand, not for outsiders who impose suffering on them, but for that enemy within us all who holds us in the bondage of our own sin. Through the Exodus Israel found freedom by political and economic liberation: political emancipation from Egypt, but not that deeper liberation from her own infidelities. Both her march through the Sinai and her entry into Canaan were bloody as she attacked any tribe weak enough to be overpowered. The land of milk and honey was seized by fire and sword. There is no hermeneutic whereby a violent marauder-Israel can serve as a literal model for Christian liberation. For Christians can find no satisfying freedom if we simply succeed in passing on our own servile afflictions to some other new and helpless victim group.[20]

Liberation theologians have been critical of the way the New Testament has led Christians to give the Old Testament texts a "spiritual" meaning. Guttiérrez writes:

> According to this hypothesis, what the Old Testament announces and promises on the "temporal" and "earthly" level has to be translated to a "spiritual" level. . . . This is a disincarnate "spiritual," scornfully superior to all earthly realities."[21]

Dussel is of the same mind:

> I should like to stress that the notion of liberation is very concrete. . . . The term "liberation" is a very Christian one, deriving from the Hebrew notion in the Old Testament. God told Moses to "liberate" his people from Egypt. The notion of liberation came down through Christianity to such thinkers as Hegel and Marx, and it was then passed along to many of today's liberation fronts. Christians often translate it into such terms as "salvation" and "redemption," but behind all these notions lies the dialectic of oppression and exodus. If we turn liberation into some abstract sort of salvation, then the term loses all meaning.[22]

Liberationists argue that the promises made to Israel were given initial fulfillment through political events. This was the inauguration of the kingdom of God. It is likewise in our own time, as we move towards the final fulfillment: the ongoing struggle between grace and sin, the hastening of the parousia, is marked and measured by historical, temporal, earthly, social, and material changes. The elimination of misery, according to this theology, is what establishes the kingdom.

Here too one must observe a propensity to reduce the divine gifts to temporal satisfaction. Yet it is a distinctive Christian conviction that the elimination of misery may not be worth it if that be accomplished by means which infect the oppressed with the savagery of the oppressors. That is why the supreme image of Christian accomplishment is not the Exodus; it is Jesus crucified. The most desired outcome of that death was the repentance and conversion of everyone who had conspired to kill him. That, in the Christian view of things, was the way in which Jesus not only survived but vanquished his enemies: by overwhelming them with his love, while they still did not love him. The Christian must interpret the Exodus in light of the ultimate Passover on Calvary, rather than the other way around. The Kingdom of God arrived, not by derring-do and military prowess, as in the Exodus and the Conquest, but in that greater show of strength by Jesus who laid down his life that his killers might live.

On that view of things, surely there are greater blessings promised to the poor than that they shall despoil the rich. More of the kingdom is to be put within their grasp during their earthly lifetimes than the overturn of political and economic and social circumstances may actually provide. Jesus' passage through our midst did next to nothing to hasten the kingdom if the kingdom be measured by the political, economic, and social revolution wrought in his time. And is that not true of our times as well?

The Inadequacy of Justice as a Social Agenda

This preference for enclosing Christianity within the horizon of Israel shows itself further in the insistence on justice as the primary emphasis in the social agenda of the Christian church. To know God authentically, the liberation school has said so eloquently, is to enact justice. Deuteronomy, Proverbs, Hosea and Isaiah and Micah and the rest of the prophets are called to witness to this summons to justice. The famous passage in Luke is commonly presented by liberation theologians as the inaugural proclamation of Jesus' mission:

The spirit of the Lord is on me
for he has anointed me
to bring the good news to the afflicted.
He has sent me to proclaim liberty to captives,
sight to the blind,
to let the oppressed go free,
to proclaim a year of favour from the Lord.
(Lk 4:16–21; Is 61:1–2)[23]

The only justice that will do justice to this kingdom, liberationists assert, is constructed right now in this conflict-filled
world we have entered, by putting down exploitation and relieving misery. "Justice is so crucial that without its advent
there is no coming of the Kingdom of God."[24] Injustice is therefore to be defeated by vigorous involvement in the political
struggle.

So far, maybe so good. But here one must beware of three
shortcomings in the way this is explained. First, there is too
little acknowledgment that if one seeks a justice which will
endure, one must operate in the political order on terms quite
different from what is conventional in ordinary power politics.
Second, even while one is dedicated to the struggle with all
one's heart and soul and strength, one's goal must be seen as
transcending the actual temporal achievements, so that great
victories can be won even if the misery continues. Salvation
must be attainable even without the establishment of a just
world order. God's greatest promise to me is not that I shall
one day be surrounded by just people, but that I can become a
more-than-just man today even in the midst of injustice. Third,
it must be recognized that if we are to love and struggle for the
rescue of our oppressing neighbors as well as for that of our
oppressed neighbors, then we shall be obliged to transact with
unjust persons, and still not retaliate. That means accepting
injustice without striking back. It means *not* dealing with persons as they deserve. And that is not justice; *that* is love after
the model of Jesus. To suffer injustice and then decline to inflict
a similar injury on our oppressors is not justice; it goes as far
beyond justice as Jesus goes beyond Joshua.

There may already be some corrective movement in this

direction. Jon Sobrino writes this: "By justice I mean the kind of love that seeks effectively to humanize, to give life in abundance to the poor and oppressed majorities of the human race."[25] This, of course, may be much more than justice. In a world where injustice has already worked much mischief, it requires much more than justice to eliminate that injustice. We would all treat everyone as brothers and sisters, perhaps, but that result can come about only if there are many who are willing to receive far less than they deserve and to give far more than others deserve. That requires a graced love far more intense than justice. To renegotiate social opportunities, to claim from the advantaged and then restore to the disadvantaged, and to do this without spite or hatred, is not simply to institute fairness: it means forgiving the exploitation of the past and acting for everyone's deepest advantage. And that is so much more than justice.

As Boff writes:

> On the other hand justice alone is not enough to maintain peace.
> There must also be a gratuitousness and a self-giving
> that transcend the imperatives of duty.
> We need love and a capacity for forgiveness
> that go beyond the limits of justice.[26]

Following his cue, one would have to say—more clearly than the liberation writings typically do—that the Christian agenda is a far more rigorous one than the demands of justice.

A Merely Political Liberation?

Precisely because we do find ourselves in a world rent by savagery and ruthless conflict, we are faced with only a few choices. We can throw up our hands in listless despair and lower our heads and hope to survive. This is the way of cowardice and denial.

Or we can take up whatever conventional weapons are needed to be formidable combatants in the hostilities. This leads to some awkward considerations of the use of force.

Dussel, for instance, draws on a distinction made by Brazilian archbishop Dom Helder Camara between "first violence" (the unjust assault by your opponent) and "second violence" (your outraged response).

> If someone wants to kill my child, I am not going to let him. If the aggressor has a knife, then I must get a knife to defend the child. If I do not, then I am an irresponsible parent. I am committing a sin.
>
> So there is a "first violence": organized, legal violence. And there is a "second" violence. . . . The second violence is the violence of San Martin, for example. He organized his soldiers and followers. When the Spaniards came to destroy the new homeland, he went out to fight them—paving the way for a new whole that is present-day Argentina. If that conflict had not taken place, there would not be any Argentina today.[27]

What Dussel does not discuss is how the "second violence" leads, in its turn, to the third and thence to the eighty-third. Also, by presenting this use of force as a specifically Christian responsibility, he does not propose an agenda much beyond that of the civil state. That is the way to leave our mark on history, but it may be an ephemeral mark because it will not hasten the Kingdom of God.[28]

The third alternative is to fling ourselves into the conflict with little regard for our own comfort or survival, but to struggle in a defiantly Christian way: risking ourselves to rescue the afflicted from their degradation but also to rescue those who exploit them from the especially degrading and destructive ruin that befalls those who fatten off the poor.

In this strange yet Christian way of entering hostilities one will encounter many enemies: both the oppressors whose advantages are threatened by any fearless proclamation of their moral misery, and those revolutionaries who are inspired by resentment and who want the satisfaction of destroying their adversaries. If we act as Jesus did, though surrounded by enemies we shall be enemies to none. That is well nigh impossible, I admit. Only the Father can make it possible. And in Jesus one sees it was gloriously possible.

When Ernesto Cardenal abandoned his commitment to

nonviolence and joined the Sandinista fighters, Daniel Berrigan challenged him: "Don't you realize that anyone who commits violence destroys not only his victims but himself as well?" Cardenal's later, laconic comment was: "Dan doesn't know what revolution is."[29] Perhaps Berrigan had in mind a revolution too radical to be the work of soldiers or of a revolutionary government.

This is not to argue that a retreat into private or individualist piety satisfies the call to freedom, to the Kingdom. What I do say is that a Christian must bring her own political agenda with her into the fray. There is too little caution in the liberation documents against accepting the secular and foreshortened agenda that is already established in the political order. It is so well said that faith must provide the motive for the struggle.[30] It must be said just as forthrightly that if the struggle be authentically Christian, faith must provide the attitudes and affect the strategies as well.[31]

Metz has written thus:

> Christianity is in its very being, as messianic praxis of discipleship, political. It is mystical and political at the same time, and it leads us into a responsibility, not only for what we do or fail to do but also for what we allow to happen to others in our presence, before our eyes. . . . it is of the very essence of the Christian faith that it is never just believed, but rather . . . enacted.[32]

Sin is rightly regarded in its structural dimensions as a political reality:

> In the liberation approach sin is not considered as an individual, private, or merely interior reality—asserted just enough to necessitate a "spiritual" redemption which does not challenge the order in which we live.[33]

But from this it does not follow, by any legitimate Christian thinking, that liberation from sin is therefore simply another name for liberation from oppression. It is as erroneous to reduce the Christian struggle exclusively to the political sphere as to reduce it exclusively to the religious sphere.[34]

Jesus, as a Jewish prophet, spoke as a figure who was

political precisely because he was religious, for he spoke in the assembly of Israel which was simultaneously a racial and a political and a religious institution. But the assembly which formed in his memory was not to be the same sort of institution. It was not composed of a single race; it was not a civil jurisdiction.

Segundo believes that the elements of the gospel which date from the days after Easter are not partisan and political in the same way as were the more primitive gospel recollections which he reckons to be more authentic. But this resistance to a partisan and political frame for Christian love may have arisen because Jesus' young church was not disposed to think of any racial, economic, and political undertaking as good enough for Christian satisfaction and endorsement. There *are* goals we hope fully to achieve in the political struggle, but they will not be our political goals. They must, in fact, be goals that are attainable even in the midst of political failure.

Christians must listen with intense interest as the liberation school develops. And we must at all times ask whether the freedom it offers is the freedom which Jesus achieved and which he offers . . . and in his own way.

BARTOLOMÉ DE LAS CASAS

I end with an anecdote about a man who is rightly regarded as a patron saint of liberation theology: Bartolomé de las Casas. He was a sixteenth-century priest who became a Dominican friar and eventually the bishop of Chiapas in Mexico. Las Casas had come as a very young man to the Caribbean from Spain, and quickly became involved as a master within the system of enforced labor there, a system responsible for the extermination of possibly 90 percent of the Indians who had lived in that region. Even after he was ordained a priest he continued to profit from this servile arrangement. But he underwent a conversion, and then became the leading protector and advocate for the Indians. He was a fearless public critic—in the political order—of what the Spaniards had done to the resident population, and vigorously rejected their right to take away the freedom of any Indian. In his sermons and his memorials to the royal court he was blunt and confrontational: as strong in his outrage as any voice to be heard in the gospels or in Latin America today.

But when he saw that his prophetic efforts were having no appreciable political effect, he made a different sort of proposal, a political proposal. He recommended that African slaves be imported in order to replace the Indians in the enforced labor gangs which were inflicting fatigue and disease on them to the point of extinction. He was not the one who founded the black slave trade, but he recommended it in several instances as a pragmatic political compromise, driven by his single-minded desire to liberate his beloved Indians.

It was years later that he underwent a second conversion. In great sorrow he deplored his earlier proposals that had relieved the Indians only to pass on the enslavement to a new victim group. In that moment he became an even worthier patron of a movement for Christian liberation. In that moment he came to understand that there is no authentic liberation unless bondage is redemptively abolished, and not just passed on.

I think that we are not carping critics to encourage our brothers and sisters who are stirring our consciences by their courageous message to take Bartolomé as the patron of liberation. But it must be the older, wiser, and more Christian Bartolomé, because only his full story does justice to the story of Jesus.

NOTES

1. Michael Novak, *Will It Liberate? Questions About Liberation Theology* (New York: Paulist, 1986).

2. Boff claims on the contrary that the liberation theologians are speaking with one voice; yet he is himself an example of independence and dissent on some issues within that group. Leonardo Boff, *Salvation and Liberation: In Search of a Balance between Faith and Politics*, trans. Robert B. Barr (Maryknoll, N.Y.: Orbis, 1984), 24–30.

3. Gustavo Gutiérrez, *A Theology of Liberation*, trans. Caridad Inda and John Eagleson (Maryknoll, N.Y.: Orbis, 1973), ix–x,14.

4. John Berryman, *Liberation Theology* (New York: Pantheon, 1987), 63ff.

5. Enrique Dussel, *Philosophy of Liberation*, trans. Aquilina Martinez and Christine Morkovsky (Maryknoll, N.Y.: Orbis, 1985), 94.

6. Gutiérrez, *The Power of the Poor in History*, trans. Robert R. Barr (Maryknoll, N.Y.: Orbis, 1983), 45; See Leonardo Boff, with Clodovis Boff, *Liberation Theology: From Dialogue to Confrontation*, trans. Robert R. Barr (San Francisco: Harper & Row, 1985), 60.

7. Gutiérrez, *Theology of Liberation*, 18.

8. Dussel, *Philosophy of Liberation*, 41; idem, *Ethics and the Theology of Liberation*, trans. Bernard F. McWilliams (Maryknoll, N.Y.: Orbis, 1978), 36–37.

9. Juan Luis Segundo, *The Historical Jesus of the Synoptics*, trans. John Drury (Maryknoll, N.Y.: Orbis, 1985), 90–92.

10. Ibid., 91.

11. Segundo Galilea, *Following Jesus*, trans. Helen Phillips (Maryknoll, N.Y.: Orbis, 1981), 3.

12. Boff, *Way of the Cross—Way of Justice*, trans. John Drury (Maryknoll, N.Y.: Orbis, 1980), 29.

13. Gutiérrez, *Power of the Poor*, 116; see also 140. Segundo draws this same view from André Myre, who writes: "'*Inner dispositions have nothing to do with Jesus' choice.* Jesus addresses himself to the lowly, the socially marginalized, the sick, the disadvantaged, the poor people who are victims of injustice, those kinds of people who have no hope in this kind of world. He announces to them that God loves them. And it must be stressed: this option, this proclamation, *has nothing to do with the moral, spiritual, or religious worth* of those people. It is grounded exclusively on the horror that the God known to Jesus feels for the present state of the world, and on the divine decision to come and re-establish the situation in favor of those for whom life is more difficult. *Jesus reveals God, not the spiritual life of his listeners*'" *Historical Jesus*, 109.

14. Ibid., 142.

15. Johann Baptist Metz, *The Emergent Church: The Future of Christianity in a Postbourgeois World*, trans. Peter Mann (New York: Crossroad, 1981), 97; Dorothee Sölle, *Of War and Love*, trans. Rita and Robert Kimber (Maryknoll, N.Y.: Orbis, 1983), 29.

16. Segundo, *Historical Jesus*, 135.

17. Boff, *Saint Francis: A Model for Human Liberation*, trans. John W. Diercksmeier (New York: Crossroad, 1982), 49–51, describes well how poverty dehumanizes rich and poor alike, albeit implying that there is no poverty except by dint of oppression.

18. Gutiérrez, *Theology of Liberation*, 159.

19. Segundo, *Theology and the Church: A Response to Cardinal Ratzinger and A Warning to the Whole Church*, trans. John Diercksmeier (Minneapolis: Winston [Seabury], 1985), 44–49.

20. Dussel, *History and the Theology of Liberation: A Latin American Perspective*, trans. John Drury (Maryknoll, N.Y.: Orbis, 1976), 144; see John Howard Yoder, "Exodus and the Exile: The Two Faces of Liberation," *Cross Currents* (Fall 1973): 297–309.

21. Gutiérrez, *Theology of Liberation*, 165–166; Boff, *Salvation and Liberation*, 43–45, has a more balanced view.

22. Dussel, *History and the Theology of Liberation*, 144. It is of interest that despite this insistence that "liberation" not be treated analogically, Dussel does make "violence" into an analogy, *Ethics and the Theology of Liberation*, 48.

23. See Gutiérrez, *Theology of Liberation*, 194ff; *Power of the Poor*, 8ff.

24. Boff, *Church: Charism and Power: Liberation Theology and the Institutional Church*, trans. John W. Diercksmeier (New York: Crossroad, 1986), 25.

25. Sobrino, *The True Church and the Poor*, trans. Matthew J. O'Connell (Maryknoll, N.Y.: Orbis, 1984), 47.

26. Boff, *Way of the Cross*, 55. See also Galilea, *The Future of Our Past* (Notre Dame, Ind.: Ave Maria, 1985), 54–55.

27. Dussel, *History and the Theology of Liberation*, 126–127.

28. Galilea, *Following Jesus*, 100–101.

29. Sölle, *War and Love*, 29.

30. Boff, *Salvation and Liberation*, 46.

31. Boff calls appealingly for "political holiness," which he describes as "loving within the class struggle." Does this mean loving across the struggle, or does it only refer to solidarity with one's allies? "A Theological Examination of the Terms 'People of God' and 'Popular Church'," *Concilium* 176 (1984): 95–96.

32. Metz, 27; Segundo, *Historical Jesus*, 71ff.

33. Gutiérrez, *Theology of Liberation*, 175. Segundo, *Faith and Ideologies*, trans. John Drury (Maryknoll, N.Y.: Orbis, 1984), 327, points out how this sort of individualized religion so easily plays into the hand of repressive governments. See also Sölle, *Choosing Life*, trans. Margaret Kohl (Philadelphia: Fortress, 1981), 80–81.

34. Boff, *Church: Charism and Power*, 25.

8

Moral Response to Terrorism

IN 1956, SHORTLY AFTER the Soviet invasion of Budapest, the European Communists acted to relieve some of the international pressure on Moscow by condemning the use of gas by the United States in the Korean conflict. According to reports the gas acted as a disabler, rendering soldiers listless and virtually unconscious, so that they could be picked up and taken prisoner without combat. I was a student in Rome then and attended a noontime rally in the Piazza del Risorgimento, where I listened with curiosity to an impassioned party leader attack this immoral new form of U.S. destruction. Her voice rose to an angry shout as she reviled the inhumane gas that would render soldiers senseless. I distinctly recall my bewilderment at her implied invitation to think of shrapnel and bullets as humane by comparison. Personally, I would have preferred to have been doped than shot and was stupefied at her denunciation of the new gas. But I realized at that moment that it was war, not this or that weapon, that was inhumane.

There is a sense in which every accusation that some new weapon of armed conflict is immoral distracts us from the fundamental ethical issues about warfare itself. There is ample documentation that the introduction of every new deadly armament has aroused objections to its moral acceptability. The Second Lateran Council in 1139 anathematized the crossbow and the longbow and forbade their use—against Catholics and other Christians.[1] Comparable outrage met the introduction of gunpowder.[2] Submarines, torpedoes, liquid fire, dumdum bul-

209

lets, biological and chemical agents, and poison gas have been the subjects of intense ethical debate in the last two centuries.

U.S. positions taken at the Hague Conference and the Washington Conference surrounding World War I elicited three quite diverse reactions. One condemned the new armaments as immoral. In this vein, one editorial commented, "America's influence at the [Washington] Conference should be thrown against the weapons that are directed against non-combatants—the submarine and poison gas." "Since a gas attack is uncontrollable, chemical warfare falls into the well-poisoning class."[3] A second position accepted the fearsome new tactical devices precisely because they would serve to deter nations from warfare: "Chemical warfare with its unlimited choice of weapons and its unlimited methods of making war intolerable, will make warfare universal, and better than any other means will bring war home to its makers. . . . Knowing that the war of the future will be brought home to every individual, the effort will be made to avoid it at all costs."[4] The third position was that the evolution of more devastating weaponry was simply the natural unfolding of warfare and that they ought be evaluated by the classical criteria of morality in war, just as they ought provoke new consideration of what warfare had always been.[5] Those conversant with the ethical debate surrounding nuclear weapons in our time and with the renewed discussion of biological and chemical weapons will find these moral judgments quite familiar.

There is a sense in which this moral concern is very near-sighted. It dwells uniquely on armaments that directly inflict bodily harm or death. Yet cryptography, radar, sonar, missile delivery, laser directional systems, and satellite photography have escalated the body count in warfare without falling subject to any similar moral condemnation before the forum of public sentiment. Indeed, astonishingly accurate delivery systems may soon obviate nuclear weaponry as the most formidable international threat.

Ethical challenge to new weapons eventually subsides in one of three ways. The new weapon may become available to all parties in conflict, in which case no one will complain of it any more. Or it may be met by a newly developed form of defense and will no longer seem so frightening. Or it may be so catastrophically destructive that no nation wishes to court retaliation in kind, and thus it goes unused. What this suggests is that ethical discourse regarding methods of warfare may not be all that profoundly principled. What appears to be moral alarm over a new and deadly weapon is often merely a tactical and temporary disequilibrium on the battlefield. Once balance is restored, the devices are either accepted as a legitimate part of conventional weaponry or they are proscribed, not so much by moral condemnation as by fear of facing them.

There is a fourth alternative. Occasionally a people will reject the use of some form of force that is available because they do not wish to undergo the moral change that affects those who take it up and use it. In this century one thinks of Gandhi, the Christian Zulu leaders, and the Arab insurgents against the Turks. This is a truly moral stand, but it is rare and carries a heavy military risk. That risk is undergone because of a perceived moral penalty that a people of uncommon integrity may be unwilling to accept: a disintegration of character that would invalidate their cause and make them the principal victims of their own use of force.

In general, however, what passes for moral judgment is the acceptance of convention. Moral judgment pretty much corresponds to self-justification. I am willing to forgo moral condemnation of my enemy for any action that I myself am prepared to perform, and I am prepared to do virtually everything my enemy can do. Thus most of what is ordinarily presented as the refined moral estimate of battle practices—a moral code of warfare—is little more than a description of what we are all willing to do and to face.[6] The sign that one has encountered one of those rare warriors who exercises true moral judgment is when that belligerent is purposely willing to face actions to which he or she is unwilling to resort.

Since World War II there have been very few declared wars yet a plethora of armed conflicts involving national military forces. At first the military was bewildered about how to address insurgency and guerrilla hostilities. Unconventional insurgency was denounced at the outset as immoral and as a defiance of the humane conventions of warfare. But in time the international legal community began to have increased sympathy for the notion that there was after all a commonalty between guerrilla warfare and conventional conflict. Even in the period of the Korean struggle, this was gaining credence within formal military circles.[7]

As this was happening, insurgents began to adopt some of the forms and usages of the military. Thus the Khmer Rouge, like the Vietcong, used a stylized bandanna to qualify as military insignia and organized themselves, as had the Chinese Communists before them, in units and echelons of command. Although neither the Geneva Convention nor the later protocols unambiguously acknowledge guerrilla insurgency as a variant upon traditional warfare and although in many areas (such as Northern Ireland) the civil power refuses to consider insurgents as anything but domestic criminals, the international trend has been progressively to acknowledge that armed guerrilla resistance is but a modern adaptation on warfare and is to be conducted increasingly within the norms of conventional armed conflict.[8] Once again, the gravitational field of conventional warfare has proved irresistible to a new form of armed strategy and has pulled the new form of belligerency into its ancient toleration.[9]

These issues of history suggest that it would perhaps be misleading to address the ethics of terrorism and response to terrorism by accepting without question the fashionable presumption that terrorism is a development so discontinuous with the traditions of warfare that it deserves unconventional moral scrutiny. On the contrary, terrorism, like the many enlargements of violence before it, is a lineal descendant of traditional warfare. It can best be understood and evaluated by analogy with conventional conflict. And I am increasingly of the opinion that it raises not old questions about new kinds of combat but new questions about all the old forms of war. It is warfare's newest and most sobering progeny.[10]

AN ATTEMPT TO CLARIFY WHAT TERRORISM IS:
Inter bellum et pacem nihil est medium

No sooner had guerrilla fighting been accommodated within the conventions of warfare than terrorism presented a similar challenge. Terrorists characteristically choose symbolic targets rather than those of narrowly military significance. They purposely ignore the conventional distinction between combatants and noncombatants, often choosing to kill or injure civilians. Their purpose is political: to terrorize, to intimidate, to dispirit a government or a people through audacious and brutal aggression. Their actions are the work either of a government that accepts no public responsibility or of a dissident group that has no political standing. There is no declaration of war, no professional military adversary, no willingness by the perpetrators to abide by conventional military constraints.

Getting a definitional clasp on terrorism is difficult. At the present time "terrorism" is so negative, so despised a term that it is frequently used as an epithet without any consistent sense of what it really is. Used in this propagandistic fashion, "terrorist" means your enemy, who is "fanatic," "radical," a "goon." This is the sort of language abuse that produces, for instance, an amusing headline that appeared recently in a Chicago newspaper: "South Africa to Crack Down on Violence."[11]

Some attempts at definition are more serious but still quite self-serving.

Terrorism is *the unlawful use or threatened use of force or violence by a revolutionary organization against individuals or property, with the intention of coercing or intimidating governments or societies, often for political or ideological purposes* (Department of Defense).[12] This definition leaves no room for state terrorism directed either to its own population or to another state.

Terrorism is defined as the unlawful use of force or violence against persons or property to intimidate or coerce a government, the civilian population or any segment thereof, in furtherance of political or social objectives (Federal Bureau of Investigation).[13] Identifying terrorism as unlawful force creates a bias in favor of unjust governments that encounter no difficulty in passing laws that

authorize intimidation by force. Apartheid, for example, is per-
fectly lawful.

*It is a tactic of indiscriminate violence used against innocent
bystanders for political effect—and it must be distinguished from the
selective use of violence against the symbols and institutions of a contested power, which is unfortunately a norm of international life* (William E. Colby).[14] According to this norm, a police officer standing on duty at an airport would be fair game for shooting by
insurgents because, unlike a civilian, he or she is for them a
symbol of a repressive government. This raises questions about
the traditional but unreflective assumption that civilians are
innocent, while police and military are not.

Terrorism would be *acts committed in time of peace that, if
committed by a soldier in time of war, would be war crimes* (International Law Association).[15] On this view of the matter, it would
not be a terrorist act for a uniformed soldier to walk into a
private home and shoot its owner dead, provided that occu-
pant were an enemy of the state. That is, after all, exactly what
soldiers do in war without being accused of war crimes, but
that does not plausibly prevent such violence from being terrorist.

*One man's terrorist is everyone's terrorist. Terrorism is best
defined by the quality of the acts, not by the identity of the perpetrators
or the nature of their cause. All terrorist acts are crimes* (Brian Jenkins).[16] But if the act, most bluntly defined, consists of homicide, arson, or house arrest, surely it makes a moral difference
who is doing it and why.

*Terrorism is the use or threatened use of violence for a political
purpose to create a state of fear which will aid in extorting, coercing,
intimidating or causing individuals and groups to alter their behavior.
A terrorist group does not need a defined territorial base or specific
organizational structure. Its goals need not relate to any one country.
It does not require nor necessarily seek a popular base of support. Its
operations, organization and movements are secret. Its activities do
not conform to rules of law or warfare. Its targets are civilians, non-
combatants, bystanders or symbolic persons and places. Its victims
generally have no role in either causing or correcting the grievance of
the terrorists. Its methods are hostage-taking, aircraft piracy or sabo-
tage, assassination, threats, hoaxes, and indiscriminate bombings or*

shootings (a working definition much used in government recently). This definition goes far to distinguish terrorism from insurgency, but it makes it quite difficult to recognize terrorism when it is a policy of a state against its own citizens.

Most definitions seem to lack an adequately large context. If one simply notices the acts themselves that we call terrorist, one thinks of abduction, extortion, mutilation, assassination, massacre, bombing, and the like. The word evokes religious fanaticism, ethnic hatred, class struggle, and a readiness to sacrifice the innocent and the uninvolved. Yet the word "terrorism," indiscriminately pointed at these acts, can obscure the fact that the ventures we call by that name are really quite diverse politically and morally.

Some terrorism is perpetrated by an ethnic and/or religious (and usually economic) minority that demands self-governance: Basques in Spain, Catholics in Ulster, Huks in the Philippines. Some expresses the nihilist rage of small doctrinal groups that fail to rally public support. Examples might be the Red Brigades, the Weather Underground, and the Armed Forces of Puerto Rican National Liberation (FALN). Some is undertaken by governments threatened by majority dissent, such as in Haiti, Chile, Rhodesia, Uganda. Some is the venture of a national minority that aspires to control the government. The National Socialists made it a strategy in Weimar Germany; the Zionists employed it in Palestine under the Mandate; the Phalange used it to reclaim its lost hegemony in Lebanon. Some emanates from a popular majority that has been disenfranchised. The Mau-Mau movement in Kenya, the FNLA in Mozambique, and some Indian uprisings against Britain could be so described. Some is the policy of a despotic or occupying power beleaguered by a resentful populace. Amritsar, Lidice, and the Ardeatine Caves are memorial names for this sort of terrorism. Some bears down on a victim group on behalf of an antagonized national majority. The Biharis in Bangladesh, the ethnic Chinese in Indonesia, and the Ndebele in Zimbabwe have been its targets. Some is practiced as a combat strategy of armed forces at war. Rotterdam, Dresden, and Hiroshima are a few reminders. And some terrorism is sponsored by governments to discredit, destabilize, and displace the government of another, uncooperative nation it wishes as an ally or as a client. The United States did this in Nicaragua, South Africa did it in Mozambique, and the Soviet Union did it in Hungary, Poland, and Czechoslovakia.

A firebombing is a firebombing; people die the same no matter who threw the torch. Yet in framing a response to an arson incident—an ethically reflective response—there is an enormous difference whether the perpetrators are an unpopular splinter group with no practical agenda, the agents of a tyrannical government, or an oppressed and outraged population that has specific grievances. The phenomenon may be outwardly identical: same explosion, same toll in lives and goods. But there are significant moral, political, and even military differences if one is to understand and respond to the phenomenon. The bombing may be morally reprehensible whoever does it. But for whoever must respond morally to the terrorist act, it surely makes a difference whether it is the work of a tyrant or of the tyrant's victims. Even at the level of military responsibility, a commander must know whether he or she is sent to cope with an unpopular clutch of mercenaries or with an aroused national people.

I am not arguing here that there is moral and immoral terrorism.[17] What I am arguing is that the background, identity, and purposes of terrorists must be known if one is to frame a moral response to them.[18]

POLITICAL JUDGMENT BEFORE MORAL ASSESSMENT:
Inter arma silent leges

An adequate response to terrorism requires a broad perspective: moral, political, strategic, and tactical. One may not restrict one's inquiry and judgment to the narrow, tactical realities. One must have political insight before framing an ethical judgment, no matter what the level of one's responsibility. This is no less true for military and police personnel who have to cope directly with terrorism. Terrorism cannot be addressed as a merely military or criminal phenomenon, for it is defined also by its political context. If a military person is to be a moral person in confronting terrorism, he or she must view it at every level. Even to describe an act as terrorist is to make a political assessment.[19]

There is a hierarchy of perspective and discourse: moral, political, strategic, and tactical. Just as a line officer needs a sophisticated understanding of the strategy before devising appropriate tactical options, the flag officer requires a discriminating grasp of political objectives in order to frame serviceable strategy. And both must be able to evaluate what they are told and what they decide in moral terms. The highest level of consideration—the moral level—requires competence on all intermediate levels, including the political.

By law and by conviction in the United States, military strategy and tactics are subordinated to civilian policy. It is likely to remain that way, for Americans are not disposed to accept a military government. Nevertheless, military leaders must frame their strategic and tactical plans in good conscience. And no moral evaluation is possible without some critical judgment of the political significance of the actions that military leaders are directed by civilians to confront or undertake.

Military action must remain subject to civilian policy. But both strategy and reality will require a military commander to operate with an educated political perspective comparable with that of the government officials who give the military their orders. Americans want no military junta running the country, but neither do they want Eichmanns serving their rulers.

An illustration of this necessity is afforded by the way the military understood the bombing of the U.S. Marine emplacement at Beirut airport on October 23, 1983. In his testimony before Congress one week later, General Paul Kelley, commandant of the Marine corps, explicitly said that his remarks would "avoid discussion of the political or diplomatic considerations of our presence in Lebanon. It is not the place of a Marine to discuss those imperatives for military employment." He then proceeded to describe the Marine presence as "conducive to the stability of Lebanon . . . we were guests of a friendly nation—not on occupation duty! . . . The Marines were warmly greeted by the Lebanese people." In that light, he interpreted the bombing: "This unprecedented, massive 'kamikaze' attack was not against young Marines, sailors, and soldiers—it was a vicious, surprise attack against the United States of America and all we stand for in the free world."[20] The general saw it as an act of terrorism. Despite his disclaimer, he was making statements that in every way assumed political assumptions and judgments.

The Long Commission convened by the Department of Defense to investigate the Beirut bombing was even more explicit in its report submitted several months later. The words "terrorist" and "terrorism" occur 178 times in the document. The original portrayal is here amplified. The Marines entered Lebanon to a warm reception by the populace, especially as they went about disarming dangerous ordnance left by the fighting of the Israeli invasion. "It was anticipated that the [Marines] would be perceived by various factions as even-handed and neutral." Only later, when they good-naturedly assisted the Lebanese army in its efforts to subdue several villages, did the U.S. military unwittingly incur local displeasure. "Although [U.S.] actions could properly be classified as self-defense and not 'engaging in combat,' the environment could no longer be characterized as peaceful. The image of the [forces], in the eyes of the factional militias, had become pro-Israel, pro-Phalange, and anti-Muslim."[21]

This report betrays the most primitive political and historical understanding. To the Palestinians still in the area, the Americans were the chief client and support of the Israelis who had seized their homeland and driven them out twenty-five years earlier as refugees without hope. To the Shiite Muslims, the United States was the guarantor of a three-decade regime of exploitation and repression by the shah of Iran. To the Sunni Muslims, the United States was the prime obstacle preventing them from displacing the Christians who continued to dominate their country as a violent minority. To the Christians, the United States was the displacer of the Palestinian refugees who had been dumped in their country to ally themselves with the growing Muslim majority with whom they, the Christians, were unwilling to share power. And to every Lebanese, the United States was the funder and protector of the invading

Israeli army and air force that had destroyed Beirut and every other city that had fallen beneath their feet.

No one who had enough familiarity with the peoples of the region could possibly imagine that the bumbling fantasy of the United States landing in Lebanon as peacekeeper would be reciprocated with anything but animosity. To them the United States has for nearly four decades been the principal destabilizer of the Middle East. Instead of vilifying the driver of the explosive-laden truck as a crazed, frantic terrorist, we should rather try to understand what long train of frustration and rejection would make that man—and any number of others ready to do the same—ready to count his life cheap. Thus, to describe his act as terrorist in the hope of degrading it morally or justifying possible reprisals is frivolous. No reliable moral estimate would be possible until one gained enough political savvy to see how the United States has come to be regarded as the major terrorist of the region.[22] The Chief of Naval Operations then serving, Admiral James D. Watkins, made this same point candidly, though generally: "Any moral framework for a response to terrorism cannot be applied in a vacuum, but must be placed in context with the political, military and other realities which necessarily impinge upon the decision making process."[23]

An Understanding of Violence, Innocence, Solidarity: *Aquila non captat muscas*

There are still other reasons why Americans must possess a sophistication that is not only political but also historical, in order to make a moral response to terrorism.

No one ever claims to have fired a first shot. The U.S. government now has a Department of Defense, whereas for the longest part of its history it had a Department of War. The change of title reflects the universal human belief that the other nation is always the aggressor, and that the United States is simply trying to restore the peace. For the Allies, World War II began at the Polish border in 1939; for the Germans, hostilities dated back to Versailles. Your military operation is an attack;

mine is a retaliation. Like virtually all other belligerency, terrorism is not perceived by its agents to be a first strike. It is intended as a reprisal. No one will ever comprehend or cope with it without reconstructing the sense of the past that the terrorists harbor.

It is important to the moral claims of the United States to assume the role of an injured defender who is intent on restoring a violated peace. The use of the word "terrorist" can be used in this same sort of self-serving way, and military people especially run this risk. When we call people terrorists, we are usually implying that they have breached the peace, that they have initiated a stream of aggressive violence. But usually the stream of violence is an unbroken one, and the people we rush to suppress may themselves be breaking out of a long and gruesome time of violence we had overlooked because it had been imposed under governmental auspices.[24]

Aleksandr Solzhenitsyn has written:

> The opposition of "peace and war" contains a logical error. . . . War is a massive, dense, loud and vivid phenomenon, but it is far from being the only manifestation of the neverceasing, all-encompassing world-wide violence. The only opposition that is logically equivalent and morally true is: Peace and Violence. . . .
>
> Any spontaneous mass guerilla movement that is genuine, in the sense of not being directed from abroad, may be caused by constant, forcible and unlawful decisions of a government, by systematic violence of the state.
>
> It is this form of established, permanent violence of the state, which has managed to assume all the "juridical" forms through decades of rule, to codify thick compilations of violence-ridden "laws" and to throw the mantle over the shoulders of its "judges," and it is this violence that represents the most frightening danger to the peace, although few realize it.
>
> Such violence does not require the planting of explosives or the throwing of bombs. It operates in total silence, rarely broken by the last outcries of those it suffocates.[25]

We must beware of treating terrorist adversaries as violators of the peace if they were roused to rage in the first place by an injustice that had tormented them for years, especially an injustice of which we were reasonably seen to be the patron and guarantor. If a man has seen his children die from malnutrition because of medical aid withheld, his village ravished by industry that underpaid and sickened the workers, his voice stifled by a dictatorship that tortured patriots, his priests shot for preaching justice and his wife raped by a plain-clothes death squad—if, after all this, he rises in wrath and bombs the vehicle of a government official with the official's innocent family inside, who has broken the peace? And can we, by military reprisal, restore the peace? Or will our reprisal only justify the rightness of his rage in his neighbors' minds and raise up ten more in his place?[26]

Apropos of those innocent family members, Americans must give thought to the peculiarity of their notion that any nation is divided into "innocent" bystanders and "guilty" militants who wear uniforms. Most of humanity throughout most of history has understood families and peoples to cohere in solidarity in ways that are incomprehensible to the rather recent Western views of the individual that date back to the Enlightenment.

Twenty years back, when a band of Africans raided a white man's Rhodesian farm and slaughtered his wife and children, the Western world was filled with revulsion at this outrageous violation of the innocent and uninvolved. From the Africans' viewpoint, however, there was no uninvolvement. Those gentle children had been washed, dressed, schooled, and conveyed abroad and entertained and cultivated by dint of the occupation of *their* land and the low-paid labor of *their* backs and the deprivation and humiliation of *their* children. It had been the white children's father's rifle that violated them and their homeland, but it was his family that lived good-naturedly on his violence. How could he be guilty and they be innocent?

Westerners have been similarly chagrined at the practice by insurgents and terrorists of lodging their militants in the midst of an inhabited and sympathetic civilian area. Some of their opponents have complained that they could not attack them there because of danger to civilians; others have gone ahead and attacked on the ground that the civilians forwent their immunity by harboring militants. Westerners might ponder instead the reality that they may really be facing an entire people, not just their mobilized members, and should ask themselves what difference this makes for their response.

There are, then, three realities that terrorism introduces into the field of belligerency that move beyond the well-staked battleground of conventional warfare:

1. Terrorism is the warfare of the desperate.
2. Terrorism is a warfare of solidarity: it may be against a whole people, not just their professional representatives.
3. Terrorism is a warfare of selective targeting.

These three aspects are present in two remarkably different ways. Some terrorism is the work of a group that lacks public support and sympathy and is flinging itself upon the representatives of an intractable people. Such would be the spoiled, bourgeois adolescents of the Weathermen or the radicalized Baader-Meinhof gang. Their terrorism is desperate because they have so little claim to authority. Their assaults are on anyone in sight because there is hardly anyone whom they can claim as their partisan. The targets they select are symbolic, for their rage is bent upon desecration.

It is otherwise when the agents of terror are a mass of people that has been denied its rightful claim to political influence. Such would be the Ulster Catholics or the blacks of South Africa. Their terrorism is desperate because they have suffered long outrage. Their terrorism is one of solidarity because there is no one in the privileged minority that has not fattened by seizing their nourishment. And their targets are chosen to frighten their oppressors into receding before their massive, yet frustrated, force.

What has been said of peoples can also be said of nation-states that turn to terrorism as a desperate measure against other states and peoples. Terrorism is always the gesture of those who feel themselves at a disadvantage. But it makes a considerable difference whether the terrorizing nation is one that is trying to subdue its rivals or one that is trying to break free of oppression.

Lest anyone imagine that the rise of terrorism has drastically altered the relative advantages in the world of conflict, it should be noted that the cybernetic revolution has made available to both governments and technologically astute dissidents new and potent access to information-based power. Although it is true that terrorism hits the most powerful nations in their soft and vulnerable underbelly, those governments are possessed of even more advantageous means of identifying, pursuing, and neutralizing their enemies, especially if they consider themselves bound by no restraints of law or morality.

The need to see all such matters in context is a moral one. It is for that reason also a practical one: to repress the terrorism of an unpopular and audacious splinter group is one thing; to deny the normal aspirations of an entire people is drastically more difficult and much harder to justify.

A Moral Estimate of Terrorism as Warfare: *Nemo me impune lacessit*

Now let us follow up the proposal that terrorism is in fact not a rejection of warfare but the resort to new and disconcerting measures that are the direct offspring of what we had previously grown familiar with as conventional warfare. To put the thesis to the test, let us see what results if we attempt to apply the traditional ethical doctrine on conventional warfare to the response to terrorism.

The tradition distinguished between the right to go to war (*jus in bellum*) and rightful conduct in war (*jus in bello*). Much of what has passed as moral discrimination between armaments and tactics in war, as defined by treaties, laws, and military codes of discipline, is little more than convention. It simply states what most warring nations agree not to do in order not to risk the same in return. We do not butcher prisoners because we want ours to survive. This is a convention, and indeed a desirable convention. But it is not a canon of morality, as if there would be clear reasons why it would be moral to protect prisoners but also moral to shoot active combatants.

This concentrates the fullest weight of moral inquiry and decision making on the *jus in bellum:* What justifies going to war in the first place? According to the Western tradition of justified warfare, there are five principal requisites for a war to be morally undertaken:

1. Action by a legitimate national authority.
2. A just grievance.
3. The exhaustion of other alternatives.
4. A reasonable likelihood of success.
5. More good foreseen than evil.

Let us see whether these criteria can be applied to counterterrorism.[27]

Action by a Legitimate National Authority

The issue here is not whether a government faced by terrorists is such an authority but whether the terrorists themselves represent a state. The international convention is that nations engage in war only with other nations. We are brought to ask, however, whether this need necessarily be so.

A problem presented by terrorism is that while it is in fact an act of armed belligerency—an act of war—it is treated legally as if it were instead an act of crime. While the terrorizing group is acting in solidarity, the nation that is the object of its belligerency acts on the fiction that it faces only individual miscreants and restricts itself to dealing with those persons who can be convicted of actual crimes. International law may need to supply a new category or, better, an extended category of warfare. If a whole people is in fact actively mounting hostilities against a nation (think of the Kurds against Iran, Iraq and Turkey, or the Mafia against Italy, or the Colombian Cartel against the United States), then the target nation ought have some deliberative and formalized way of declaring the terrorist group as a whole its adversary.[28] Thus, for instance, the Irish Republican Army Provos as a group might be declared by Great Britain to be its adversary at war. Any member of the belligerent group, not just one who was convictable of violent acts of terrorism, would be at risk of capture.

In the international legal community, the first moves have

already begun to accommodate terrorism and its opposition within the conventions of warfare, just as had been done years before for insurgency. But in the meantime sovereign nations are left relatively free to decide whether to acknowledge terrorist enemies as formal belligerents. To date few have been willing to do this.[29]

Furthermore, since terrorism is often undertaken by peoples who are in arms precisely because they have been denied the opportunity for national self-determination, they cannot be represented by a recognized government. The nations they oppose use this as an excuse to deny them legitimate recognition as conventional belligerents, but this is often a self-serving exercise of political self-interest. That way, the dissidents can be classified as criminals instead of as belligerents. Israel, for example, consistently refuses to acknowledge the right of the Palestinian people to national recognition, or the Palestine Liberation Organization (PLO) as their legitimate representative, though Israeli polls have consistently shown that more than 90 percent of the Palestinians resident in the homeland consider the PLO their rightful representative: a degree of support probably greater than what Charles de Gaulle's government in exile in London enjoyed from the French during World War II and twice as strong as any Israeli party has enjoyed from its people since 1948.

It is the legal convention among nations that we recognize established governments as representing the national populace. But there are some countries where this is not true. Is our first obligation of fellowship to the unpopular government or to the people? Are there ways in which we can render the government its formal due while also supporting the people's just claims on our aid? And if this is impossible, then should we not on occasion withdraw our recognition of a government and establish our links of fellowship with other, more credible representatives of the people? If a government is our terrorist adversary, could we not declare war on that government without declaring war on the population? For that matter, could we not declare war on a non-national group that has in effect entered into systematic hostilities against us? These are possibilities worth considering.

Current moral inquiry on the subject of terrorism has been puzzling over the acceptability of preemption. This may not be the best way of approaching the question. It is only by regarding terrorist activities as distinct acts of criminal violence that one could speak of preemption. The criminal law does not easily permit authorities to move against persons who are contemplating a crime. But if a group is described and declared to be at war, then an action to fend off their intended strike is not preemption but part of a continuing campaign. Once again, the ethical picture depends on the model one chooses to use. If terrorism is merely a crime, then it must be dealt with by according due process to individual persons for individual actions. If it is a state of belligerency, then it must be dealt with by warfare and by the restraints appropriate to warfare.

For any response to a terrorist group to be ethical, then, a nation must acknowledge popular leadership in its adversaries as pragmatically as it recognizes de facto governments after coups, and it must consider the group as a whole as its true challenger.

A Just Grievance

As in the criterion of legitimate authority, the question here is not so much whether a government has a just grievance in defending itself against terrorists but what grievances the terrorists are wanting to redress.

The criminal law gives little sympathy to grievances behind violent acts. It need not be so between warring parties. Before taking action against terrorists, a government must satisfy its conscience about what motivates its adversaries. What is the grievance that has roused them to a violence that is often costly and risky to themselves? Is their cause just though their method wrong? If so, should our response be a redress of their grievances instead of a reprisal? We have no easy way of acceding gracefully to criminals. Still, we must learn to yield to belligerents who are rising against injustice and oppression.[30]

Patience and magnanimity are peacekeeping virtues. They are required to pursue the norms of a just war. The vice that defeats these norms is hubris. It is an act of hubris to refuse to visualize the character, motivation, and popular constituency of one's adversary.

When we can bring ourselves to recognize no fair grievance, then we are obliged to suppress a terrorist movement. The discernment of justice will be sensitive to whether the terrorists are a group that attempts to manipulate a larger people or a group that has been manhandled. A military junta and a national population would not have the same benefit of doubt. A dissident minority patronized by an imperial power would have grievances more suspect than the national population they opposed.

A nation that must address a terrorist adversary, then, has the highest moral obligation to discern what the terrorists have experienced and what are their complaints. That nation must, ironically, make a reflective moral appraisal of the grievances of its adversary before allowing itself to respond with the use of force. In the face of passion and anger, the offended and affronted government is morally compelled to use patience and dispassionate objectivity. Granted the heroic difficulty of such objectivity, it may be that nations should turn to detached, judicious outsiders to render their opinion before any decision is made. A moral decision to move into engagement against terrorists requires mighty patience and discernment of grievances. The first alternative always to be considered is the satisfaction of terrorists' demands, and nothing could usually be less agreeable to their target nation.

The natural instinct of all victims of terrorism is outrage and the desire to retaliate. But leaders of state and of the armed services, perhaps more than any other citizens, have the duty not to operate on instinct, especially this sort of instinct, for it is most likely to increase the force of the vortex of violence. Secretary of State George Schultz has given voice to the retaliatory instinct in its simplest form: "Our goal must be to prevent and deter future terrorist acts, and experience has taught us over the years that one of the best deterrents to terrorism is the certainty that swift and sure measures will be taken against those who engage in it."[31] The classic embodiment of this instinct is to be found in Israel, where retaliation has become, in the words of one former head of military intelligence, "a conditioned reflex."[32] Other senior Israeli personnel have privately admitted that the policy of instinctive, escalated reprisal has done nothing to stem the virulence of terrorism or to bring peace within their grasp, but it has become a habit from which they seem unable to free themselves. The history of the State of Israel is the world's best contemporary example of how incessant resistance to injustice cannot be repressed by reprisals.

The Allied bombing policy during World War II, in reprisal for the German bombing of English cities, was a similarly terrorist destruction of the German civilian population. The result of this reprisal was the increased conviction among Germans that they could not capitulate. The earlier German bombing of Rotterdam, in its turn a retaliation for the unexpected military defense by the Netherlands, simply stimulated the creation of the Dutch resistance movement. Reprisal is so rarely an end to things and so often a renewal of the cycle of violence.

I am not making the case that terrorists should be given satisfaction simply because they have indulged in violence. My point is that terrorists should not be denied redress and satisfaction simply because they are terrorists. It is in the national interest not to be blinded by outrage but to ascertain whether we are dealing with people who are themselves the victims of earlier, and possibly more grievous, injury: injury that we may have inflicted or conspired in or from which we can give them relief. To fail in this inquiry out of anger is to fail in one of the primary duties of patient statecraft.

When there is no justice in terrorist demands, then the next alternative is measured retaliation: purposefully restrained, with the promise of harsher reprisal to follow. Should that not stay the hand of terrorism, then is the time to declare that belligerency has begun. After that, the strategy is not to await further strikes in order to strike back but to move to capture or to destroy the terrorists. Nothing could be clearer at this point than the difference between a small band of destructive criminals, such as the Colombian drug network, and a great national populace, such as the combined peoples of Central America. It is conceivable that the former could be dispersed and destroyed. It is inconceivable that the latter could be and unthinkable that the United States should undertake it.

Reasonable Likelihood of Success

The only success is peace, and the only steady ground under peace is justice. A nation must ask whether a belligerent response to a terrorist attack will quench hostility or only foment more determined resistance and widespread sympathy.[33] Will it enlarge the conflict? Will it rupture the relations we now maintain with the sponsoring group? They may only be civil and formal, but even so they may offer an access to reconciliation that rupture would remove. Would a belligerent response lead to confrontation with a more formidable patron power?

Every nation must ask its people, especially its military and its police, to absorb outrage when no reasonable advantage is likely to accrue from a hostile response. It must be endured. Once again, one sees the difference between an adversary group of terrorist criminals and an adversary nation. The one group may much more easily be neutralized by armed response than the other, which ultimately cannot be either squelched or destroyed. It must be rendered peaceable, and this is not deftly done by belligerent response.

On the other hand, the principal service of war is to make people once again prefer peace. Not until the two peoples loathe the war more than the price they must pay for peace will they cease their hostilities. And there are some injustices so despicable that men and women will count their lives forfeit in resisting them. It is this sort of readiness to sacrifice oneself that we must be noticing in our terrorist adversaries, especially if they are an entire people. There is little reasonable likelihood of success against such a people except by coming to terms.

More Good Foreseen Than Evil

The primary risk in responding to terrorism is the moral danger to the respondent: What brutalization of character do we incur if we enter into comparable hostilities or, on the other hand, if we stand idly by? By striking out at terrorists, one may seize the advantage. By striking out intemperately, a nation may sacrifice the advantage of moral sympathy from other nations. The difficulty in applying this criterion for justified belligerency is that one must compare such incommensurables: human life with property, urgent needs of the moment with long-term values, individual welfare with the common good.

The ultimate good is the creation of peace. Every response to terrorism must have as its desired outcome that the terrorist people would eventually become allies. Thus we must measure how far we can go in destroying their dignity and driving them into insensate and irredeemable hostility.

When terrorism is an act of covert warfare initiated by another state and all parties know that, we face a severe conflict. Do we wish to suppress public mention of the true source of the violence in order not to exacerbate what remains of our public relationship, or is the crisis so acute and our opportunity to prevail so likely that we would choose a public showdown? What response is vigorous enough to maintain the respect that may discourage further attempts at terrorism yet not so headlong that we are entrapped into needless forfeiture of life and property? Is there a response available that might cope with the terrorist program itself but that, once introduced into accepted usage, would find us as an especially vulnerable and exposed potential victim?

THE GOAL: PEACE NOT CAPITULATION:
Opus justitiae pax

Many conflicts come to apparent cloture through the capitulation of one party to another, however peace is not really created and a resentment is left to fester until another even more violent day.

The criteria for rightful entry into belligerency against another power offer an array of challenges to those in public office who must determine how to respond to terrorism. The just war test meets the terrorist situation well: well enough to lead to the expectation that terrorism will eventually be seen not as an anomaly in international relations but as one more of the degenerate progeny of conventional warfare.

Recall the three distinct reactions that weapons development early in this century had elicited. Some thought the new devices were horrendous and therefore immoral. Others thought they were so horrendous that people would become more reluctant to resort to them. Still others thought that they were indeed horrendous but that they only brought out more clearly how horrendous all warfare had always been. The realities of terrorism may justify all three conclusions. Terrorism is indeed savage and inhumane. It is a moral quagmire into which a nation steps at its peril, for it may be as bottomless as quicksand. And yet it brings to the light the essential character of warfare, which, despite conventions and mutual restraints, is a form of inhumane savagery that threatens at any moment to break loose into uncontrollable destruction. Inquiry into the nature and ethical imperatives of terrorism is sound only if we do not imagine that it is inhumane by contrast with war, which is humane. Conventional warfare is conventionally inhumane.

There is a double paradox about peace being the desired outcome of belligerency. On the one hand, you may not be preserving the peace by refusing to fight. Thomas Jefferson, who had explicitly renounced any resort to warfare, eventually sent the navy to suppress the Barbary pirates. He explained, "Against such a banditti, war had become less ruinous than peace, for then peace was a war on one side only."[34] Yet on the other hand, armed intervention can destroy the possibility of peace when its target is a resolute group of men and women who believe themselves to be defending their families, their homes and homeland, their faith and their freedom: in short, the precious things people are willing to die for. Every decision to use force or to abstain from force can be justified only by its realistic claim to make peace more possible.

NOTES

1. John Hewitt, *Ancient Armour and Weapons in Europe* (London: Henry and Parker, 1855), 158.

2. See, for instance, the passage where Hotspur quotes a dandy he disliked in Shakespeare's *1 Henry IV* 1.3.59–64.

And that it was great pity, so it was,
This villainous saltpetre should be digg'd
Out of the bowels of the harmless earth,
Which many a good tall fellow had destroyed
So cowardly, and but for these vile guns
He would himself have been a soldier.

3. St. Louis *Star* and Norfolk *Virginian-Pilot*, quoted in "Viper Weapons," *Literary Digest*, 24 December 1921, 8–9. See also "The Herald of Gospel Liberty," quoted in "Christian Consciousness and Poison Gas," *Literary Digest*, 8 January 1921, 38: "The whole 'gas' enterprise is only another leaf out of the book of militarism which has been written into the history of our nation just at the present time by those who make profit and gain out of war—but it is a page that ought to arouse every Christian conscience to a quick and defiant resentment in behalf of the honor and nobleness of America, against which it ought not for a moment be possible to bring even the suggestion of such inhuman practices, no matter what the rest of the nations of the world may do."

4. "Chemical Warfare," publication of the Chemical Warfare Service of the U.S. Army, quoted in "Viper Weapons."

5. One journal welcomed chemical warfare as possibly "making war humane. . . . The real reason for the instinctive aversion manifested against any new art, or mode of attack is that it reveals to us the intrinsic horror of war. We naturally revolt against premeditated homicide, but we have become so accustomed to the sword and latterly to the rifle that they do not shock us as they ought when we think of what they are made for" ("Fighting with Fumes—A Humane Innovation?" *Independent*, 10 May 1915, 227–228).

6. All too often the law is accepted as possessed of intrinsic moral value rather than as a conventional norm that should, but may not, correspond to a moral imperative. For instance, some define terrorism as immoral simply because it operates outside the law. "Terrorism, that is, international and politically motivated terrorism, is impermissible use of political violence. . . . It is impermissible morally because it is not restrained by the rule of law or the laws of war" (Ernest W. Lefever, in "Terrorism: A National Issues Seminar," *World Affairs* 146 [Summer 1983]: 104). This has been enunciated even more bluntly and crudely by C. E. Zoppo: "Custom is law, law is morality. . . . Politics basically defines what is moral" ("The Moral Factor in Interstate Politics and International Terrorism," in *The Rationalization of Terrorism*, ed. David C. Rapoport and Yonah Alexander

[Frederick, Md.: University Publications of America, 1982], 137,144). Leszek Kolakowski makes this corrective observation: "The worst atrocities committed by the Soviet government against its own people, including the genocide during Stalin's regime, have been for the most part entirely legal" (*Harper's*, 269 [October 1984]: 46).

7. See *The Law of Land Warfare*, U.S. Department of the Army Field Manual 27–10 (Washington: Government Printing Office, 1956). This manual has enjoyed an extended existence and has been much cited in judicial proceedings.

8. The 1977 Geneva Protocols attempt to draw international irregular conflicts into the ordinary regulations of Geneva and even to extend these provisions (regarding prisoner of war status) to domestic belligerents. The language of the protocols remains hedged, however, and has left it up to signatory nations to decide whether to accord the status of belligerent to terrorists. Typically they will not. In some countries, however (Vietnam, Northern Ireland), captive insurgents have been in fact treated as prisoners of war or as political prisoners even though they may not have been awarded that status formally by the protocols or by the government. See the protocols in Dietrich Schindler and Jirit Toman, *The Laws of Armed Conflicts* (Geneva: Henry Dunant Institute, 1981).

9. Stanley Hauerwas is persuaded that the crossbow and longbow were outlawed because they constituted a new and formidable handicap to the way knights fought in battle. It was thus as much a class issue as a moral one since the newer forms of archery gave too much advantage to the peasants and threatened the entire equestrian order. Even without this suggestion, one might observe that much of the outrage against guerrilla warfare, and subsequently against insurgent terrorism, has been turned by the affluent upon the poor.

10. See Harry G. Summers, Jr., "What Is War?" *Harper's* 268 (May 1984): 75–78.

11. For two splendidly opposed views of who are the terrorists in South Africa, see Paul Rich, "Insurgency, Terrorism and the Apartheid System in South Africa," *Political Studies* 32 (1984): 68–85; Keith Campbell, "Prospects for Terrorism in South Africa," *South Africa International* 14 (October 1983): 397–417.

12. DOD Directive 2000.12.

13. "Stuart Taylor, Jr., "When Is a Terrorist Not Necessarily a Terrorist?" *New York Times*, 12 December 1984, Y14.

14. William E. Colby, "Taking Steps to Contain Terrorism," *New York Times*, 8 July 1984, E21.

15. See Alfred P. Rubin, letter to the editor, *New York Times*, 28 July 1984, Y22.

16. Brian M. Jenkins, "Statements about Terrorism," *Annals of the American Academy of Political and Social Science* 463 (September 1983): 12.

17. There are, however, some intellectually serious moves in that direction. See, for example, Robert Young, "Revolutionary Terrorism, Crime and Morality," *Social Theory and Practice* 4 (Fall 1977): 287–302; H. Odera Oruka, "Legal Terrorism and Human Rights," *Praxis International*, January 1982, 376–385.

18. Aleksandr Solzhenitsyn writes:

The great world organization of man was unable to bring forth even a moral condemnation of terrorism. A selfish majority in the United Nations countered such a condemnation with yet another effort at dubious distinction by asking whether any form of terrorism was in fact harmful. And what is the definition of terrorism, anyway? They might well have suggested in jest: "when we are attacked, it's terrorism, but when we do the attacking, it's a guerilla movement of liberation." But let's be serious. They refuse to regard as terrorism a treacherous attack in a peaceful setting, on peaceful people, by military men carrying concealed weapons and often dressed in plain clothes. They demand instead that we study the aims of terrorist groups, their bases of support and their ideology, and then perhaps acknowledge them to be sacred 'guerillas.' (The term 'urban guerillas' in South America almost approaches the humoristic level.) "Peace and Violence," *New York Times*, 15 September 1973, M27.

19. Arthur Wolffers observes, in the reverse direction, that a political or judicial understanding of terrorism implies moral judgments: "Philosophische Überlegungen zum Terrorismus," *Archiv für Rechts und Sozialphilosophie* 66 (1980): 453–468.

20. White Letter No. 6–83, Headquarters U.S. Marine Corps, 4 November 1983.

21. Report of the DOD Commission on Beirut International Airport Terrorist Act, 23 October 1983 (20 December 1983).

22. "We must recognize that the real problem facing the United States in the Middle East is not crazed terrorists driving stolen vans but the widening gulf between America and the Arabs" Augustus R.

Norton, "The Climate for Mideast Terrorism," *New York Times*, 26 September 1984, A23.

23. Admiral James D. Watkins, "Countering Terrorism: A New Challenge to Our National Conscience," *Sea Power*, November 1984, 37.

24. John F. McCamant gives an interesting illustration of how selective the public view can be of terrorism:

> How far the antiseptic view of government permeates the U.S. culture was demonstrated by reports on the 1982 elections in El Salvador. Newspaper editorials waxed enthusiastic about the large turnout of voters and exclaimed what a wonderful example of democracy the elections were. President Ronald Reagan said that we in the United States should be inspired by the Salvadoran example. It had been public knowledge for some time that some 30,000 civilians had been killed for political reasons over the previous two years, mostly by government troops, and that six leaders of the opposition Revolutionary Democratic Front were dragged by government troops from their last meeting in San Salvador in November, 1980, and brutally murdered. Yet the 200 observers brought in for the occasion still reported that the elections were free and fair. The public imagination seemed incapable of putting human rights violations together with political processes. "Governance without Blood: Social Science's Antiseptic View of Rule: or, The Neglect of Political Repression," in *The State as Terrorist: The Dynamics of Governmental Violence and Repression*, Contributions in Political Science 103, ed. Michael Stohl and George A. Lopez (Westport, Conn: Greenwood, 1984), 12.

25. Solzhenitsyn, "Peace and Violence."

26. See William F. May, "Terrorism as Strategy and Ecstasy," *Social Research* (Summer 1974): 277–298.

27. This has been done, interestingly and competently, by Watkins, "Countering Terrorism," 35–37. He had essayed the same argument earlier, in his commencement address that May (1984) at the U.S. Naval Academy.

28. Recent legislation against organized crime has moved somewhat in this direction by considering the entire enterprise as a conspiracy and thus under a criminal cloud from the start.

29. See Alfred P. Rubin, "Terrorism and the Laws of War," *Denver Journal of International Law and Policy* 12 (Spring 1983): 219–235.

30. For two differing partisan estimates of how the Carter and the Reagan administrations related the defense of human rights with opposition to terrorism, see remarks by Elliott Abrams and Robert A. Blair in *World Affairs* 146 (Summer 1983): 69–78,114–116. Walter Laqueur has some sobering conclusions on how little terrorism has actually abated even when attention has been given to its expressed grievances and also how little terrorism itself has accomplished; see *Terrorism* (Boston: Little, Brown, 1977), 215–226.

31. Hon. George Schultz, Address to the Park Avenue Synagogue, New York City, quoted in *New York Times*, 26 October 1984, Y6.

32. Thomas L. Friedman, quoting Aharon Yariv, in "Israel Turns Terror Back on the Terrorists, But Finds No Political Solution," *New York Times*, 4 December 1984, Y8.

33. For a study of the delicacy and weight of public opinion regarding terrorism, see Albert Legault, "*La dynamique du terrorisme: Le cas des Brigades rouges*," *Études Internationales* 14 (December 1983): 639–681.

34. Letter to John Wayles Eppes, 11 September 1813, in *The Writings of Thomas Jefferson* 9, ed. Paul L. Ford (New York: G.P. Putnam's Sons, 1898): 396. Jefferson is also remembered to have said that "an insult unpunished is the parent of others." See note 31 above.

Moral Wisdom and the Civil Order

9

The Inability of Law to Accomplish Its Own Purposes

MOST PEOPLE ARE AWARE that the highly antagonized debate over abortion in America has found its principal focus on a question of law: Shall we have legal barriers that protect the unborn by restraining their mothers' freedom to abort? Both parties to the debate have turned their sharpest attention to this as a matter of law. Partisans of free choice considered their struggle largely successful when *Roe* v. *Wade* and *Doe* v. *Bolton* in 1973 legitimated abortion on demand at any time during pregnancy. Prolife advocates have been laboring mightily ever since to overturn those enactments. The course of the conflict has been punctuated by the passage of various new laws and regulations and the handing down of a lengthening series of court decisions.

I want to argue that many on both sides may be seriously misled. Abortion is one of those issues that will never be resolved by law.

Prolife people ought to ask themselves what one stands to gain from a satisfactory change in the law. They have been reminded from all sides that a practice which is engaged in each year by a million and a half women is not likely to be stopped by a statute. Indeed, in the days before 1973 when American laws made abortion under most circumstances a criminal act, those laws led to relatively few prosecutions. Frequent comparisons have been made to the Constitutional

Amendment which forbade the manufacture, possession, and use of alcoholic beverages, and which eventually was repealed because the support which brought it into being was not strong enough to sustain it against the long tide of popular rejection. All of this raises the question: Would it really be possible to restrain abortion by the force of law?

The Difference between Law and Moral Wisdom

But first one should review what criminal laws are all about. The common and statutory traditions of law in our culture owe much to the tradition of law in the Bible. Not so much to the New Testament, which offers very little support for a system of law, and indeed raises strong doubts about whether lawmaking ought ever be an enterprise of Christians. Christian statesmen of later ages, however, o'erleapt the New Testament and took much comfort in the Jewish scriptures, a large part of which present codes of law.

The Hebrews, whether they were enjoying their own independence, or (as was more often the case) when they were living under the sovereignty of some superior power, virtually always operated as a unit unto themselves. Even when the Assyrians, Babylonians, Persians, or Romans governed them, they were not assimilated into a general citizenry any more than were most other ethnic groups. Instead they were expected to discipline their own social and public and religious life, provided only that they remitted their taxes on time. The ruling power would reach into their legal affairs only to control certain acts considered to affect the imperial security.

Many Christians today quite fail to realize that what we have preserved for us in books like Exodus and Deuteronomy is not what we would understand as religious law. It was, of course, taken as standing on God's authority, but it was not a religious law as distinct from civil law. Neither was it a merely civil law. It was the only law the Hebrew had, and it treated in a unitary fashion of all matters of their public and private welfare.

In ancient Israel, and later in Judah and Judaea, the function of the law was not merely to redress damages or to assure justice, but to protect the peace. The chief of clan, tribe, or nation had the maintenance of that peace as his or her principal responsibility. When someone rode down the street and trampled your young daughter, it was not understood to be simply her injury, or even yours. It was a grievance between your two families or clans or tribes. What began as a personal injury in a single household might quickly fester into a blood feud between two whole peoples. The ruler's knack—which came to be called wisdom—was to devise and impose a solution that did not merely punish offenders, but managed to send all parties home with the sense that their dignity and claims had been adequately honored. They never developed our distinction between crime and tort, or between criminal and civil proceedings, for every unresolved personal conflict was also a potential menace to the public peace.

This talent of the ruler was exemplified in Solomon. The story of his judgment between the two ladies of the night quarreling over a single infant was often told as an example of the shrewd insight a ruler needed to keep the people in peace.

The purpose, then, of the national law and of its application through judgment was that this nation of rival tribes and proud families could survive its normal traffic of dispute and outrage and still hold together in a confederation of kinship.

The law's purpose went even beyond social tranquillity. It was also Israel's way of maintaining peace with the Lord. Since the law was God's command, to violate it was to incur his wrath and his punishment. And God, like one's neighbor, was understood at first to deal with whole families and clans, not just individuals. Thus if one person's crime was an outrageous enormity, God might well retaliate with a broad swipe and exterminate an entire village or tribe in order to cleanse his land. Capital punishment among the Hebrews was intended, therefore, less as a deterrent or punishment for grave crime, than as a measure of self-defense for the entire people, who could be put at risk for a single person's sin. It was in everyone's interest that individuals abide by God's law, and it was also in everyone's interest to eliminate serious offenders before God's wrath began to scourge the entire countryside.

The earliest Christian church communities, like the Jewish synagogue communities they imitated, had a single law—civil, religious, social—for all purposes. It was when the Christians surprised even themselves by taking gentile members into their midst that they could no longer continue as a unitary society under a unitary law. The new Christians did not see their loyalties combined in the same way the old believers had: one God meaning one religious fellowship, one circle of companionship, one ethnic identity, one residential society, one law governing all obligations. The newcomers looked to their church for their religion but did not always choose to re-identify themselves in the civic order as totally absorbed into a minority enclave.

This Christian arrangement did not turn against their Jewish tradition. The prophets had insisted loudly that any settlement of a dispute that was not a just settlement yielded a worthless and fragile peace. By claiming the right to criticize and even to reject unfaithful kings and their unjust enactments of either self-aggrandizement or favoritism in light of a higher law, the Hebrew prophets were implying that national law and legitimacy must always face a higher moral scrutiny.

Christians pursued that insight and accepted a dual loyalty: to civil law and to moral duty. And the two claims could be at odds. The function of the civil law was still to keep them at peace. It might keep them at peace with the civil power and with their fellow countrymen of every belief and none, though without necessarily offering them peace with God or with their consciences.

Within the church they now encountered, not a law, but a wisdom about God's claims on them and what they needed to do in order to enhance their own personal lives. By analogy they often called these new claims "law": the law of Christ, the law of love, the law of the church. But in fact this new society had no right or ambition to enforce among them anything similar to what they had understood as law. The risk of flaunting this Christian claim was not to encounter God's wrath—for their God was now understood to have no wrath—but to incur their own spiritual self-destruction.

This was a "law" that could not be enforced, for it operated by conversion instead of by coercion.[1] The moral "law" kept them at peace with their fellow-believers and with their God. Indeed, they came to realize that they must defy civil rulers and civil laws which they understood to violate God's claim. As a Christian community they codified for themselves what they understood as a new "law." And while they were at it, they moved some distance away from the traditional strictures of their ancestral Jewish scriptures, to frame a code of conduct that was understood to represent God's newer and sometimes more stringent claims on them through Jesus and the apostles.

This is the tradition which has largely shaped classical Western political thought. We would misunderstand it entirely were we to suppose that it envisions two spheres of law: one public, civic, and secular; the other private, ecclesiastical, and sacred; each sovereign in its own territory. There is a rule of law in the hands of those who govern. There is as well a community of moral discourse and wisdom in the hands of all who wish to share in it: a discourse to which religious teaching makes a constant contribution. Those who frame and enforce the law will achieve their purpose, an enduring and endurable public peace, only if their laws are just. Violence may be quelled briefly by measures that are unjust, but the enduring peace will not be fostered except by equitable laws equitably enforced. Thus, though the power to levy the law belongs to those who govern, the power to judge the law belongs to all who share in the public forum. Those who wield the sword have the prerogative of rule, but also the onus of answering to those who wield moral judgment.

THE PRINCE AND THE FRIAR: EXPONENTS OF LAW AND WISDOM

The claims of the criminal law and of moral preaching, as two contributions to peace-keeping, are well portrayed before our imaginations by that most improbable source of jurisprudence, Shakespeare's *Romeo and Juliet*. The two main characters in the play are usually taken to be the idiot teenagers who, like a pair of adolescent Clouseaux, stumble from tragedy to tragedy until both are dead. I am much more taken by two other characters: the Duke of Verona and Friar Laurence. They represent in parable the state and the church, the law of the state and the wisdom of faith.

They are both responsible for the peace of Verona, which as we enter the play is an exceedingly unpeaceable city. The duke arrives in the opening scene with the militia to put down one of the periodic riots between the Capulets and the Montagues. Out of patience amid the wreckage that pride and blood-lust have strewn upon his streets, the duke loses his temper and reviles both families—the leading aristocrats of Verona—because they have made it unsafe now for citizens to walk the streets. He lowers a solemn threat on them all: who next riots in Verona will pay with his own life.

Only a few scenes later the duke must call out the troops once more, for the same demonic brawling has erupted all over again. As he arrives in wrath and armored might, outraged and ready to levy heavy justice, he is stopped by the discovery that the prime surviving offender is no knave but Romeo, scion of the Montagues. Here the duke flinches at his own threat. Having galloped up, frothing with indignation and the sentiments of a hanging judge, in one instant he diminishes to a wimp. Instead of carrying through with his threat, he banishes Romeo indefinitely to nearby Mantua. It is at this point that the Montagues and the Capulets can wink across the piazza at one another. They know what kind of duke they have. They know there will be more deaths, there will be no peace, because their ruler has no nerve to use the weapon he possesses to keep Verona at peace: his power to coerce. The strength behind the duke's law is armed might, and he has not got the nerve to use it. Instead, he lectures the populace. And he is a failure as a preacher.

The other character is a mendicant friar. It is his vocation as a free preacher to berate the great families as sinful, riotous villains who victimize the entire town with their arrogant hatred. His calling is to rebuke them, to appeal to them, to transform their hearts. Yet, instead of preaching Christ's message incessantly, the friar sets about scheming and politicking. He is an amateur pharmacologist, and also an amateur at statecraft. When the two adolescents reveal to him their passionate

and flighty love, he agrees—*sans* banns, *sans* premarital coun-
seling, *sans* license—to marry them. He then conspires in a
scheme that is intended eventually to corner the families and
coerce them into acquiescing in what they would never otherwise accept. Instead of preaching conversion, he tries to force
the families to accept his will without any real change of their
character.

In the end both peacekeepers must confess that they have
failed. The interesting thing is that each has failed precisely by
shrinking from his own duty and resorting instead to its opposite. The statesman gives sermons when he should be using
force. The churchman uses political stratagems when he should
be using moral confrontation.

Consider for a moment the inadequacy of either task . . .
on its own. Even had the duke been faithful to his mission, he
would have suppressed violence but not uprooted it. People
would be afraid to riot: but only afraid, not unwilling. He
would be obligated to unremitting vigilance because the same
smoldering hatred would have abided in those two noble
homes and hearts and would flare up again once his back was
turned. The friar, on the other hand, had a more trying task
because it is far easier to punish and suppress violence than it
is to purge it from people's minds and characters. His task was
less likely of success than that of the duke, but his goal was a
peace more ambitious and more enduring. The statesman was
to protect the peace by stopping violent acts; the churchman's
mode of peacemaking was to stop violent wishes.

Now I take these two figures as a parable of the diverse
callings of the church and of the state, and also of the difference
between the criminal law and religious obligation. The law has
as its purpose the preservation of minimal peace: not so much
by changing people's character or conscience or motivation,
but simply by suppressing their more destructive forms of behavior. It is the mission of the church, and of those who hold
prophetic office within the church, to appeal to people's inner-
most commitments and, in the precious instances when they
succeed, to turn them from violence to benevolence.

All too often, however, we witness the same malfeasance
as in Verona. The two public services are confused with one

another. Those who are meant to govern lack nerve, and those who are called to preach lack nerve as well. The tasks of coercion and of conversion are so very different. Yet both require the same courage, and both aim together at peace.[2]

THE LIMITS OF THE LAW

The goals of both citizenship and faith converge, in that each one hopes for our common peace. And though each of us may have different responsibilities in the civil or the religious establishments, we all have a stake in the courageous and authentic pursuit of the respective contributions of both coercion and conversion. But I want to dwell now on the grave frustrations that are usually visited upon any conscientious person who accepts responsibility for the formulation and enforcement of the civil law.

The first frustration of the lawperson is that law cannot reach the roots of civil disorder. What is it that causes larceny? Greed. What draws people to abuse their children? That is more complex and puzzling. We are increasingly anxious to understand what twist in the spirit would lead men and women to exploit the young. Whatever it is, it lies deep: well beyond the reach of the law to set it right. What spawns rape, that pathetic and predatory act of violence? Who knows? We know only that the sanctions of criminal justice cannot remedy those deep troubles within the human character, nor would we wish our civil officers to be given access to people at that level of derangement. The law gives access to symptoms of disorder, not to the sickness. One's most urgent efforts in the field of criminal law must be sandbag levees against the flood, always in peril of washing away at the next mighty surge.

The enforcer will also be stymied when the law itself is calculated to protect some socially accepted form of exploitation. One of the recent decisions on abortion by the Supreme Court, *Thornburgh*,[3] illustrates this problem. Pennsylvania was forbidden to require abortion providers to supply a mother with information about pregnancy development, or medical and psychological risks associated with abortion, or her legal entitlements to financial support. The Court feared that such information would "serve only to confuse and punish her and heighten her anxiety." This enactment of law treats abortion without parallel or precedent among surgical procedures, in that any information which could lead a client to reconsider submitting herself and her offspring to surgery is to be withheld, rather than shared.

The real interest being protected here, of course, is that of the medical fraternity. Absolutely no higher scrutiny or advocacy of third-party rights must be permitted to interfere with the "privacy of the informed consent-dialogue between the woman and her physician." Yet as anyone in the know is aware, the typical mother going to an abortion never goes to "her physician" but to an unknown abortionist who has forfeited his obstetrical practice; she has no "dialogue" with him because she never even sees him until she is on the surgical table; and there is no "professional judgment" because he has left the career of healing and chosen that of a technician. The irony rises to the surface of the law when Justice Blackmun, whose own career has included long paid advocacy of the medical establishment, describes in awed respect the decision to be made by a woman "with the guidance of her physician,"—intensely "personal," "intimate," "private"—and then declares it a violation of the United States Constitution to require anyone to tell her his name. This is but one illustration of laws framed to protect the powerful at the expense of the powerless.

A third frustration for the law is that even when effectively enforced, its power to deter is so limited. The statistics for crime enforcement in our country are notoriously inadequate. I shall try, however, to use them cautiously enough to give at least a fair impression of the measure in which crimes in our land fail to be resolved by conviction under law.[4]

Interestingly, one of the crimes that most often leads to the sentencing of an offender is murder. About 25 percent of all reported murders in the U.S. actually lead to the conviction of an adult offender (statistics for juveniles are more elusive).

The statistics go down from there. The figure for forceable rape is 16 percent. For theft it is 6 percent.

Consider further the crime of rape. In America, 66 percent of reported rapes eventuated in an arrest, yet only 16 percent subsequently yielded a conviction. More significant still—and more discouraging—is the estimate that perhaps two to three-and-a-half times as many rapes occur as are reported to the police at all. If accurate, this would imply that possibly only about 5 percent—one out of every twenty rape offenses—leads to the conviction of the guilty party.

Surely no one would want to plead this as an instance of an effective law. Therefore, to the responsible administrator behind the law, it must be disheartening to see that despite honest enforcement, one cannot claim that this particular form of human violence is being significantly repressed.

A fourth frustration for law enforcers is that sometimes the very people who support the existence of a law are among its violators. When I was a newly ordained priest in 1960, my first summer assignment was to a parish in Killeen, Texas. The older priest to whom I was apprenticed had the custom of reciting his daily prayers from the breviary while driving across the flatlands of the parish at ninety miles-an-hour. It was my view that anyone who drove that fast should be praying, but not that he should be reading his prayers from a book. Now I am quite certain that this good priest supported the state laws against speeding. It is just that he did not observe them. Imagine the trooper in hot pursuit who pulled him to the side of the road, only to find a beaming and amiable clergyman, all smiles and support of him in the courageous and regular performance of his duties. What really can be said of the power of the law to curb behavior when some of its regular violators would never want the statute repealed?

Some observers admit that the law is ineffectual as a deterrent, yet they argue for its power to punish after the fact. *But a fifth problem for anyone applying the force of the law is that its actual power to punish may be quite superficial.* What does it mean to punish? If you throw your wife down a flight of stairs, what can anyone do to punish you? You have already morally disabled yourself. What can one do to a person who defrauds widows of their savings? You could put that person in jail. You could take the person's own money away. You could give the person a whipping as North Carolina, I believe, was the last state to do. You could execute him. But is that a truly significant punishment, when the crime itself has already done far more damage to the criminal than society itself could then impose?

If a woman is a liar, what can you do to her that is more hurtful than what she has already done to herself? If a man is a tyrant, and thus is morally maimed, does this not dwarf the significance of any pain you might want to inflict on him as punishment?

A sixth frustration is peculiar to our form of government. *Our form of democracy presumes selfishness, yet it requires altruism without being able to provide it.* We cannot live together in a free community unless we are willing to inconvenience ourselves for the common good, for our neighbors. There can be no peace if we merely coexist as aloof strangers, each one out for his or her own survival. There will be times when each of us could not survive without the readiness of our neighbor to extend himself or herself and help us, to sustain us when we falter, to hold us up to standards when we would otherwise defect. And yet everything about our laws seems to assume that the average citizen cannot really be relied upon to forfeit much of his or her own convenience if a neighbor is in the lurch. Merely to observe the criminal law one must be possessed of generosity and social responsibility; yet the law, if it has the bite necessary to do much good, cannot assume good will. It must relentlessly demand minimal performance, whatever one's disposition to care for others.

Seventh, and lastly, the law seems to require religious conviction as its nearest ally, yet in our democratic tradition the law has turned its back on faith and faith's commitments as none of its concern. It is only when people's hearts and minds are touched and they undergo moral conversion that they can find the motivation to observe the law. And the major force for moral conversion is usually the example and the appeal of a religious community.

Take, for instance, the progress of commitment to civil rights in our country. What were the major milestones of our faltering journey towards justice for blacks? First there was the

Constitution, and then its Bill of Rights, the first Ten Amendments. Later, after our Civil War, there were what I call the Amendments Greater Still: the Thirteenth, Fourteenth, and Fifteenth, which brought an end to chattel slavery. Then one must scan across a period of many years, perhaps to 1954: *Brown* v. *Board of Education*, the court decision which made segregation unlawful. Lastly one remembers the Civil Rights Acts of 1964 and 1971, which went further to prevent discrimination.

But is it not truer to say that the great markers along that road were moral and religious ones? The Quakers and the Christian abolitionists in the early nineteenth century accomplished what Jefferson and Madison had not the nerve to do. Martin Luther King, Jr., had an effect upon the nation that went beyond what Abraham Lincoln achieved (and Lincoln's voice as a moralist had perhaps stirred Americans even more than his obstinacy as a statesman). I expect that there must be religious people still to come who will bring to fruition the legal changes sponsored by Lyndon Johnson. The freeing of the blacks, still incomplete, is more truly a series of religious events than one of legal procedures. Sometimes the conscience moves before the law does. Sometimes the conscience is slow to keep up with the law. But without conscience, justice will never be a plentiful yield from just laws. Law does not produce law's own goal, which is peace through justice. For justice is a disposition of character, and the law cannot govern character.

LAWS THAT FAIL TO GOVERN

I have mentioned these incapacities of the law, not because law is not worth the effort but because it is important that those who sponsor and enforce just laws do so with full awareness of the limits of their work. On the one hand they must strive with the full effort of their endurance to secure laws that are fair. On the other hand, they must often admit that many laws are simply paper.

In 1967 the President's Commission on Law Enforcement and Administration of Justice cited the observations of a jurist:

> If we are deeply disturbed by something which we know to be happening, and feel that we ought to be doing something to prevent it, this feeling can be partly relieved by prohibiting it on paper.

A national law enforcement officer was quoted in a similar vein:

> The criminal code of any jurisdiction tends to make a crime of everything that people are against, without regard to enforceability, changing social concepts, etc. The result is that the criminal code becomes society's trash bin. . . . [S]ociety legislates one way and acts another way.

The Commission concluded: "There is surely some truth in [the] comment that these laws 'survive in order to satisfy moral objections to established modes of conduct. They are unenforced because we want to continue our conduct, and unrepealed because we want to preserve our morals'."

Is it thinkable, though, that we should dispense with laws which criminalize acts we regard as severely unjust, even when those laws fail of their purpose? The President's Commission was arguing that laws in certain matters were particularly unenforceable: drunkenness, gambling, abortion, and extramarital sexual behavior. (The Commission adds the astonishing observation: "The absence of a complaining victim appears to mark many ineffective criminal laws." One would be stupefied by a public supposition that alcoholism, gambling, abortion, and sexual promiscuity are victimless crimes, at a time when voices with rising volume are telling us of the personal devastation wrought by all these crimes. The operative word, of course, is "complaining.") Even if one accepts the premises of the Commission, one would have to ask whether those are matters any less successfully controlled by law than are drug abuse, auto theft, or rape. Would we dispense with criminal sanctions against these actions simply because the law has not been a success in eradicating them?

What of other instances where full and effective enforcement may be lacking, not because the law is unsupported, but because even when it is supported, law is not enough? Think of our laws on purity of food and drugs, on the rights of workers to bargain collectively, on seating restraints for babies in automobiles, on regulating bankruptcy, or on licensing physicians. These are not thoroughly effective laws, but they have a purpose even beyond effectiveness. They are part of our public profession of justice. They are what we, as a people, are willing to state out loud as what we promise one another.

The law will always fail if it is unsustained by the common conscience. But that is no reason for repealing the unsuccessful law. When the laws had finally been passed for the enforcement of civil rights in our country, were blacks then assured of fair or friendly treatment? Certainly not. Are they today? Not near the point of satisfaction. The struggle for such freedoms as Abraham Lincoln may or may not have wildly imagined is only underway; it has not been brought to the completion of its purposes. Yet, is it thinkable that any of our laws for fair employment practices, for fair access to public facilities, for fair access to education, for the freedom to marry whom one chooses—is it thinkable that because these laws have as yet not changed human hearts, we should therefore abrogate them? Is it thinkable that because only one rapist in twenty is brought to justice, we ought to repeal the laws which declare this to be a harsh and dreadful crime? I think this is not thinkable.

Why? Because the law can have a further purpose: not to transform people, but to declare and disavow publicly what we commonly believe to be unfair or damaging. You probably cannot tell the moral character of a people by reading their laws. But you can learn something about a people's character by finding what laws they lack.[5]

If one accepts this view, then one would be willing to condone the readiness of the duke in *Romeo and Juliet* to preach to the people, but he would still fail because his reticence to act deprived his words of their rightful force, just as the unwillingness of the friar to speak deprived his stratagems of their moral integrity. The duke and the friar were meant to be allies, though each had a distinct priority among his public duties.

Would Law Eliminate Abortion?

Now all this can be illustrated by a particular public issue in our country today. There is at present a fierce conflict underway between those who support abortion as a freely available alternative and those who support the right of the unborn to survive. There is in our country today, despite the attempts of the press and broadcasting media—sometimes ignorant and sometimes purposeful—to conceal that fact, an ongoing consensus which holds that most abortions which are legal are nevertheless unjust. By a decisive majority the adult American public has persistently believed that abortion should be a crime for all except two reasons: to protect a mother from death or severe injury to her physical health, and when pregnancy has resulted from criminal intercourse, i.e., incest or rape.

I take it that in the long run the law will have to run along the rails of the public consensus. The present law (or, more precisely, the present prohibition on laws) will give way. If and when the matter of abortion is once again released to the political process, if the law conforms to public opinion as it has been expressed consistently since the early 1960s, then abortion will be legally permissible in only about one percent of the millions of cases recorded each year in the United States.

But what, I then ask, will be the benefit of that? What would be the effect of such a change in the law? There would surely be a reduction in the body count. Estimates vary enormously about how many abortions were performed before legalization. My own estimate after repeated study of the documentation is that abortions have increased approximately five times over since *Wade* and *Bolton* in 1973. The coercive force of a restored law would persuade some women to carry their children to term. Also, the public debate has now raised the issue in people's consciences as it had not been raised before, and this could deter some women who previously might have sought abortions. On the other hand, the effect of public permissibility during the years since legalization, and the easy availability of abortion during that time, plus the technical and medical developments that make it a brief and relatively safe procedure for the mother, would all pull in a contrary direction and combine to motivate more women than before 1973 to resist the law and have an abortion anyway. The factors pull both ways. Still, I would reckon that the net result of recriminalization might imaginably be the salvage of nearly one million American infants each year. And that is a result of formidable proportions.

But is it enough? A restoration of legal protection for the unborn might do very little to reach the sources which motivate so many women and men today to eliminate their unborn offspring.

CAN LAW PLUCK UP OFFENSE BY THE ROOTS?

What are the motives that lead women and their male partners and abortion personnel to be willing to destroy unborn children?

A first motive has been highlighted by California social scientist Kristin Luker.[6] She conducted a series of lengthy interviews with committed activists on either side of the controversy. She discerned a different profile in the people who gave so tirelessly to the struggle for abortion freedom and those who worked as generously for the survival of the unborn. One of the most salient differences she observed was that prochoice activists expected that life should not deal them an unjust hand, and that they must not be expected to carry unwanted burdens too long or too heavily. The prolife people, by contrast, understood some hardship as written into the script of life. They saw suffering—even chronic suffering—as something we have no right to avoid or to evade on demand.

One of the sources of the widespread readiness to relieve oneself of an unwanted child is precisely an anger at being trapped. The attitude reaches out much more broadly than to the issue of childbearing. Americans today are tending to believe that suffering is something we should not have to endure, whether it be a migraine headache or Parkinson's disease or an unsatisfactory school board. We expect, more and more, the right to get our way. It may be no coincidence that the profession we turn to for surest relief is the same profession that staffs abortion clinics.

Christians should respond in a characteristic way to this suggestion that the burdensome be eliminated, for it has been our traditional belief that the more helpless someone is, the more we need to be helping her. The worst crimes or sins are the ones with the most helpless victims. That, however, is not the perspective of the growing readiness today to terminate the lives of the chronically ill or to extinguish the lives of handicapped infants. The argument is being made consistently for all three of these victim groups—not on their own behalf but on behalf of those who would eliminate them—that they count for little and that the taxpayer ought mourn their passing with short sorrow. This, I would argue, is an attitude of soul that the law, by itself, can do little to heal.

Another motivating attitude associated with the willingness to abort is a readiness to set aside kinship loyalty. The Christian tradition has invited men and women to cleave to one another, for better or for worse, until death. The bond between spouses has been understood as similar to that between parents and children: a tenacious attachment that would forfeit self-satisfaction for the benefit of one's kinfolk. My perception is that many abortion decisions represent a backing away from—and, in quite a few instances, a renunciation of—that kinship bond.[7] A change in the law would have a limited effect on those sources, those motivations, those deep roots of rejection of the unborn child.

We have nothing better to do with our lives than to foster life. That is a persuasion that we grow precisely by enhancing the growth of others: in particular, those who have most need of us. Everything in our tradition has nourished in us a belief which the law could hardly have produced: that we mature by raising others. Yet ours is an era and a culture that will not be known for its welcome to children.

When a man and a woman preside over a household peopled by children, every time you visit them you are struck by how the children have grown. One is tempted to annoy the children by remarking, "Oh, Rachel, how tall you are!" or "How Bobby has grown!" The fact, however, is that their parents are growing at an even faster rate than the youngsters. We grow by affording growth to others. We have a need to be burdened by people we did not want: boat people, children, ethnic strangers. Our life is drawn out to full measure precisely by having to accommodate ourselves to the uncontrollable needs of others to whom we are committed. The prochoice movement has echoed the agenda item of our culture: that one has a right to freedom of choice. Our own tradition, which fastens its attention more on need than on choice, finds it amusing that anyone should identify freedom of choice with parenting. What could be a worse warrant for child-rearing than an insistence on getting just what you want? What could set you up for a bigger fall than to expect your child to satisfy your roster of hopes? Children exist to destroy hopes . . . and then to replace them with enhanced hopes.

The attitudes of character that cause us to be so reluctant to open our lives to risk and jeopardy by welcoming children, who by their nature arrive without our knowing in advance what claims they will put upon us with their needs—these attitudes are what give us life and growth. Children are the quintessential strangers. When I preside at weddings, I like to use a ritual I learned from a priest working in the inner city of Detroit. Before witnessing the marriage promises of a couple, he puts to them a series of questions in the hearing of the congregation. One of those questions is: "Are you prepared to create a home that has a welcome for strangers; and in particular, for those strangers who will arrive as your own children?" If he were to give them time enough to think about it, they might not give their assent. But child-welcoming, like marriage, is something you can grow into.

I doubt, however, that we are doing much to invite men and women into the generosity of character that would induce them to offer a sacrificial welcome for children. Yet it is, I would argue, a quality of character without which we may not find it possible to grow out of our native selfishness into love.

LET THE LAW BE JUST: STILL IT WILL NOT BE ENOUGH

Those who have argued and worked strenuously for freedom of abortion choice share one attitude in common with those who work and argue just as strenuously for the protection of the life of the unborn. Both have had their attention fixated upon legal and constitutional remedies. I think that is illusory. The supporters of abortion freedom have been told by some of their most astute allies that they took excessive comfort from enactments which enjoyed the support of only a minority of public opinion and which affronted an ancient moral conviction in the Anglo-American consensus. On the other hand, many allies have reminded those in the prolife movement that they are far too ready to direct the full force of their energies exclusively to a change in the law ... and they may wind up with too little to show for all their struggle.

Would a change in the law actually reduce the present incidence of abortion? Yes, to some extent. Would it make a moral difference? Would it affect the mind and conscience of the nation? Yes, to a considerable extent. By taking away any protection of law whatever from the unborn, by deleting any of the benefit of doubt that humans traditionally enjoy before the law when their survival is at stake, the U.S. Supreme Court did in effect imply what its moral position was. The unborn were now negligible.

The law, both common and statutory, is understandably the product of prevailing political, economic, and social forces. But constitutional principles are and ought be more removed from that ebb and flow. They follow such basic moral courses that their articulation has a different function in aligning the moral commitments of a community. Thus, when the Supreme Court struck down all legal restraint of abortion by invoking the supremacy of personal maternal privacy, its claim that it was not involved in moral discourse was frivolous. Large portions of the national public drew the conclusion that if abortion was now so openly acceptable by constitutional right then it must be moral. Reverse that ruling, and the public would be invited to reconsider its moral inference. People would no

longer be as free to assume that they have the moral encourage-
ment of the public culture in the destruction of their unborn
children. That would be a change, a moral change, a powerful
moral change. And I am deeply persuaded that our country can
have no conscientious or enduring peace until we have laws
that protect unwanted, unborn children: laws that do their feeble best to allow them life.

But a change in the law will only be an overture towards
a real welcome for the young. For that we need an insurrection
of consciences. For that we need the startling example of fathers and mothers who nourish their young at high cost, and
show that thus they themselves grow. For that we need a religiously inspired alliance of women and men who know that love
of the helpless cannot be coerced.

The law by itself is unable to accomplish what the lawmakers have in mind. A transformation of minds, a somersault of
values, is needed. The prospect, for those of us who fear we
shall destroy ourselves if we stand by and acquiesce in the
extermination of the young, is daunting. We must support the
just and dutiful application of coercive power by those who
rule. But our firmest reliance must fasten upon the courageous
appeal of those whose duty it is to preach. And it is the duty
of us all, without exception, to preach a welcome for the helpless.

True justice is guaranteed by law only in a nation whose
people have undergone changes of heart. Those who accept
the obligation to protect the unborn should be the first to ensure for them the further shelter of conversion. The appeal to
law imposes on us an appeal to conscience, rather than relieving us of that further and more arduous duty.

NOTES

1. For excellent reflections on the relation between morality
and law, conversion and coercion, see George F. Will, *Statecraft as
Soulcraft: What Government Does* (New York: Simon & Schuster, 1983).

2. See chapter ten below.

3. *Thornburgh, Governor of Pennsylvania, et al.* v. *American College of Obstetricians and Gynecologists et al.*, 106 S. Ct. 2169 (1986); 476 U.S. 747 (1986).

4. For information on the incidence and resolution of major crimes in the U.S., see The President's Commission on Law Enforcement and Administration of Justice, *Task Force Report: Crime and Its Impact* (1967); *Task Force Report: The Courts* (1967). The quotations given are to be found in the latter volume, chap. 8. See also Milton S. Eisenhower (chairman), *The Rule of Law: An Alternative to Violence. A Report to the National Commission on the Causes and Prevention of Violence* (Nashville: Aurora, 1970). See also *Uniform Crime Reports: Crime in the United States*, 1965–84. Also D. Chappell, "Forcible Rape and the Criminal Justice System," in *Sexual Assault: The Victim and the Rapist*, ed. M. J. Walker and S. L. Brodsky, (Lexington, Mass: Heath, 1976).

5. See chapter eleven (6) below.

6. Kristin Luker, *Abortion and the Policies of Motherhood* (Berkeley: University of California Press, 1984).

7. See chapter eleven (5) below.

10

The Statesman and the Churchman

Two households both alike in dignity,
In fair New York where we lay our scene,
From ancient grudge break to new mutiny,
Where civil blood makes civil hands unclean.[1]

FOR SOME YEARS NOW abortion has been adding further agitation to the recurring brawl among Americans over church-state relations. The national elections of 1984 put the matter into very sharp prominence. That campaign is long past but the disagreement is not, and there may be wisdom to be had from a review of what was then at stake and how it was presented by some who went most public on abortion as a political matter.

The late President Kennedy is frequently thought of as having defined a middle position for Catholics that appeals to Americans who imagine the papal submarine ready to land the First Lord of its Admiralty in Chesapeake Bay when the White House is properly occupied. Kennedy, however, will not have made an enduring contribution. His 1960 campaign speech to the Houston ministers made it clear that he shared their inadequate view: the only way that a church could visit moral imperatives upon communicants who are civil leaders would be as "instructions on public policy" imposed by church officials. Even were he cognizant of a shared moral vision within the church that might secure his agreement, Mr. Kennedy's pledge to be a chief executive "whose fulfillment of his presidential oath is not limited or conditioned by any religious . . . obligation" would support the view of those who claim there was no ethical influence of the Christian consensus discernible in his political decisions.[2] His religious commitments were so profoundly private as to yield no known effects beyond weekly attendance at worship. He would have been an unlikely inclusion in any later edition of his own *Profiles in Courage,* for we know of no matter on which his conscience stood staunchly enough before God to risk great political sacrifice.

Mrs. Geraldine Ferraro was, understandably, the front-line skirmisher in the 1984 campaign, but her salient exposure then was not of a character likely long to outlive that election. She candidly stated that her religious beliefs bore no influence upon her governmental service. The mettle and independence of mind to which an inquiring public might have ascribed this, however, had to be discounted when one learned that she was simply subject to another obedience: the National Organization for Women, whose moral imperatives for the political order have been more specific, immensely more dogmatic, and more peremptory than any religious body could dream of imposing. If Mrs. Ferraro will be remembered long after that Election Tuesday it will be for her remarkable request that the electorate frame their political opinion of her, not on her public record as a legislator, but on her devout religious conviction that what she had been voting for is immoral.

Mr. Reagan and Mr. Mondale, of course, were also antagonists in center fray. Theirs, however, was an insubstantial contribution to this perduring issue. Mr. Mondale, the clergyman's son, spoke stirringly of his own faith and prayer, but stood upon a platform that truculently offended the consciences of many Christians less persuaded than he that their religious perspective must go blind when it gazes upon partisan choices. Mr. Reagan, who wished schoolchildren to enjoy a freedom to worship of which he was deprived, announced a religious agenda that bore no resemblance to any known Christian priorities. The hands were the hands of Christianity, but the voice was the voice of the right wing of the GOP.

There were some prominent ecclesiastics whose interventions will also prove in the longer campaign to have been indecisive ambushes. The egregious snub by Cardinal Krol (late of

Philadelphia) of his fellow bishops' policy against "political partisanship" and taking "positions for or against political candidates" undoubtedly recommissioned him from a chaplain into a combatant. His decision, in the last presidential election year before his own retirement, to toast Mr. Reagan with many a public "Nastrovia!" isolated him effectively, not only from the other bishops, but from what lay Catholics expect by way of propriety in their officials. He had gone the way of the ethnic alderman.

More likely than any of these as the antagonists to watch in years to come were The Honorable Mario Cuomo and His Excellency John O'Connor. Both men were striving to be public servants and faithful Catholics (an ambition less difficult as governor and more difficult as archbishop than most people are likely to imagine). Both men had long records in governmental service (Admiral O'Connor had more years towards his civil pension than did Governor Cuomo). Both men were likely to be in office beyond that November, and both could reasonably aspire to an enhancement of station in the future. Indeed, O'Connor changed from purple excellence to scarlet eminence not long thereafter. Both became inextricably enmeshed in this controversy, and this controversy was destined to go active in many electoral seasons yet to come.

THE PUT-DOWN OF CATHOLICS

One reason the issue will stay current is that now it is the American Catholics who are going to keep it alive. For one thing, Catholics have begun to bridle at the tiresome fact that they alone, among the nation's religious communities, come to civil office under suspicion. In 1960, when two candidates were contending for the presidency—each of rather desultory allegiance to the creedal and moral heritage of the Catholic and Quaker persuasions, respectively—John Kennedy underwent endless, hostile interrogation, while not a single voice was raised about how the most pacifist of our Christian communities could manage to produce a commander-in-chief of our armed forces.

In recent days Catholics, whose polled views on abortion match, within a very few percentage points, those of the national population, are viewed with mistrust when they deal with that issue in government, while Jews, whose polled views on abortion run exactly opposite the popular consensus, are never put on the defensive. Catholics begin to notice this.[3]

They are similarly impatient at the obnoxious portrayal of them in the media as an authoritarian populace that yields its political judgments to hierarchical control, when in fact they have a long tradition of debate and civil independence far more nonconforming than what is common in NOW, B'nai B'rith, or the average black Protestant congregation.

Catholics have also become lately aware that, with some artifice and purpose, they have been officially designated as the dissidents in the abortion controversy. When the National Abortion Rights Action League was being put together in the late 1960s, its founders realized that in order to promote a program which transgressed the sentiment and ethical convictions of the American majority, they would have to select a target group of villains. Their choice was the Catholic bishops.[4] The editorial board of the *New York Times* later took up the same policy which, as one member explained it, was "not to let the Catholics get away with suppressing abortion." Most Catholics are coming to know what the New York literati have ignored: that the resistance to abortion, which Michael Harrington called one of the "few genuine social movements of the 1970s,"[5] had been a widely ecumenical and lay uprising. Even to the extent that Catholics were involved, tens of thousands of women had borne the heat of the day before the evening hours when the bishops became active.

In sum, Catholics are tired of the insult, and have lately begun to notice that the doctrine of their opponents, that any transcending religious allegiance is a threat to full American citizenship, is itself more of a religious tenet than a political viewpoint. And, as I say, they are tired of it. So for them this great matter of political duty and religious conviction must be brought closer to resolution than it has thus far.

How the Archbishop and the Governor Agreed

What is most notable in the exchanges between Governor Cuomo and Archbishop O'Connor was not their differences, but the alarming matter on which they agree.

The Archbishop said that he was merely reiterating "the formal, official teaching of the Catholic Church." "All I can judge, as a formally, officially appointed Catholic teacher in the Catholic faith . . . is that what was said about Catholic teaching is wrong." "It is my responsibility to spell out for Catholics what the Church teaches." He referred to "what you can be a good Catholic and believe." And he referred the entire matter to higher authority: "So Geraldine Ferraro doesn't have a problem with me. If she has a problem, it's with the Pope."[6]

The global impression given by Archbishop O'Connor was that within the Catholic Church moral edicts are officially asserted by the bishops: doctrines to which, as a matter of loyalty, all Catholics are expected to conform. They would fail to do so at their peril.

Governor Cuomo framed the issue in essentially the same terms: "It's a question of loyalty." He said he rejected abortion because he accepts the church's teaching authority, he accepts the doctrine of the bishops. He testified convincingly that he is "attached to the Church first by birth, then by choice, now by love." "To be a Catholic," he wrote, "is to say 'I believe' to the essential core of dogmas that distinguishes our faith," and repudiation of abortion is one of those "articles of faith."[7] "There is a Catholic law on homosexuality. There is a Catholic law on birth control. There is a Catholic law on abortion. I accept the Catholic law."[8]

I cannot and would not speak for other religious bodies, but the depiction given by the prelate and the politician of moral discourse within the Catholic Church is seriously inadequate. What it portrays is in fact the least authoritative sort of teaching.

When I was a boy my mother told me one day that cherries and milk taken together would produce a stomach ache, I took it on her authority. I never had enough desire for cherries and milk *ensemble* to put her teaching to the test, so I cannot vouch for it myself. To tell the truth, I doubt very much that she ever did, either. She was passing on some hearsay. And hearsay is the weakest form of authority.

But when a recovering alcoholic stands up at an Alcoholics Anonymous meeting and tells them that drunks who will not admit their failure to themselves are liars, or when an ex-junkie tells a high school audience that dope kills those who use it, or when a savvy educator describes to parents what happens to children when they are allowed to run the family: that is not hearsay. That is strong authority at work. These teachers are vouching for what they pass on, from long, accumulated experience of themselves or of others they have worked with closely. And those who take it in are not merely accepting it because of the impressive status or character of the person holding forth. For this moral tutelage to "take," the learner must have her or his eyes opened, and look out over his or her own experience, and see there what was not seen before but now can be perceived once it has been cogently pointed out.

The alcoholic in the back row at the A.A. meeting does not go home and tell his wife that the speaker said that anyone with his drinking behavior is a drunk. He says that *his* eyes were finally opened and now, with the speaker's help, he sees what everyone else but himself had long seen but he could not bear to see. The man says this as something he owes to a wise and helpful mentor, but now it is something he is vouching for himself. He is devoted to the recovering alcoholic who pressed home the truth for him, but he would never think of his acceptance of that insight as an act of allegiance, or loyalty, or submission to authority.

Ironically, though, the sharing of moral insight in this way is the highest form of moral authority. Authoritarianism, by contrast, is found in people who should have moral authority but do not, who have to fall back upon their office instead because they have failed to pass on a conviction so that others could make it their own.

THERE ARE NO CATHOLIC LAWS

Judgments of good and evil focus on whether any course of action will make human beings grow and mature and flourish within their persons, or whether it will tend to make them indifferent, estranged, and stunted. When we are evaluating human behavior we have little to draw on except our own experience, that of our forbears, and whatever wisdom we can wring from our debate with others. We believe that God's Spirit guides us in those debates, but we should remember enough gaffes in the past not to get too cocky about that guidance. Some of our most enduring insights came owing to people we had thought dead wrong, so we are reminded that the Spirit has an elusive way of breezing in unlikely places too. All of this is about common human experience, though from an uncommon perspective. What we are trying to unpuzzle are things like economic policy and childbearing and immigration and private property and agricultural output and infant mortality and drug use and educational access and fidelity and acceptable forms of struggle against injustice, and so much else about which we must frame moral judgments. With our fellow communicants we have shared commitments and assumptions: beliefs that we are happier giving than getting, and that there is no greater love than to put down your life for your neighbor, and that your neighbor always turns out to be the most unlikely person.

One might say there is nothing specifically Christian about this way of going about it. True enough. That may be why it is so strange to call any of our moral convictions "religious," let alone sectarian, since they arise from a dialogue that ranges through so many communities and draws from so many sources. And when debate and dialogue and testimony do fructify into conviction, and conviction into consensus, nothing could be more absurd than to expect that conviction and consensus to be confined forcibly within the enclosure of a person's privacy or a church's walls. Convictions are what we live by. Do we have anything better to share with one another?

Catholics, of course, believe that moral misadventure is

damaging and destructive of our ability to cleave to another: to our fellow humans or to God. When we call it "sin" we see it less as defiance and disobedience than as self-abuse. The strong language we sometimes use is a warning, not of church discipline or divine punishment, but of the sickening and impairment of one's moral self that may put a person beyond the reach of a church which has no power to punish and even of a God who has no ability or heart to do so.

When we say lying is a sin, what we mean is that people who tell lies become liars, and liars wander off into the tundra of a truthless wilderness beyond the reach of personal intimacy. When I learned how lethal racial hatred was, I did not learn it as much from the sermons of Martin Luther King, Jr. as from the video clips of Bull Connor. But King had seen Connor first, and it was his sermons that cued us to look at what we had previously ignored. I learned that it was lethal when I heard of the four youngsters killed in the Montgomery Baptist church bombing: not from looking at the mangled bodies of the four children who died there, but from imagining the mangled selves of the adults whose readiness to destroy others whom they resented had backfired upon themselves and deadened them. This is how moral discourse proceeds within the church.

We do not have a religious law on abortion, any more than we have a law on embezzlement or a law on gossip or a law on child abuse. We have a wisdom on these matters, a commanding wisdom.

Our convictions, if they have any sense behind them, should be accessible in some measure to others whose grounding is not in our faith. In fact, one of the better tests of our moral discourse ought be our ability to plead its soundness to others besides ourselves. And even if others cannot find their way along the path of our reasoning, they may join us as allies in causes which they reach by their own, somewhat different reasons. Thus we have been energetic partisans in promoting the National Labor Relations Act, the Civil Rights Act, and the Equal Employment Opportunity Act, and also in opposing the Right to Work Laws and the Anti-Miscegenation Laws. Moral discourse begins at home, but when it grows up it has to make its way in the world.

Bishops can contribute to this moral discourse and they sometimes do. When the discourse swells to a consensus, the bishop will then usually give it voice, but he could no more imagine himself as its source than imagine he put up all the buildings he is called to dedicate. Our moral discourse is more of a folk phenomenon: ever dynamic, ever incomplete, for no consensus is so established that it may not be revised, ratified, or reinforced.

If bishops do wish to teach within this tradition, they must first enter it thoughtfully enough to learn from it. Then they can begin to vouch for it, and to speak with moral authority. It will never be adequate for a teacher to state that something is right or wrong. He or she is obliged to portray it so that we can all see the issue clearly enough to vouch for it ourselves.

MORAL STANDS ARE NOT OBEDIENTIAL

Now this is what Archbishop O'Connor did not do. If all he could do is invoke "official doctrine" then he failed. If he must cite the pope to make his point that abortion deals in death, then the pope was ill-served, and so are we and so is the issue itself. There was not that note of true authority in his voice. By this I do not mean the authority of his appointed office, but the authority of one who has seen what abortion brings upon those who resort to it and those who make their living by it, the authority of one who can appreciate and feel the confusion and anguish of the women involved, and the savage injustice which destroys children before they can come even to share our taste of human anguish. It would be an authority that knows also the duty every Christian must accept to extend help to both mothers and fathers and their children. Instead of such authority, we heard what sounded like a sectarian house rule, a call to close ranks and join in a vote of confidence. The archbishop emerged with the mien and manner of a party whip, when what we needed was the authenticity of an eye-witness. When he told of the official teaching, he did it with the conviction of a red-neck sheriff reciting his legal rights to a black he has just arrested for rape: not quite spoken from heart to heart.

If this way of proceeding were authentically Catholic, and if Catholic civil servants took it as their moral imperative in political life, non-Catholics would have every reason to take fright. Catholics, however, would have even graver cause for alarm, to see their community's moral discourse amputated, with only an authoritarian stump remaining in the place of true moral authority.

Representative Ferraro said that "as a Catholic," because she has the "gift of faith," she believed abortion is the destruction of a "baby,"[9] but she went on to say that she felt "very uncomfortable" even discussing her religious views, which are "very, very private," and irrelevant to her in legislative decisions because not everybody shares them.[10] Mr. Cuomo's position was essentially the same, though its incoherence was less glaringly stated. He stated that he took it on faith that abortion is evil. Unlike Mrs. Ferraro, he was willing to act on that belief in his governmental duties, but he insisted that the strategy and tactics must be left to his own judgment.

I would fear that any moral assessment of a common human experience which is taken on faith alone is no conviction at all, but only a sectarian mystery that should not be let outside to roam the streets and threaten people. If these were true convictions, Mrs. Ferraro and Mr. Cuomo should be as unable as the rest of us to say how much they derive from the unbroken Christian tradition that extends back through New Testament days, how much they rest on their own verification of the teaching, how much they are ratified by the inadequacy of arguments to the contrary, how much they have been sustained by evidence from other sources of conscience.

The governor spoke with conscientious eloquence about his resolve to rally support for the dispossessed. The unemployed and homeless, the drug-addled, the desolate poor, the deserted mothers: all these have in him an effective advocate, ready to confront and to oppose whatever political forces would continue to make them society's victims. His advocacy has brought him into conflict with conscientious citizens and politicians who read it all differently. But he has a stomach for contention and is not likely to flinch from struggle. His pluck and readiness to venture forth are not paralyzed when his first patrols report contact with hostile forces. He is a politician, and contest is what politics is all about.

Why, then, did he speak so differently about abortion? He pleads strong convictions on the subject. He and his wife have chosen not to resort to it. But on this subject the tone of his voice is somehow altered, the readiness to protect the victims is relaxed, his pluck goes limp. Here the public is forced to make an assessment. Either the governor's view is dependent upon the say-so of his ecclesiastical superiors, in which case it lacks authority in both their mouths and his, or it is a statement of moral vision like those others he has stood by so forthrightly, in which case it is unthinkable he would not want to pursue it in season and out of season in the political forum.

The governor stated that his positions on these other issues derive from his own conscience. Reporters pressed him about his courageous veto of a recent bill on capital punishment, and he insisted that he acted, not on religious grounds, but out of a pragmatic knowledge that capital punishment simply does not work. Perhaps he is telling the truth. Maybe the only kind of religious moral enlightenment he is aware of comes from bishops during election years. But if a communicant of a religious community that has turned enormous energies to discerning our moral duties towards the poor, the laborers, the refugees, war victims, handicapped, elderly, and other disadvantaged people can remain unenlightened, unmotivated, and perhaps even uninformed by the traffic and earnestness of all that discussion, then perhaps the only effect his church has had on him is restricted to those few hierarchical utterances to which he affirms his loyalty.

THE PRELATE

It is perhaps regrettable that abortion had to be the specific point of contention which opened that round of the religion-and-government fracas, for the latter matter may be receiving distorted attention due to the way in which the former has been so misrepresented and misunderstood.

Archbishop O'Connor, unfortunately, mismanaged his treatment of abortion in two significant ways. Along with several other bishops he not only fell into the trap of presenting abortion as a "Catholic issue": he hoisted it as the decisive issue in that year's elections. In doing so he deviated from a wiser policy of the American bishops as a whole. Their corporate statement issued that spring, "Political Responsibility: Choices for the 1980s," set forth a broad moral agenda:

> Christians believe that Jesus' commandment to love one's neighbor should extend beyond individual relationships to infuse and transform all human relations from the family to the entire human community. Jesus . . . called us to feed the hungry, clothe the naked, to care for the sick and afflicted and to comfort the victims of injustice. His example and words require individual acts of charity and concern from each of us. Yet they also require understanding and action on a broader scale in pursuit of peace and in opposition to poverty, hunger and injustice. Such action necessarily involves the institutions and structures of society, the economy and politics. . . .
>
> As citizens we are all called to become informed, active and responsible participants in the political process. It is the laity who are primarily responsible for activity in political affairs, for it is they who have the major responsibility for renewal of the temporal order . . .
>
> We hope that voters will examine the positions of candidates on the full range of issues as well as their integrity, philosophy and performance.[11]

Archbishop O'Connor seemed to have made abortion a preemptive issue: a single test for candidates. This is not an illegitimate approach. I expect that in 1968 Mr. Cuomo, for instance, did not investigate the full program of George Wallace: his racism alone was enough to disqualify him for the Democratic presidential nomination. But Catholics in particular have such a broad moral agenda that they would find it especially difficult to limit their requirements to a single issue, even one as overwhelming as abortion. The bishops' alphabetical list included abortion, arms control and disarmament, capital punishment, civil rights, the economy, education, energy, family life, food and agricultural policy, health, housing, human rights, mass media, and regional conflict in the world. To demand but one of these, as the archbishop seemed to do, was to be too easily pleased.

Furthermore, he tried to short-circuit the teaching process. That is a frequent episcopal temptation. When they were issuing their letter on nuclear warfare and peace, the bishops wrote it in such a way that few ordinary Catholics could be expected to read it. It was long and it was heavy. It was addressed primarily to the Executive and Legislative Branches of the federal government. But this is not how bishops should operate, though it has become a predilection of virtually all church professionals now located in the District of Columbia for that purpose. In the end their efforts have questionable political effect, because they deliver no votes. The appropriate constituency for the Catholic bishops is the Catholic community, their people. Only if the people are brought to a changed awareness of some moral matter—such as nuclear warfare—will their changed political expectations weigh in politically with the government.

Archbishop O'Connor did not try to foreshorten his task by appealing in that fashion over the heads of his people, but he did appeal to voters to assess candidates according to their records or stands on abortion. Had he succeeded in sharing his convictions on that subject with his people, there would be no need to argue the obvious: that they choose candidates accordingly.

The reliable polls show that a majority of Catholics accept abortion legally for two so-called "hard cases": first, to save the life of a mother, or to preserve her from seriously crippled physical health; and second, when pregnancy has resulted from rape or incest. Considerably fewer Catholics—not half—would legitimate it when the offspring is handicapped. In all three instances Catholics report opinions that vary by only a few percentage points from the general population. The challenge facing the archbishop and anyone else who considers these exceptions to be unprincipled and unjust was and still is to plead their views more cogently and effectively before the

Catholic people, not to appeal in their name for a more stringent law than they are really prepared to support.[12]

On the issue of abortion itself, then, the archbishop had propounded too narrow a political program, and had advanced beyond the point where his constituency was prepared to support him.

THE POLITICIAN

On the abortion issue Mr. Cuomo was likewise unconvincing, and also in a pair of ways. He wrote well of the need for political consensus.

> Our public morality, then—the moral standards we maintain for everyone, not just the ones we insist on in our private lives—depends on a consensus view of right and wrong. The values derived from religious belief will not—and should not—be accepted as part of the public morality unless they are shared by the pluralistic community at large, by consensus.[13]

But then the governor steered his argument into confusion. There is nowhere to go now legally, he insisted, because no consensus exists in support of the Catholic bishops' view. "Indeed, the bishops have already confronted the fact that an absolute ban on abortion doesn't have the support necessary to be placed in our Constitution."[14] True, but irrelevant. Everyone knew that a total prohibition on abortion would not wash politically, for want of support. Only about one-fifth of the population then or now would favor such a law. The question that was active was not whether all abortions be outlawed, but whether all abortions should be lawful, as had been the case since 1973.

Here the governor had his facts wrong. Forget the 300 Catholic bishops. What the adults among the 50,000,000 Catholic laypeople wanted was in reasonably close consensus with what their fellow citizens wanted. Mr. Cuomo writes that "our view is in the minority."[15] The bishops' view, maybe, and Mr. Cuomo's view, but not the Catholic people's view. The fact is that adult Americans reject legalized abortion-on-demand.

They reject government funding for abortions except to save a mother's life. Mr. Cuomo writes: "Catholics, the statistics show, support the right to abortion in equal proportion to the rest of the population."[16] Exactly, but only about 20 percent of them support abortion-on-demand as a right. How the governor became so misinformed is a matter for grave concern, though it must be admitted that most other readers of the *New York Times* have labored under the same difficulty.

There was and is no national consensus for the position of the U.S. Catholic bishops. There was and is a massive and persisting consensus, however, against abortion-on-demand— our present law—and if Mr. Cuomo ignores that consensus he ignores Catholics, Methodists, Lutherans, Mormons, Baptists, Presbyterians, Orthodox, Mennonites, and a host of other citizens. It is not the bishops but the laity—the voting laity of every church—who will call him to account.

And they will not ask after his own childbearing choices, nor into the excellent supportive programs he means to institute to relieve some of the misfortunes which impel people towards abortion. They will be looking at what he does when he takes up the gubernatorial pen, to see if there be any reliable sincerity in his claim that he, like them, regards the extermination of the unborn as infamous. They will not judge him politically by his professed beliefs; they will judge him by his political performance, which they are likely to assess as prochoice. His claim that strategy and tactics must be left to his professional judgment is entirely legitimate. But it is precisely his strategy and tactics that have given rise to public objections.

The spirited yet fateful interplay between these two men was reminiscent of two literary figures from *Romeo and Juliet* I portrayed in the previous chapter: Prince Escalus, the Duke of Verona, who was responsible for enforcing the city's peace, and Friar Laurence, whose duty to the public peace was to expound it. The friar is to blame for he never had the nerve to confront the families and teach their consciences to repent. The duke is to blame for he never had the nerve to act with strength and rule the unruly town. Each of their vocations is essential; and each is incomplete. The sad sum of it all is expressed by the duke: "Mercy but murders, pardoning those that kill."[17]

The prince and the preacher do bear a telling resemblance to our other tale of the politician and the prelate, and another most distressing and tragic breaching of the peace.

NOTES

1. Apologies to William Shakespeare, Prologue to *Romeo and Juliet*.

2. John F. Kennedy, speech to the Greater Houston Ministerial Association, 12 September 1960, *New York Times*, 13 September 1960.

3. James Tunstead Burtchaell, C.S.C., *Rachel Weeping and Other Essays on Abortion* (Kansas City: Andrews & McMeel, 1982), 105–121.

4. Bernard Nathanson with Richard Ostling, *Aborting America* (Garden City, N.Y.: Doubleday, 1979), 51–52.

5. *New York Times*, 18 September 1979.

6. *New York Times*, 10 September 1984.

7. Governor Mario Cuomo, "Religious Belief and Public Morality: A Catholic Governor's Perspective," manuscript of a speech delivered to the Department of Theology at the University of Notre Dame, 13 September 1984, 1,4.

8. *New York Times*, 14 August 1984.

9. Hon. Geraldine Ferraro in a House debate on Federal funding for abortions for the poor, in the *New York Times*, 13 June 1984.

10. *New York Times*, 14 August 1984.

11. *Political Responsibility: Choices for the 1980s*, A Statement of the Administrative Board, U.S. Catholic Conference (Revised edition, 22 March 1984), 3–5,7. See also the statement by Bishop James W. Malone, president of the National Conference of Catholic Bishops, *New York Times*, 10 August 1984.

12. Judith Blake and Jorge Del Pinal, "Predicting Polar Attitudes toward Abortion in the United States," in *Abortion Parley*, ed. James Tunstead Burtchaell, C.S.C. (Kansas City, Kan.: Andrews & McMeel, 1980), 27–56.

13. Cuomo, "Religious Belief," 7.

14. Ibid., 12.

15. Ibid.

16. Ibid., 14.

17. *Romeo and Juliet*, 3.1.202.

Critique

11

Moral Crititque

1: THE GOD OF OUR CALCULATIONS

A review of *Pentecostal Catholics: Power, Charisma and Order in a Religious Movement,* by Meredith B. McGuire (Temple University Press) and *When Bad Things Happen to Good People,* by Harold S. Kushner (Schocken).

Joseph Fichter's *The Catholic Cult of the Paraclete* has stood since 1975 as the most professional yet appreciative study of the charismatic movement. Meredith McGuire, whose sociological scrutiny yielded more than a decade of attention to the movement, has produced a study that must stand at the center of the plentiful publications on modern pentecostals. The perspective is that of participant-observer, sympathetic yet sober. Her attention is fastened upon four features of the movement: strategies for recruitment and allegiance, dynamics of prayer meetings, attitudes involved in faith healing, and authority style in an exuberant community.

McGuire sees the movement attracting persons whose dependence on a firm sense of order is no longer served by their church: a vernacular liturgy left in large part to local adaptation; moral issues on which there is heated and public dispute; entire segments of the layperson's creed lobotomized out of existence: the church ostensibly failing to provide an authoritative and

279

simple way to salvation. And in public, before a cynical and secularized society, the church seems to offer a limp and unimposing presence. To such a clientele, now more middle-aged than the earlier waves of young converts, McGuire sees the charismatic movement holding up a reassuringly secure vision. Its doctrine is homely yet definite, its authority imperturbable, its moral teaching without quibble.

Increasing deviation in perspective and emphasis will probably strain relations between the movement and the large church, which has hitherto been acquiescent. McGuire sees in the group a growth of sectarian qualities: a contempt for society at large, a sense of privileged access to the truth, a creed that claims dominance over all other sources of understanding, a leadership which requires total allegiance. Differently from Fichter who saw in the movement the more fluid and less totalitarian qualities of a cult, she observes that its steersmen are growing increasingly hostile towards competing navigators, and are heading in a more sectarian direction.

Also noted is the privatizing of religion among charismatics. Few social activists are drawn into membership nor, once committed, do charismatics tend to involve themselves actively in the economic, social, and political order. Ethical concerns are explicit in respect of individual behavior or marital relations (e.g., male dominance and female submission). But matters of a more social ethic are expounded with less bite. Ministries of the movement are mostly devoted to its own membership.

> Interaction in the public sphere is defined as far less important than key aspects of the private spheres: personal devotion, family life, and the prayer group. . . . In essence, the pentecostal movement among Catholics represents the celebration and enhancement of the privatization of religion. [This] enhances the segregation of 'opinions' on social issues from the sphere of religious experience and meaning, [and] makes it highly unlikely that the movement will produce any significant effort for socio-economic change, at least in developed countries. Theodicies provided by the Catholic pentecostal belief system legitimate members' middle-class comforts and allow them to ex-

press their concern for less comfortable members of society by prayer. (213)

To a theologian, McGuire's soundings into the implicit charismatic understanding of God give much to reflect on. The pentecostal is familiarized with a Lord who is attentive to the most everyday occurrences. He or she looks to Jesus to relieve high blood pressure, to find lost car keys, and to secure employment. Pain, poverty, and illness are interpreted as sequelae of sin or the work of Satan or evil spirits. Thus healing prayer begins with the exorcism of demons and an appeal for the alleviation of sin, so that serious sickness can then be relieved.

This Lord of Pentecost is expected to incline his ear to the most earthy and particular supplications. This could betoken a belief in God's exquisite care: if no lily flowers but under the watchful divine eye, surely God cares distinctly about your sister's shingles and the current price of your GM stock. Yet somehow that God does lack something of the grandeur of the sparrow-eyeing Lord. There is a diminishment in any presumption that God is at our beck to remedy our paltriest concerns.

The church is ready to acknowledge miracles when they show forth the divine benevolence and testify to special men and women whom the Lord has possessed by the Spirit. But the craving to construe every auto accident and upturn in the financial cycle as a skirmish between Jesus and Satan for possession of each one of us has too little in common with our received faith in the Almighty. It is the gospel writ tiny.

It is no copyright of charismatics, of course. This God so widely worshiped has troubled many a soul. For if an influenza fever broken or sunshine on a wedding day or a new furnace donated to a convent are, to true believers, to be taken as signs of God's periodic affection, then spina bifida at birth or the hit-and-run death of a young father of three or dry rot in the basement beams must be darkened by God's wrath. If all the give-and-take of welcome and dread events is spoken by God in a decipherable stream of good and bad news, if weal and woe mean blessing and curse, then this is a puzzling world and that is surely a God you would want to be wary of.

Harold Kushner was not wary. When his firstborn was diagnosed at three to suffer from a wasting terminal illness, the young rabbi felt his faith buckle. "Like most people, my wife and I had grown up with an image of God as an all-wise, all-powerful parent figure who would treat us as our earthly parents did, or even better. If we were obedient and deserving, He would reward us. If we got out of line, He would discipline us, reluctantly but firmly. He would protect us from being hurt or from hurting ourselves, and would see to it that we got what we deserved in life" (3).

But when days go dark and humans suffer, this theology invites people either to begin blaming themselves or, if they can find no equivalent fault, to begin hating God.

Alerted by his own misery to the many ways good folk in his flock could be stricken, Kushner choked on the God-defending theodicies he had been taught: that God would prove fair in the long run, that suffering ennobles or purges those who bear up under it, that no one is given a heavier burden than he or she can bear, that early death is to rescue the innocent from a depraved world. These seemed either to deny reality or to imply an unworthy deity, and they also undermined outrage at injustice in the world.

After Aaron Kushner died at fourteen, his father had wrestled the ancient problem through and he brought out his quickly popular book on God and suffering. What makes it so worth reading is the author's sensible rejection of theory after theory devised to explain how the slings and arrows of outrageous fortune all bespeak a mysterious but eventually decipherable purpose of a fair-minded God.

Kushner's own theological answer is, sadly, almost as flawed as the ones he disallows. Ironically, it is constructed on a profound misunderstanding of Job. That book (*sans* the prologue and epilogue of a later editor who flinched at the daring of the first edition) was published to correct a teaching derived from the great prophets. Whereas more ancient thinkers had explained unmerited prosperity or suffering as retribution for others' deeds, shared out across a tribe or down the generations of a family, Jeremiah (31) and Ezekiel (18) rejected that explanation. In their view, the Lord would be no more ready than any good person among us to favor or to afflict one person on another's account. Every one suffers for his or her own sins. Both Job and his visitors abide by this prophetic teaching. His adversity convinces them that he must be guilty of some awesome offense, but it enrages him because he knows that is not the case. The Lord, roused to hurricane force by all this theological bickering, rages onto the scene. He demands why, when he had never thought it needful for them to understand how the tides flow or when the mountain goats breed or whence comes the morning dew, they should be so cocksure that he had unriddled for them the far greater mystery of suffering. Enough for them to know that he knows what he is about. Job's answer, and the book's sign-off for theologians is:

> I had better lay my hand over my mouth . . .
> You have told me about great works that I cannot understand,
> about marvels which are beyond me, of which I know nothing.
> (40:4;42:3)

Job, of course, helped provoke the turmoil which led to the Wisdom of Solomon and its breakthrough doctrine that the just would survive injustice and death and would journey, not to the underworld helter-skelter with the unjust, but to the heavenly court to join the Lord's own retinue. Latter-day Judaism subsequently set aside this theological development, but Christians received it, through the Pharisees, as an insight of the living tradition. Job's point is that believers ought never imagine that God's governance and justice are simple enough for them to comprehend in their application. Rabbi Kushner has somehow turned this around. The author of Job "believes in God's goodness and in Job's goodness, and is prepared to give up his belief . . . that God is all-powerful. Bad things do happen to good people in this world, but it is not God who wills it. God would like people to get what they deserve in this life, but He cannot always arrange it. Forced to choose between a good God who is not totally powerful, or a powerful God who is not totally good, the author of the Book of Job chooses to believe in God's goodness"(42–43). Kushner has the book balking at precisely what it was written to vaunt: a Lord whose goodness and justice bear upon us in ways that transcend any of our daily calculations and interpretations.

Kushner's theology and that which McGuire discerns among charismatics stand starkly opposed to one another. But they are mirror-images of one another in that they both diminish God, and in so doing they both miss some elements very central to Christian and erstwhile Jewish speculation on God's governance.

First, one cannot safely pick and choose what in the world will serve as signs of God. One person will cultivate posters with starlit mountain lakes and inscriptions from the Psalms, and will luxuriate in a God of elegant bounty. But another will be gripped with loathing for a God who drowned his young sister in exactly such a lake. Both are really picking out things and events which they, according to some prior notions of their own not found in nature or history, had already decided are revealing. However, they are not receiving the revelation from what they behold; they are identifying it according to what they have already accepted. The church does not see nature or history offering any consistent or decipherable vision of God. She points straightaway at Jesus' death and resurrection. Jesus, who dies for those who kill him, displays in himself and on behalf of his Father an absence of all wrath, an inability to punish, a relentless love. In him God is deciphered for us. Elsewhere God is suggested ambiguously, by persons or scenes or events.

Second, one thing which God apparently does not create *ex nihilo* is the character, the inmost *ego* of a human. That, unlike freckles or a musical ear or a gentle temperament, is not ours; it is *us*, and we must somehow share the authorship of our very selves. Everything else we have; but that, we are. God creates us, but this most inward center of God's creature, or self, we must then co-create. In that way we are identical with who we are. All else—the corona of endowments and influences—is given to us. But our moral personality is who we have managed, through choices or the forfeiture of choice, to become.

Third, we need time and opportunity to become. We cannot imagine the possibility of growth to human maturity, into transforming love, in a world where events are not haphazard. Any of the tidier worlds our imaginations might fashion, where people could expect a fair reward for their efforts, would be deprived of the most precious advantage our world now affords us: the possibility of virtue. Appetite for reward would outcrave desire for our neighbor's welfare. Strangely, in just such a just world we could never become just. It would be in our interest to give our neighbors their due, but precisely because of this self-interest we could never develop the strenuous and loving zeal for their dignity and their needs which is the virtue of justice. Just acts would be guaranteed, but just people could never ripen. We would be surrounded by justice but unable to possess it. The God whom McGuire reports and the God whom Kushner portrays would both be loving, perhaps, but not loving enough to allow us to become so. Ironically, the only world imaginable wherein we can grow to the full stature of human maturity is the one in which both good and bad things—and evil things—can happen to both good and bad people, and the best people can be crucified.

2: FROM QUACKERY TO DIAGNOSIS

A review of *Educational Guidance in Human Love: Outlines for Sex Education*, by the Sacred Congregation for Catholic Education.

Shortly after his great *Dictionary* was published, Samuel Johnson was approached at a social gathering by a lady of fashion. "My dear Doctor Johnson," she said, "I do commend you on your magnificent dictionary. What I especially appreciated," she confided, "was that you did not include any of those vulgar or obscene words." "Oh, Madam," replied Johnson, "You looked?"

When the Vatican released its recent guidelines for sex education the American press seems to have read them with an equally prurient eye. The *New York Times*'s coverage is not untypical. According to its correspondent, the document describes extramarital and homosexual relations and masturbation as moral disorders, and calls for governments to restrain pornography and overly explicit sex in entertainment. As a summary of either the contents or the emphasis of the thirty-six-page instruction, this is distorted. The *Times* has culled the publication for anything that would exemplify what it calls "the stern orthodoxy represented by Pope John Paul II."

The document is dull but not damning. It appears to have been drafted by an educator rather than by a bishop. Either the educator is as poor a teacher as many bishops, or his (or her) native pedagogese has been further encumbered with the curial style. The final text lumbers along heavily. An example of its turgid prose: "Friendship is the height of affective maturation and differs from mere camaraderie by its interior dimension, by communication which allows and fosters true communion, by its reciprocal generosity and its stability" (92). Plentiful quotations from John Paul II are not entirely helpful, for his style is sometimes as impenetrable as that of his mentor, Edmund Husserl.

That the Vatican is promoting sex education at all is worthy of note. Pius XI had condemned it, but Vatican II later encouraged it. A lengthy footnote performs some historical revisionism by explaining that the pope was only speaking of the programs of his day. The public programs of our day, however, are probably more defective than what the pope was opposing.

On the whole this is a positive document. It repeats over and over that love is to be the characteristic of authentic sex. The purpose of rightful sexual communion—and therefore the theme of sex education—has to be personal maturity. "Sexuality, oriented, elevated and integrated by love . . . is achieved in the full sense only with the realization of affective maturity" (6). Sex education aims at "the harmonious and integral development of the person towards psychological maturity" (34).

Sexual intercourse, in the view of this instruction, is possessed of twofold value: an intimate communion of love between the couple and the fostering of children. In the numerous passages where these two values are proposed side-by-side, it is the unity which is placed ahead of fecundity. Augustine and Aquinas had not even mentioned conjugal communion as having anything to do with sex, and Pius XI had ranked it as subordinate to procreation. The stress in this present Vatican document is remarkably similar to the stress in the writings of German writer Herbert Doms that brought his condemnation under Pius XII. "Love and fecundity are meanings and values of sexuality which include and summon each other in turn, and cannot therefore be considered as either alternatives or opposites" (32). This blend of the unitive and procreative offers a distinct improvement on some of the papal emphasis on fertility sometimes heard in recent years. It is surely more healthy than the sterile fixation on satisfaction for the couple (or, often enough, for the individuals)—without a thought for children—which is dominant in our culture and in the most influential sex education programs.

The instruction is strewn with encouraging *obiter dicta*. At one point it explains how arduous and demanding a fully human integration of genitality, eroticism, and love really is. Then, instead of complaining that society has made this goal practically unattainable, it supposes that while not too many may attain it fully, more people than we might imagine reach it reasonably well (42).

The "problems" portion covers less than ten percent of the text, and it is couched in sensible terms. Masturbation is linked with immaturity, and is deficient by "not being at the service of life and love" (98). Homosexuality "impedes the person's acquisition of sexual maturity" (101). Educators are told not to disturb people who are troubled in these ways with heavy accusations of guilt. And they are also warned not to whitewash this sort of sexual activity as a likely path to sexual integration or maturity.

Sex education is essentially a prerogative of parents, the statement says outright several times. Educators and clergy are only the collaborators of the parents. In an age when virtually every parental responsibility is declared to be beyond the competence of most layfolk, and child development is increasingly bound over to professionals anointed for expert service, this has a hardy ring to it.

Contraception is dealt with in a single paragraph. Young

people should be made knowledgeable about natural methods of regulating fertility, and they should learn why artificial contraception does not harmonize with "responsible marriage, full of love and open to life" (62). Not adequate, but not a harangue either.

If one were to fault the instruction, it might be for adopting too mild a tone. Standard sex education today tends to be morally bankrupt. It begins with a biological description of genital function and fertility (known in the trade as the "organ concert") and it ends with indoctrination in contraception, abortion, VD, and, lately, AIDS. Basic to this pedagogy is the belief that youngsters will not accept moral ideals, and should at least (or at most) be helped to cut their losses. Such a counsel of despair is far sicker than the document implies with its flaccid complaint that "excessive weight is given to simple information, at the expense of the other dimensions of sex education" (37).

This is a document on sex education. It has been issued by the teaching center of practically the only community in the world which still believes that men and women can pledge themselves to one another for better or for worse until death. I found it astonishing that it contains not a word about fidelity. Surely it is lifelong fidelity and unconditional self-giving that Christians believe make the promises of sexual union believable.

Is this one more in a series of nay-saying, repressive utterances on the church's most scolding subject? Not at all. Clearly the Vatican has not yet absorbed all the insights on masturbation disclosed in *Ms.* The testimonies on the gay scene uttered in the *Village Voice* have not yet brought round the magisterium. The newer wisdom on recreational sex elaborated in *Hustler* is still under advisement. The Vatican may also be backward in not adopting the liberating norms worked out by Anthony Kosnick and the other authors of *Human Sexuality*, whereby about the only discouraged form of sex is doing it with a Doberman.

But compared with *Casti Connubii* (1930), which is never once cited in this document (a typical 1930 passage: "Among the values of marriage, childbearing holds the first place"), this is an improvement. Compared with the condemnation of Dr. Doms by the Holy Office in 1944, because of his view that the production and rearing of children might not be the purpose of marriage to which all other purposes are subordinate, this is an improvement. Compared with *Humanae Vitae* (1968) which identifies contraception, rather than an aversion to children, as the principal adversary of Christian marriage today, this is an improvement. Compared with the 1975 Vatican *Declaration on Certain Questions Concerning Sexual Ethics*, which was one long peeve, this is positively congenial.

Awhile ago I spent several hours with a couple of distressed parents. Their eldest child—thirty years old, a military officer, and a Ph.D—had recently told them his girl friend had taken up residence with him. Their youngest children were still in their teens, and the parents did not know whether they should break the news to them, since they look up to their elder brother and since the parents are reluctant to disturb their innocence. But as our conversation progressed it became clear to me that the children had probably known what was going on before their parents learned, and had spared *them* as long as possible. It was the elders that everyone was protecting, for they may have been the ones most likely to have trouble coping.

When documents like this issue from Rome, it is ironic that one reads them, not in search of insight or clarity or challenge, but in the wistful hope that maybe the folks over there are understanding things a little better now. Like parishioners who humor an autocratic pastor who gives them no credit for faith-filled judgment, and who is really protected by them from anything he could not cope with, layfolk and their *soi-disant* servant-leaders in the church are happy enough when the Vatican backs itself out of an old impasse and shows signs of glimpsing what had long been plain to many others. This may be faint praise, but on the subject of sex anything more effusive would be forced. The world is sick on sex and on marriage, and Rome is still working its way from quackery to diagnosis.

3: Healing Nature

A review of *Toward a More Natural Science,* by Leon R. Kass (Free Press).

Like Lewis Thomas, Leon Kass is so thoroughly educated in the reflective disciplines and so articulate a writer that he is a security risk within the medical establishment. With the M.D. of a practitioner and the Ph.D. (in biochemistry) of a scholar, he is withal a humanist who tends to ask, not what or how, but why and whether.

His essays are strewn with enviable one-liners, such as the following:

Trendiness has replaced tuberculosis as the scourge of the intellectual classes. (44)

We stand in much greater danger from the well-wishers of mankind [than from our enemies], for folly is much harder to detect than wickedness. (62)

It is hard to claim respect for human life in the laboratory from a society that does not respect human life in the womb. (125)

Modern science is guided overall by this moral and political intention: a lifting up of downtrodden humanity. Never mind the question how a science invincibly ignorant of and in principle skeptical about standards of better and worse can *know* how to do *good* for mankind. (131)

It is far from clear that leisure is most fruitfully used when stacked up at the end of a life in which work is regarded as the main source of dignity. (304)

It is probably no accident that it is a generation whose intelligentsia proclaim the meaninglessness of life that embarks on its indefinite prolongation and that seeks to cure the emptiness of life by extending it. (316)

Leon Kass has been a publishing bioethicist now for almost two decades. Those of us who have been following the steady formulation and reformulation of his distinctive viewpoint in a series of scattered articles thought it was time for him to sit down in his Luce chair at Chicago and write a comprehensive and coherent statement of his philosophy. He resembles Stanley Hauerwas in that he has become a foremost exponent of a distinctive and very valuable point of view in ethics without ever having set forth a comprehensive and orderly exposition of his theory. In this book he has given us a coordinated compilation of his essays: a fugue, though not yet a symphony.

Modern science has been determined that its methodical scrutiny of physical objects be objective and uncontrovertible. Taking mathematical physics as a most reliable model, science assumed that objects are best explained in terms of their most basic components and most rudimentary forms. Hens, huckleberries and humans would make surest sense by studying the lowest forms and functions they all have in common. Kass disputes this as a reductivist claim of science to explain the complex by the simple. On the contrary, the more highly organized the living being, the more its basic components and functions are governed by its advanced needs and purposes. Higher beings can be understood only in the light of their own advantaged and enlarged agenda. The simple can be understood better insofar as it is bound into the complex.

Despite Darwin's reluctance to designate species as "higher" or "lower" except in respect of the struggle to survive, it was Darwin's work that best drew attention to the outbreak of distinctive life forms. The first organisms were possessed of rudimentary nutrition, growth, and reproduction. This was followed by three successive transformations: the emergence of sensitivity and awareness; the emergence of locomotion, and with it, desire; and finally, the emergence of speech and intellect (271).

Kass sees in this stratified array of creatures an internal teleology comprising five elements: "(1) orderly coming to be, reaching an internally determined end or completion; (2) an organic and active whole, a unity of structure and function, with parts contributing to the maintenance and functioning of the whole; (3) directedness, activity pointing toward a goal; (4) serving and preserving one's kind. Implied in all of these notions is a fifth element, the notion of 'good' or 'well' or 'fit' or 'successful' or 'perfect'" (257).

This leads Kass to affirm that organic beings can be seen to be whole or blighted, successful or frustrated, functioning rightly or poorly—on their own intrinsic terms. This in turn begets a strikingly effective notion of health on which the Kass theory stands. The traditional warrant of medicine—to conserve health and to cure disease—gains its meaning from the wholeness and sound function and integrated unity of the natural human being, the organically conjoined body and soul (11).

Health, then, is an objective condition, not an arbitrary or choosable one. We may decide that for our purposes the health of the mosquito is a bane for us. But even when we exterminate the mosquito we must realize that its welfare may have been sacrificed to ours, but not altered. The female mosquito's innate purpose and nature require blood meals. And our own health, no less than that of the mosquito, is in function, not of what one thinks or wants, but of what one is.

One might try turning Kass's principle back in his face. If the higher powers are more integrative and governing, then the highest of them all, the human intellect and will, ought be able to designate by desire and choice what is best for itself and for inferior powers and inferior living beings. In its typical form, this argument would claim that health is what our desires and interests dictate, and that disease is simply what we have chosen to be rid of. Kass replies that well-being and health is not a mere choice, however. It is an inborn intentionality of every material being. Medicine therefore does not exist to serve the patient's pleasure or preference; our health is what our bodies require, not what we request. Nor do the physician and surgeon simply make their technical skills available for hire, for their profession limits them to applying their skills for the body's own needs to function well.

The World Health Organization has defined health as "a state of complete physical, mental and social well-being" (160). Kass deplores that as a coarse description of happiness, not health, and one which far exceeds the training and arts of the medical practitioner to supply. That agenda is too broad for medicine, for the doctor's rightful yet restrained duty is to assist the human body to be fit and available to sustain life's further powers and pursuits.

The point is taken further still. Even the prolongation of life is a false goal for medicine. To the extent that the physician's primary duty, to protect and to restore health, fends off premature death, it will save lives, but that will always be its provisional effect. We all age and die. Medicine is to make us healthy while we live and thus it protects life . . . but only for awhile.

Confusing life with health distorts our view of what medicine is to do.

> We go after the diseases that are the leading causes of death rather than the leading causes of ill health. We evaluate medical progress and compare medicine in different nations, in terms of mortality statistics. We ignore the fact that we are largely merely changing one set of fatal illnesses or conditions for another, and not necessarily for milder or more tolerable ones. We rarely stop to wonder of what and how we will die, and in what condition of body and mind we shall spend our last years, once we are able to cure cancer, heart disease, and stroke. . . . That their prevention may enable the prospective or actual victims to live longer may be deemed, in many cases, an added good, though we should not expect too much on this score. The complete eradication of heart disease, cancer and stroke—currently the major mortal diseases—would, according to some calculations, extend the average life expectancy [of a mature adult by only a couple of years]. (162–163)

While there is reasonable hope of restoring a patient to a healed and recovered state, therapy is still possible, and that therapy is likely to prolong life because it sustains healthy functioning.

> But when reasonable hope of recovery is gone, [the physician] acts rather to comfort the patient and to keep him company, as a friend and not especially or uniquely as a physician. I do not want to be misunderstood. Mine is not an argument to permit or to condone medical callousness, or euthanasia practiced by

physicians. Rather, it is a suggestion that doctors keep their eye on their main business, restoring and correcting what can be corrected and restored, always acknowledging that death will and must come, that health is a mortal good, and that as embodied beings we are fragile beings that must snap sooner or later, medicine or no medicine. (163)

Nature's own needs are inborn, given: to be discerned, not decided (98). Likewise with the human health which medicine serves. Kass observes that many who scorn the ethical suggestion that "unnatural" intervention into human reproduction is questionable will themselves appeal to "nature's way" when it suits their purposes (107).

There is something refreshingly wry in Kass's warning that the use of science always raises questions of political and moral import quite beyond those of technique or method. Failure to engage in appropriate moral inquiry is, he sees, usually self-serving. One likes, for instance, to speak of "the control of nature by science," but that is a cover-up. Science provides power, but it is humans who wield that power, and they wield it over other humans.

Kass much prefers the ancient teaching that science is for understanding nature, not for controlling it, and that its use must minister to nature (25–28,131). The moral duty of medicine is to discriminate between intervention that enhances nature and that which violates it.

The existence of human life in the laboratory, outside the confines of the generating bodies from which it sprang, also challenges the meaning of our embodiment. People like Mr. and Mrs. Brown [parents of Louise, the first child born of *in vitro* fertilization], who seek a child derived from their flesh, celebrate in so doing their self-identity with their own bodies, and acknowledge the meaning of the living human body by following its pointings to its own perpetuation.... But life in the laboratory also allows other people—including those who would donate or sell sperm, eggs, or embryos; or those who would bear another's child in surrogate pregnancy; or even those who will prefer to have their children rationally manufactured entirely in the laboratory—to declare themselves independent of their bodies, in this ultimate liberation. For them the body is a mere tool, ideally an instrument of the conscious will, the sole repository of human dignity. Yet this blind assertion of the will against our bodily nature—in contradiction of the meaning of the human generation it seeks to control—can only lead to self-degradation and dehumanization. (113–114)

Kass would see it as natural, not merely conventional, that sex and childbearing be enclosed within the confines of marriage and family. Programmed reproduction by medicine will weaken the family, "the only institution in an increasingly impersonal world where each person is loved not for what he does or makes, but simply because he is" (33–34).

Wide and profound and tough, then, must be the scope of moral consideration governing research and therapy. Even to know what a disease is, we must first know what human nature is and what its enhancement requires: a vast and subtle inquiry for which medical folk are ill-trained and ill-disposed (168).

Yet despite the aggressive challenge Kass raises to the moral naïveté and willfulness of scientists and practitioners, he flinches when he gets down to particular normative issues. In *The Medusa and the Snail* Lewis Thomas argued that the study of classical Greek is probably the ideal undergraduate preparation for medical studies, and that anyone who has majored in "pre-med" or taken the MCAT exams should be denied admission to medical school. One day I was telling a friend about this modest and delicious proposal. It turned out that he was a professional acquaintance of the author, and told me that before being chancellor of Sloan-Kettering Thomas had indeed run a medical school, and had admitted the same science-and-grade-crazed applicants every other school took. When studying Kass's essays one occasionally has the disheartening sense that his trenchant and rigorous principles similarly often lead him to only hushed and hesitant conclusions.

Take, for instance, his abundant consideration of eugenic prenatal diagnosis and of its supporting rhetoric—"the very language used to discuss genetic disease leads us to the easy but wrong conclusion that the afflicted fetus or person *is* rather than *has* a disease" (89). To those who claim that the defective are eliminated for their own good or for that of society, he asks which of us would be retrospectively grateful to have had our lives forfeited to someone else's view of our social worth. It is all too easy for anyone in power to believe that what is better for him must be better for the rest of us (93).

Some of his most sarcastic comment is reserved for those who aim to better the world by ridding it of the handicapped:

> After all, how many architects of the Vietnam War or the suppression of Solidarity suffered from Down's syndrome? Who uses up more of our irreplaceable natural resources and who produces more pollution: the inmates of an institution for the retarded or the graduates of Harvard College? And which of our genetic mutants display more vanity, self-indulgence, and the will-to-power, or less courage, reverence, and love of country than many of our so-called best and brightest? It seems indisputable that the world suffers more from the morally and spiritually defective than from the genetically defective. (46)

> It is ironic that we should acquire the power to detect and eliminate the genetically unequal at a time when we have finally succeeded in removing much of the stigma and disgrace previously attached to victims of congenital illness, in providing them with improved care and support, and in preventing, by means of education, feelings of guilt on the part of their parents. (84–85)

Kass admits that his own view of nature, as pointing to a fullness, a perfection, tends to award human rights only to the fully outfitted individual. It has been used to justify abortion, infanticide and slavery.

> There is another notion of nature, less splendid, more humane, and, though less able to sustain a notion of health, more acceptable to the findings of modern science: nature not as the norm or perfection, but nature as the innate, the given, the inborn. Our animal nature is characterized by impulses toward self-preservation and by the capacity to feel pleasure and to suffer pain. On this understanding of nature, man is fundamentally like the other animals, differing only in his conscious awareness

of these inborn impulses, capacities and concerns. The right to life rests on the fact that we are self-preserving and suffering creatures. Yet on this understanding of nature, the fetus—even a 'defective' fetus, not to speak of a child, 'defective' or no—is not potential, but actual. The right to life belongs to him. For this reason, this understanding of nature does not provide and seems even to deny us what we are seeking, namely, a justification for genetic abortion, adequate unto itself, which does not simultaneously justify infanticide, homicide, and enslavement of the genetically abnormal. (98)

Following on these insights, he finds that the use of a physician to abort an unwanted child is as alien to medicine as is the use of a physician to administer execution by injection. Neither pregnancy nor crime, after all, is a disease (235). The entire use of medical technique to manufacture or to eliminate children on demand may have dehumanized the doctors themselves (111–112).

But what, after all this insight and indictment, is his moral judgment on the question of the engineering of reproduction? Merely that we do not now possess sufficient wisdom to exercise such dread powers or to determine standards for their use. "In the absence of standards to guide and restrain the use of this awesome power, we can only dehumanize man as we have despoiled our planet" (78).

Dr. Kass had led himself to the point where a simple assertion of immorality would follow. But he shies away from that, almost as if he could not oppose his fellow M.D.s that boldly.

The ethical issues in prenatal diagnosis to detect the genetically defective, as the author clearly sees, direct us to the morality of abortion itself. But this pivotal problem he then excuses himself from resolving (81–82). The assignment of trimestral status-lines by *Roe* v. *Wade* is a biological embarrassment, he notes, for it does not correspond to any real transformations during fetal development (109). There has also been sleight-of-mind among those who with uneasy conscience and heavy heart have gone along with abortion only because women were demanding it (125). There is a radical contradiction in the extirpation of the unborn by the very hands dedicated to bringing them to birth. "If medicine is constituted by the task to assist living nature in human bodies to the work of maintenance and function and perpetuation, then one must wince at the monstrous because self-contradictory union that is the obstetrician-abortionist" (235). Kass states openly that "any honest biologist" must be "inclined" to the view that a human life begins at fertilization.

Kass however cannot bring himself to ascribe to this youngling any right to life that we must respect. The newly implanted blastocyst is only *"potentially* a mature human being," deserving of our respect. Indeed, the closer he draws to the nub of this entire moral issue of what abortion is and does, the more his prose fibrillates. He is "inclined," but he takes no step. He agrees with uneasy conscience and heavy heart, but he agrees. He winces, but he cannot say nay. He asks for restraint, not for refusal (105–106).

Leon Kass is one of the most intrepid and free-minded theorists contributing to bioethics. All the more disheartening that he cannot quite bring himself to levy any clear moral repudiation of any practice that is actually widespread and conventional among the very profession whose moral judgment he finds so wanting. I know of no ethicist who both demands so much and forgoes so much from his colleagues who are called to save life but are tempted to master it instead.

4: Gazing Steadfastly at the Holocaust

A review of *The Nazi Doctors: Medical Killing and the Psychology of Genocide,* by Robert Jay Lifton (Basic Books).

In 1948, when Alexander Mitscherlich published the first account of the complicity of physicians in the Nazi extermination programs, his German medical colleagues retaliated by ostracizing this distinguished psychiatrist personally and buying up his book to keep it out of circulation. Leo Alexander shortly after the Nuremberg doctors' trial introduced Mitscherlich's reports and his own to the American public, but it is more recently that such a torrent of publication on the Holocaust has become available. One hopes that Robert Jay Lifton's study may not suffer from the ennui this surfeit has begun to impose on the nation's readership.

How did men and women trained, sworn, and professionally fulfilled as healers ease into the task of mass murder? Through nearly a decade spent reading the archival records and interviewing former Nazi physicians, imprisoned physicians who worked under their orders, and the survivors of their ministrations, psychiatrist Lifton found that most Nazi doctors were quite ordinary: "neither inherently evil nor particularly ethically sensitive" (4). Yet, if they were banal people, their work was demonic, and Lifton wanted to know what grotesque shift enabled healers to be killers.

It has become a convention, much sponsored by Elie Wiesel, to insist that any comparison of the Holocaust to other acts of murderous inhumanity dishonors the Jews who perished at Nazi hands. Lifton is not of that mind. His insights into the motivations of Nazi doctors aspire to "raise broader questions about human behavior, about ways in which people, individually and collectively, can embrace various forms of destructiveness and evil, with or without the awareness of doing so" (417). Genocide and its fellow plagues are possible within any nation and any person, and the psychic paths to such murderous behavior had better be widely known than imagined to have perished with the Third Reich.

German doctors showed an early affinity for the Nazi movement. Forty-five percent of them were party members, much more than in other professions. In the SS they outnumbered teachers proportionately seven to one. Six months after the Nazi takeover the German Chamber of Physicians acknowledged the new era by recommencing the cycle of its official journal, the *Deutsches Ärzteblatt*, with a new issue No. 1, and the swastika on the cover. They enthusiastically supported government measures progressively forcing Jewish colleagues out of practice and out of the country, and raised no protest when one Jewish doctor, Karl von Ossietzky, was imprisoned, denied access to his Nobel Peace Prize, and brought to an early death from aggravated tuberculosis in captivity.[1]

There were three inaugural ventures to eliminate undesirables: the mentally handicapped were sterilized; mentally defective children, and then adults, were killed; then the chronically ill and habitual criminals were killed. Each program was expanded somewhat by preferential though unsystematic inclusion of Jews, even when they were not designated as mentally ill or as criminals.

From the outset it was a strict policy to entrust sterilization and extermination exclusively to physicians. In fact the order from Hitler which initiated the exterminations simply authorized doctors to administer a "mercy death" to whomever it would, in their professional judgment, benefit. The program was inaugurated through a formal visit by the Führer's own physician to Leipzig for a personal examination of one congenitally blighted child called Knauer. Five years later the pace had quickened: Josef Mengele and his colleagues were sorting out as many as 20,000 arrivals a day, and deciding which of them death would, in their professional judgment, benefit.

Doctors were not technically needed for diagnosis or for lethal injections or gassing. But their responsible and visible involvement lent public credibility to the annihilation. Apart from some disgruntled parents and a few wrathful churchmen who quickly protested the elimination of handicapped children in the early days, most people gave way quietly. Many would have supported Herr Knauer's encomium of Hitler's doctor who made that historic house call:

> He explained to me that the Führer had personally sent him, and that my son's case interested the Führer very, very much. The Führer wanted to explore the problem of people who had no future—whose life was worthless. . . . From then on, we wouldn't have to suffer from this terrible misfortune, because th Führer had granted us the mercy killing of our son. Later, we could have other children, handsome and healthy, of whom the Reich could be proud. . . . He was a savior to us—the man who could deliver us from a heavy burden. (115)

There was, of course, nothing even remotely therapeutic in the Nazi doctors' treatment of victim groups. The clinical facilities in concentration camps aimed only to extend the useful labor-time of inmates before they were starved or gassed to death. The medical experiments, later reckoned to be amateur and worthless, simply used and destroyed human subjects for the career ambitions of their medical captors. Despite this, it was standard procedure for physicians to follow the entire sequence of procedures "as if" they were functioning as healers. First a physical examination, then a meticulous medical record, then admission to a medical facility, then "treatment" by poison chosen and administered personally by the physician or by medical corpsmen under the doctor's direct orders and supervision, then personal verification of death, then the signing of a falsified death certificate, then sympathetic notification of next-of-kin. All this was done with an observant use of medical symbolism: white lab coats, red cross insignia, etc. Lifton observes that the retention of the full though fictive therapeutic pantomime engendered in the doctors themselves the feeling that they were continuing their professional pursuits. It was the medical profession, not the public, that was most profoundly deceived.

After seeing this pattern of complicity established in the early extermination programs, Lifton devotes the large part of his book to Auschwitz, and to lengthy studies of three principal doctors there. Then he sets forth his theory. The Nazi physicians and their coopted prisoner doctors were able to turn from healers into killers by what he calls "doubling." They divided their selves into two partial identities, each incomplete but each able to function alone. The healer self remained, and could display attentive concern, affectionate compassion, and professional integrity. The "Auschwitz" self, however, lacked those components and was ruthlessly and contentedly devoted to killing. Off duty, and in unanticipable, momentary episodes on duty, the healer self could appear with medical solicitude. But the healer self bore no guilt for the carnage that was the work of the "Auschwitz" self, and indeed deplored that work as an unavoidable, bloody ordeal.

The book describes the strategies used to numb the conscience of the doctors so that they could live so divided a life without breaking under the contradiction.

(1) Redefinition of the profession. Health, the natural goal of the profession, was redefined as the physical soundness of

the *Volk,* the racial collectivity. The welfare of any personal patient had value only insofar as it benefited or threatened the genetic nation. The killing of one person could, for the public health, be considered a therapeutic imperative. An entire block of prisoners could be gassed when a few of them had contracted typhus: this was then a public health measure "to prevent mass death." The entire Jewish people could be eliminated as a "gangrenous appendix in the body of mankind."

(2) Vocabulary. "The language of the Auschwitz self, and of the Nazis in general, was crucial to the numbing. A leading scholar of the Holocaust [Raul Hilberg] told of examining 'tens of thousands' of Nazi documents without once encountering the word 'killing,' until, after many years he finally did discover the word—in reference to an edict concerning dogs" (445). The entire killing program was concealed—from the executioners even more than from their victims—in a disguise of euphemisms, like "euthanasia," "mercy killing," "disinfection," "resettlement," etc.

(3) Bureaucracy. "The numbing of the Auschwitz self was greatly aided by the diffusion of responsibility. With the medical corpsmen closer to the actual killing, the Auschwitz self of the individual doctor could readily feel 'It is not I who kill.' He was likely to perceive what he did as a combination of military order ('I am assigned to ramp duty'), designated role ('I am expected to select strong prisoners for work and weaker ones for the "special treatment"'), and desirable attitude ('I am supposed to be disciplined hard and to overcome "scruples"'). Moreover, since 'the Führer decides upon the life and death of an enemy of the state,' responsibility lay with him (or his immediate representatives) alone. As in the case of the participant in direct medical killing ('euthanasia'), the Auschwitz self could feel itself no more than a member of a 'team,' within which responsibility was so shared, and so offered to higher authorities, as no longer to exist for anyone on that team" (444).

(4) Wartime exigency. Hitler's memo authorizing the killing was dated on the first day of the war, on the belief that the extraordinary claims of a national struggle would bring many to condone what they would otherwise condemn. A frequent

theme of the Nazi doctors was that they were doing no more in the camps than they might be doing in combat.

(5) Initiation. Unwilling newcomers were broken in by initiation into murder, peer pressure, and an abundance of alcohol. Once one had been blood-bonded into the fraternity by actually doing some killing, the outsider became an insider, and initial revulsion subsided into acceptance.

(6) Justification. Many medical personnel took pride in some life-related exception: rescuing a few individuals from death (for a time, mostly), medical research, a competent pathology lab, etc.

(7) Routine. When day followed day according to an unvarying pattern, the conscience encountered no unsettling new events to penetrate its numbness.

(8) Technical perspective. Acquiescence in the Final Solution invited the individual practitioner to forgo consideration of the overall endeavor and focus his attention on the efficient accomplishment of his assigned tasks. "From top to bottom, each perpetrator's part in solving the ['Jewish Question'] can thus be looked upon as essentially technical. And the pattern can be insidious: for technology does not require the conceptual level of scientific thought, but tends to create a focus on maintenance and function. . . . [This] enables one to kill promiscuously and without pain" (494–495). (These findings closely match mine in chapter 3, *"Die Buben sind unser Unglück,"* in *Rachel Weeping and Other Essays on Abortion* [Kansas City: Andrews & McMeel, 1982]).

Lifton declines to identify this "doubling" as one of the classical psychoses, like schizophrenia or multiple personalities. He analyzes it as a character disorder that is moral, not merely emotional—and he is explicit in saying that though his outlook and profession are psychiatric he is writing a moral essay here. One of his most striking observations deals with the many physicians he had interviewed: "none of them—not a single Nazi doctor I spoke to—arrived at a clear ethical evaluation of what he had done, and what he had been part of. They could examine events in considerable detail, even look at feelings and speak generally with surprising candor—but almost

in the manner of a third person. The narrator, morally speaking, was not quite present" (8). This casts a shadow over his
later view that doubling "tended to be more a form of adaptation than a lifelong pattern" (423).

The shadow becomes still darker when one examines the
Deutsches Ärzteblatt for 1983, commemorating that special issue
fifty years earlier. Lengthy portions of an original article by the
vibrantly Nazi editor of that unique period were reprinted ap-
provingly. No disapproval of the events of 1933 was expressed.
" 'Would it have changed anything,' one article asked, 'if the
physicians' organizations had resisted the pressure of the new
administration and if they had not acquiesced voluntarily?' The
only insight presented: it was totally a question of social security and insurance technicalities; the offers of the new administration were irresistible."[2]

But one cannot finish reading this book and conclude that
the perversion from healer to killer is a German phenomenon,
or even a medical one. This reviewer was especially struck by
a pattern of evidence which the interviews assembled, and
which may deserve even more prominence than the author
gives them.

One of his fellow physicians at Auschwitz was unwilling
to repudiate Dr. Mengele's lethal medical experiments. "One
must be aware that in the Auschwitz milieu, where thousands
were being killed continuously, such a thing [Mengele's killing
a few twins] was nothing at all extraordinary" (322). He repeatedly invoked "the conditions" or "the atmosphere" of
Auschwitz, as a context so remote from the normal world that
ordinary ethical norms did not apply. One inmate doctor said
that "Auschwitz was 'a different planet' whose rules totally
reversed those of ordinary society: according to those rules, 'we
were there to die and not to live.' And 'to be able to accept
being where we were, we had to switch . . . to a different kind
of mentality'" (375–376).

It was not quite that in the enclosure of enforced violence
no ethical vision was possible. Once one consented to ignore
the evil of the entire undertaking, one felt free to apply a near-
sighted moral judgment to particular aspects of the undertaking. A lady on a guided tour of a medical facility where handi-

capped infants were being starved to death asked with outrage why they were not being killed by injection, because that would be more merciful (62). The children were ordinarily cremated; their ashes were then mixed together and a portion sent to each family, as if they were the actual ashes of their child. One staff member found this to be his sticking point: the killing itself might be forgiven, but not this impiety (75). One mental hospital chief complained to the Ministry of Justice that if they wanted him to eliminate all handicapped youngsters, they should make it legal (81). A doctor who arrived as chief administrator of a mental hospital where the killing was underway wrathfully rebuked the staff because nurses were being allowed to do the work indiscriminately. He insisted it be more methodical, with doctors' examinations, daily rounds, medical records, clinical decisions about which drugs to be used . . . and a more efficient death rate (100–101). One death doctor recalled that it was the killing by groups that offended him: "I had imagined it would be done as an individual procedure, . . . one by one. Well, . . . it was done as a mass affair. . . . I think in human terms it is different whether you take care of someone who has to go this way as an individual" (105). The doctors discussed how they might make their killing "more humane." "Dr. B. told how Mengele 'was the only one among the SS doctors who concerned himself with the practical [aspects] . . . of gassing'; the 'overburdened' facilities and 'technical . . . mistakes' made the whole process 'even more inhuman,' so that 'as perverse as it may sound, he took the trouble to look into these matters . . . for humanitarian reasons'" (322).

Why, indeed, might this sound perverse? Lifton points out that the Nazis managed symbolically and legally to normalize a genocidal universe. Within its inexorable flow of events doctors came to say yes, and not to question the entire endeavor. "One seeks instead the most 'humane path' within the going project" (497). As some doctors said, "I'm not here because I want to be. . . . I can't change the fact that prisoners come here. I can just try to make the best of it" (450). Once one accepted the overall context of murder, then one was freed from moral responsibility for all but the details.

Lifton sees that the German medical establishment may

be as ready today as it was in 1933 to be put under a spell and enlisted in assigned tasks within someone else's moral-free zone. But as a contemporary comparison he prefers to point to the nuclear arms race, which is a moral horror that has for most of us become normalized.

One is struck that he did not think to draw the seemingly more imposing parallels with another large and normalized project which is no mere threat, because each year it extermi- nates more lives worldwide than the death toll in all of World War II, and in America alone it has a higher body count than did Auschwitz at its point of highest output. It is managed entirely by physicians, with full observance of routine as if it were therapeutic: physical examination, meticulous records, clinical environment, white smocks. It has been given legal authorization and despite some muffled misgivings, is acqui- esced in by the medical profession—indeed, its legalization was endorsed by their national association. The same numbing strategies are employed: health is redefined as a concern of someone other then the person to be "treated," but a public therapeutic imperative nevertheless; an entire vocabulary has been elaborated to avoid all reference to death; bureaucracy removes moral responsibility from those involved, since the physician is doing what the family wants and the family is submitting to a strictly medical decision; emergency population needs make it a time for special ethical allowances, on behalf of the community's future; opinion within the profession is divided almost entirely according to whether one has been blooded by the "procedure" or not; the carnage is justified by desirable side-effects, such as making it available to the poor; routine has made it an accepted part of daily necessity; and moral concerns are now reduced to how the whole endeavor might be most humanely done, not whether it ought be done at all. Throughout the literature in its support, there is the same reluctance to regard the moral worth of the overall en- deavor, but only the gutsy determination "to make the best" of what is inevitable. Once again, healers double as killers.

The only person of heroic character in the entire book is a young French inmate physician, of vigorous Protestant convic- tions, who was told by the chief physician that she had to join in the medical "work" in Auschwitz. "She explained that such activities were 'contrary to my conception as a doctor.' He then asked, 'Can you not see that these people are different from you?' 'And I answered him that there were several other people different from me, starting with him!' . . . She rebuffed two additional approaches: one from Dr. Samuel advising her to take part in experiments because 'there are executions,' to which she replied, 'If I did them, I would commit suicide afterward.' The second approach was from Mengele: 'Of course I told him I did not want to do it'; afterward, 'he told others that he could not ask me to do what I did not want to do'" (298). She was the only doctor in the book who asked, not how to do it, but whether she should, for she gazed steadfastly at the entirety of the proposal.

5: A DEATHLY ESTRANGEMENT

A review of *The Psycho-Social Aspects of Stress Following Abortion*, by Anne Speckhard (Sheed & Ward).

Anne Speckhard writes as a social scientist who is critical of traditional abortion studies in her discipline. These studies had commonly inquired into the psychic turbulence women incur by using abortion to deal with what they felt were overwhelming problems. But they tend to study abortion only as a coping device, while ignoring the possibility that it may also be a new source of stress in its own right. Speckhard finds their accounts too individualistic. By examining only the emotional aftermath wrought by abortion in the mothers themselves, scholars have been too ready to ignore how it may have estranged these women from their crucially important natural support communities.

Speckhard conducted extensive interviews with thirty women for whom abortion had been a highly stressful memory. The typical woman had become pregnant while in a long-standing sexual partnership, which then unraveled; she was fifteen to twenty-four years old at the time of the abortion, and still in the process of achieving independence from her family-of-origin; and she was knowledgeable about birth control but not using it.

The women reported emotional reactions already well described in earlier literature: intense guilt, anger (primarily at the abortion providers), depression, fear of discovery, loss of ability to experience emotions, and painful reactions when encountering pregnant women or small children.

More original is her report of behavioral aftereffects not well noticed in other studies: eating disorders, extreme weight loss or gain, drug or alcohol abuse and addiction, sexual promiscuity, a prompt repeat (or "compensatory") pregnancy, and flashbacks, nightmares, hallucinations, and "visitations" by the aborted child.

Attitudes also had changed. At the time of their abortions 35 percent of these women considered abortion as their right, while another 27 percent had not even regarded it as a moral issue. But in the aftermath, 96 percent now regarded it as wrong.

Speckhard's most valuable finding, however, is that abortion compounded the stress of those women by estranging them from their most important loyalties. Fearful that their sexual activity and pregnancy would strain their parents' loyalties beyond the breaking point, they confided neither in them nor in any friends they thought might tell their families. Thus they underwent both the crisis and its aftermath isolated from their closest natural supports.

They did find emotional companionship in other friends who supported their choice of abortion, but that support went bad later. "Many subjects reported that friends who had been enthusiastic supporters of the abortion decision were unwilling to listen to any accounts of the stress produced by the abortion. It appeared to be a protective strategy on the part of friendship systems to avoid having to deal with the pain of abortion" (83). The decision to abort meant they were refusing to make a commitment to their sexual partners or their children, and the decision to do it furtively hid them from their original families. Their isolation from family was therefore stark and complete.

Abortion was also religiously alienating. The typical subject, although religiously inactive (perhaps because she was inactive), had thought of God as punitive and vengeful. "Such a perception led to a great deal of fear and anxiety, as it was not uncommon for these subjects to report a fear that God would punish them for the abortion by denying them future fertility" (89).

These women were to find eventual peace in surprising company: not with their families or their friends, but in prolife groups or in ardent religious communities. "In these social systems subjects found members who allowed them to discuss freely their feelings of grief, guilt, loneliness, anger, and despair. They also found that members of these systems were not adverse to discussing the details of the abortion experience, particularly with reference to concerns over pain that the fetus may have experienced and damage that may have occurred to the subjects' reproductive organs. In other systems these concerns had not been validated" (83).

They found religious reintegration by accepting the church's negative appraisal of extramarital sex and abortion, by embracing a greatly modified view of God as cherishing, and by discovering the possibility of forgiveness as a final resolution for their fault and the stress that had followed.

Speckhard's findings seemed to confirm this reviewer's earlier observation that women at risk for irresponsible pregnancy and abortion have tended to be too weak either to confront their sexual partners or to reveal themselves in crisis to their dissenting families and friends. They have tended to be acquiescent and passive, victimized by families that turned a blind eye towards what was going on, and victimized by partners who wanted sex but not partnership.

One of the primary sources of moral teaching is our communal insight into how certain actions tend to destroy us personally: those who lie, who embezzle, who seduce, wither. They are enfeebled in their characters, their persons, their selves. And we also see what course of action is followed by those drawn towards sanctity. For those who have the eyes to see it, faith can show us the moral valence of actions by the sight of what happens to those who perform them.

Recollections by women who destroyed their children and were later transformed are a valuable source for reflection by those who believe that we have nothing better to do with our lives than to make room for the most helpless. This is not merely social science research. It offers us a window of insight into one of the ways that those who kill, die . . . and can be raised to new life.

6: The Law as Conscience

A review of *Abortion and Divorce in Western Law: American Failures, European Challenges,* by Mary Ann Glendon (Harvard University Press).

Among all the twenty nations of Europe and North America included in this study (and the seven Warsaw Pact countries which receive only adjunct notice), the United States stands alone in denying absolutely any shelter of law to protect the unborn from abortion. Glendon, the scholar of comparative law whom Harvard Law School persuaded to come across the Charles from Boston College, surveys the results of the recent two-decade period in which virtually all developed nations revised their abortion laws. At one end of the spectrum are countries that exempt abortion from prosecution only if the mother's life is endangered. Next come nations which allow it for the so-called "hard" reasons: endangered maternal health, handicapped fetus, or pregnancy resulting from criminal intercourse. Then come regimes where abortion is allowed for various lesser, specified kinds of hardship, but only during the early months of pregnancy (this is the most typical category). Further over are countries which allow elective abortion in early pregnancy but restrict it thereafter. Standing alone at the radically permissive end of the spectrum is the United States, where abortion on demand is effectively legal at any time up to birth.

Scholars of a more pragmatic turn of mind disregard this kind of categorization by enactment. They observe that in actual fact abortion is liberally available in virtually all these countries, with little or no criminal jeopardy. Indeed, they view some of the ostensibly rigorous laws as less than sincere; for combining pious rhetoric about the preservation of the unborn child with statutory vagueness, these laws actually end up allowing abortion almost as permissively as does the much less ambiguous American law. It is the argument of this book, contrary to this pragmatic view, that systems of law are not to be assessed merely by what behavior they coerce.

Glendon applies to abortion law six other, larger points of comparison:

1. In no other country does one find "the same studied rejection of efforts to preserve the fetus that characterizes the United States Supreme Court's abortion decisions" (22–23). Even the most pro-choice regimes typically mandate consultation with a social worker, a waiting period for reconsideration, or a gestation limit beyond which abortion is forbidden.

2. Whatever their specific laws, other countries supply realistic dissuasives from abortion via more generous social benefits for mothers and enforced child support from fathers. In our country where one of every four preschool children lives in poverty, social programs providing income supplements and day care and other aids to child-rearing at levels comparatively lower than other developed countries may amount to a pro-abortion enactment that reinforces *Roe* v. *Wade*.

3. The U.S. stands virtually alone in characterizing the freedom to abort as a "right" of privacy. Privacy, which in the Anglo-American tradition has been described as a right to be left alone, is described on the Continent as a right to develop one's personality. There it is a freedom *for*, not *against*. Privacy in that context could be no excuse to abandon one's own. Our courts, by contrast, have developed a notion of privacy that gives individuals rights over against those to whom they are linked by bonds of promise and bonds of blood, whereas the continental jurisprudence explicitly sustains privacy as a shelter around the family, not as a segregator within it.

4. American abortion policy is extraordinary in that it was imposed by the Supreme Court and not allowed to be be framed by the give-and-take of the political process. The polarization of society over this issue of abortion was not limited to our country, but in other lands the legislative compromises,

while acquiescing in a perceived determination to have abortion as a legal option, nevertheless continued to assert the protection of unborn life as a public value.

5. The U.S. Supreme Court claimed specifically that the unborn could not be accorded status before the law as human persons. It said the question of their true identity had never been settled, but then resolved the question implicitly by stripping them of all protection of law or benefit of doubt. Other national jurisdictions, by contrast, have openly described abortion as the taking of human life, even while decriminalizing it in certain circumstances.

6. The presupposition to American abortion law has been that the body politic is an assemblage of separate and warily independent individuals, by contrast with the stand in other nations that solidarity within the society and the family (and the churches) binds people accountably to sacrifice for their own.

On this much larger view of law and its manner of application within a field of larger social forces, the United States stands out even more starkly as offering the least legal protection for the unborn child.

Glendon then moves to a parallel study of how, compared with the same countries, we provide for those who stand to lose most from divorce. The law touching this matter has also undergone recent relaxation, allowing effectively for "no-fault" divorce in most of the study countries. The U.S., once again, emerges on the radical end of the legal spectrum by defining marriage as a relationship terminable at the will of a single party, with no right to demur granted to the other partner.

Once again the author notices that in many countries the newly permissive statutes continue to assert wistfully the desirability of fidelity and the stable family. Not so in America. Rather than complimenting the Anglo-American legislation for its laconic consistency, she finds that in this country the respondent partner has no claims to use as a strength in negotiation. As a result, the financial burden of raising the children falls disproportionately upon the custodial parent. Her (it is usually her) standard of living sinks, while that of the unencumbered ex-spouse rises. Unfettered judicial discretion in awarding custody and fixing child-support can expose loyal parents to accepting inequitably low child-support as the price of not having custody contested. American law guarantees no minimal or scaled support; it rarely enforces actual payment; and it poorly compensates those whose child-support never arrives.

In a word, by taking no stand on behalf of filial and spousal vulnerabilities that emerge from a broken family, and by treating all concerned as solo individuals, with the children relegated to subsidiary status alongside the parents, the law makes paltry provision for the welfare of the most exposed survivors. Glendon thus portrays the United States as "unique among Western countries in its relative carelessness about assuring either public or private responsibility for the economic casualties of divorce" (105).

The reviewer confesses to periodic amusement at the sight of some book which an undergraduate, in anxiety not to miss any point of significance, has highlighted in its entirety. He must confess that after reading this excellent thirty-page concluding essay, he had filled practically every margin with glosses and emphasis marks. It is a very competently crafted piece of legal history which, in accord with the author's own view of the law as one among a culture's social forces, is eloquent and broad.

Glendon concludes by asking: Why this American difference? Why has American law come to enact that marriage and pregnancy could be terminated at will with no responsibility for the victim-parties? She sees this as a result of the notion that the state deals only with individuals, not with collectivities or other social unities. The only subject of the modern Anglo-American state was the self-reliant individual. When the single republican virtue of individual liberty was cultivated in isolation, and the close-knit associations that nurtured the other necessary, companion virtues were disregarded as "factions," the national purpose was narrowed. "When the Founders debated and worried about what they called factions, it was no doubt difficult even to imagine a world in which small towns would become suburbs, urban neighborhoods would be up-rooted, religion would be banished from the public square, craft associations would be confined to a narrowly economic role, and individual choice would render family ties increasingly fluid, detachable, and interchangeable" (118).

Hobbes, Locke, and Mill in succession gave rise to the belief that the purpose of government was to protect individuals from one another. Law could not pretend to be the instrument of moral wisdom or of anyone's vision of a sound society. This doctrine was pursued, in an age when most of our republic's legal traditions were being consolidated, by Oliver Wendell Holmes and others who denied to the law or the lawmakers any notion of right behavior. Since no one's account of justice could be imposed on anyone else, the law must simply conform to behavior.

This view took firmest hold on the Anglo-American scene, especially so in this country with its lack of tradition and its pluralist society. Continental jurisprudence never took this dogma so closely to heart, partially because customary law continued as a retardant to statutory and common law, and partly because intellectuals like Rousseau had taught so successfully that the law must be framed with a traditional wisdom so as to lead the people to virtue, and hence it was an instrument of education and persuasion, not merely of coercion.

This latter view leads Glendon to sympathize with continental codes today that hold up a high purpose for any major sector of law, even when the actual statutes may not live up to the ideal. In light of this expressed value, she argues, there is hope for better judicial interpretation in the present, and the seed is sown for a better law in a better day. The American dogma has been that all matters of wisdom and morality are private, and therefore inappropriate to the counsels of the state; that the doings of citizens within their families are also private, and hence to be left to the individuals and their own strengths; and that the state can assume no responsibility to foster the family or its inner loyalties and bonds, because those are private and moral matters. This doctrine Professor Glendon considers to be specious. The very claim that relations between parents and children are private is itself a moral statement.

We need to make the effort to understand what the totality of our legal regulations relating to family life is saying about our society and the way we view families, individuals, human life, dependency, and neediness in all its forms. . . . Because the role of law in the constitution of culture is so much more limited than that of the mores, it also behooves lawmakers to be solicitous of, or at least to try to avoid damaging groups such as families, churches, and local communities where values are formed, maintained and transmitted. (142)

NOTES

1. Harmut Hanauske-Abel, "Medicine under National Socialism," International Physicians for the Prevention of Nuclear War *Report* 4,2 (September 1986): 11–15.
    2. Ibid., 12.

Index

317